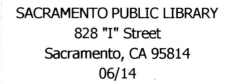

JAMES WEBB

I HEARD MY COUNTRY CALLING

★ *A Memoir* ★

SIMON & SCHUSTER

New York London Toronto Sydney New Delhi

Simon & Schuster
1230 Avenue of the Americas
New York, NY 10020

First Simon & Schuster hardcover edition May 2014

SIMON & SCHUSTER and colophon are registered trademarks of Simon & Schuster, Inc.

For information about special discounts for bulk purchases, please contact Simon & Schuster Special Sales at 1-866-506-1949 or business@simonandschuster.com.

The Simon & Schuster Speakers Bureau can bring authors to your live event. For more information or to book an event, contact the Simon & Schuster Speakers Bureau at 1-866-248-3049 or visit our website at www.simonspeakers.com.

Interior design by Ruth Lee-Mui
Jacket design by Jackie Seow
Jacket photographs courtesy of the author
Insert photographs courtesy of the author

Manufactured in the United States of America

10 9 8 7 6 5 4 3 2 1

Library of Congress Cataloging-in-Publication Data

Webb, James H.
  I heard my country calling : a memoir / James Webb. — First Simon & Schuster hardcover edition.
    pages   cm
  Includes index.
1. Webb, James H.   2. Legislators—United States—Biography.   3. United States. Senate—Biography.   4. United States. Department of the Navy—Officials and employees—Biography.   5. Authors, American—United States—Biography.   6. Marines—United States—Biography.   7. Vietnam War, 1961–1975—Personal narratives, American.   8. Navy Cross (Medal)—Biography.   9. Silver Star—Biography.   10. Purple Heart—Biography.   I. Title.
  E840.8.W395A3   2014
  328.73'092—dc23   2014007267
  [B]

ISBN 978-1-4767-4112-3
ISBN 978-1-4767-4116-1 (ebook)

For Hong Le

*Who was not a part of my life during the period covered by this book,
but whose wisdom, encouragement, and inspiration
are forever on every page. Anh Yeu Em.*

Author's Note

This book is a memoir. As I write about the early years of my life I mention many historical events. But I would like to emphasize that the book is not intended in any way to be an historical polemic, and that the events are mentioned in order to outline how the societal momentum and the foreign policy actions of those years affected me and my family. I have made considerable effort to ensure that each historical detail is properly documented, and it is my belief as well as my hope that such documentation is precise.

The book also contains a lengthy quote from *Born Fighting*, an earlier book I wrote. The bulk of this quote is from a government report on the economic conditions of the American South during the presidency of Franklin D. Roosevelt. I wish to express my appreciation to Random House, my earlier publisher, for their cooperation.

Descriptive phrases regarding the terrain and challenges in the An Hoa Basin in Vietnam similar to those on pages 268 and 269 were first used in an article entitled "Heroes of the Vietnam Generation," which I wrote for *The American Enterprise Magazine* in August 2000, and which has been frequently quoted in other publications.

Contents

I vow to thee, my country, all earthly things above,
Entire and whole and perfect, the service of my love;
The love that asks no questions, the love that stands the test,
That lays upon the altar the dearest and the best;
The love that never falters, the love that pays the price,
The love that makes undaunted the final sacrifice.

I heard my country calling, away across the sea,
Across the waste of waters, she calls and calls to me.
Her sword is girded at her side, her helmet on her head,
And round her feet are lying the dying and the dead.
I hear the noise of battle, the thunder of her guns,
I haste to thee my mother, a son among thy sons.

—From Sir Cecil Spring-Rice,
"I Vow to Thee, My Country," 1912

Chapter One

JANUARY 3, 2013

The Senate wing of the U.S. Capitol was completed in 1800, renovated in 1811, burned by British troops during their rampage of Washington in 1814, and reconstructed for the first time in 1826. In 1850 Senator Jefferson Davis of Mississippi introduced legislation to significantly enlarge the Capitol. This enlargement was finally finished in 1868, following the Civil War, during which then former senator Jefferson Davis rather ironically had become president of the Confederacy. As the country has grown and evolved from that time, so has the Capitol, as well as the sprawling grounds that surround it. A series of modernizations moved the Library of Congress and the Supreme Court out of the Capitol building into their own mammoth neoclassical structures. These modernizations also brought about a vast complex of six separate office buildings where the members of the House and Senate and their ever-growing staffs now carry out their obligations, and where, every now and then, one of them becomes forever remembered for some embarrassing personal escapade or political scheme.

The building and the grounds that surround it are a wonder to behold, extending eastward beyond the Supreme Court building and westward past the Washington Monument, all the way across the Mall to the Lincoln Memorial and the very edge of the Potomac River. There are few places in the world that can match the quiet splendor of these landmarks, especially when they are lit up in the dark of night for the world to see. This is not a craven political statement; rather it is the frank, almost unwilling admission of one who was raised from his earliest days to mistrust any form of elitism and to make fun of pretentious symbols.

Even the deepest cynic cannot deny the transcendent power of this place. It is almost as if those who designed and built the Capitol had opened up their hearts in a form of romantic innocence, risking the chance that they would be rejected by future generations for having been corny Harlequin-romancers if they were proved wrong, in the gamble that they might remake the world's comprehension of American-style democracy if they were shown to be right.

And they were not wrong.

If you are a thinking American, it is a humbling experience to spend time inside the dark, cool confines of the building itself. During my time in the Senate I walked through this building every day, indeed sometimes a half-dozen times a day, and still after all those years its majesty overwhelms me. No matter how many times I traversed its passages, no matter how burdened I felt under the weight of the laborious or silly issues of day-to-day politics, the history that lives inside this building always rescued me from the temptation to feel as though we in the Senate were mindlessly treading water rather than working to solve the problems of the country. History was being made here, whether or not we felt the truth of that as we barked and quibbled among ourselves on any given day.

When I stop and think about why I continue to feel this way, I usually end up remembering my father, the first Webb after generations in the Appalachian Mountains to finish high school and then the first to finish college following twenty-six years of intermittent night school. The Old Man would have been busting his buttons to see me walking these halls as the equal of giants whose names he had known only through history books and newspapers. I still roll my eyes and laugh to myself, imagining the daily phone calls I would have received had my father lived to see me become a member of the U.S. Senate. Truly he would have irritated the hell out of my staff. He would never have left me alone. He would have called me every day, bursting with ideas, providing advice, challenging me with crude jokes, and quoting from the key phrases of editorial writers who hated me.

James Henry Webb Sr. was not an easy man to please. He gave me no slack in the days of my boyhood as our family moved from town to town, from military base to military base, and I from school to school to school. Complaints were not in order. My siblings and I grew up with certainties that he, and especially my mother, could never have imagined: there was always food on the table; I never lacked for clean clothes; from the time I was twelve, there was always a job somewhere if I knew how to hustle. And he never let us forget that we were living in the greatest country on earth, a country that our rock-hard ancestors had pioneered, one stark mountain and one wide river and one war at a time.

When it hurts, just grit your teeth and take it. Don't you ever back down. Never start a fight, but if somebody else does, never run away. If you run from a bully you will never stop running, but if you fight he won't risk coming back at you again. Stand up. Fight back. Mark him. Give him something to remember every morning when he looks into the mirror. Then even if you lose you win. And by the way, if you ever run from a fight I will personally beat your ass.

My father was not exactly a mellow guy. He did not spare the rod. But he taught me early that there is no substitute for moral courage, whatever the cost, and that the ultimate duty of every leader is to take care of the people who rely on him when otherwise they would be forgotten or abandoned. Courage in the face of those above you and loyalty to those below you were my father's inalterable standards, the only true way to measure the worth of another human being.

I had fought my way into the Senate based exactly on those principles. I was not recruited to run for political office, which was one of the odd attractions of running in the first place. I took the gamble precisely because I could not accept the idea that a country such as America should be governed by a club of insiders who manipulate public opinion in order to serve the interests of hidden elites who hold the reins of power. I did not solve this problem in a mere six years, but I did nudge it here and there, even as my concerns about it only grew stronger.

I knew what my dad would be saying to me at this moment if he were still alive. He would be aggravated beyond words that I had declined to run for reelection. He would not be able to resist sending a verbal barrage my way on the very day that I was heading to the Senate floor for the final time in order to congratulate the person who would now be taking my seat:

What the HELL is going on in your brain, Sonny Boy? After you fought so hard to get here, what are you doing walking away from it, just when you reached the top of your game? There are no instant replays in life! You are not coming back! Didn't I teach you a damn thing?

I would have listened to him for a while, nodding now and then as a measure of respect, finally telling him to stop being such an irritable, cantankerous bastard. We had argued with sharp, combative humor for decades about everything from poetry to baseball to history, and especially about the unpredictability of my so-called career. But for me, in this imagined debate the answer would have been easy:

Dad, seriously. We're talking about an institution with a 6 percent approval rating, and I can't figure out why anybody would want to be in that 6 percent.

• • •

On this final morning the corridor in front of my Russell Building office was eerily quiet. I was arriving without a briefcase, and indeed without portfolio. I did not belong here anymore. I had already become an interloper in a place that until yesterday had been my personal fiefdom and even my second home. No staff members greeted me. Actually I did not even have a staff anymore, as of this very morning. But none of that really mattered. I had not come here to be escorted, briefed, coffeed up, or attended to. All I wanted was to walk through my personal office spaces one last time, in the rare calm of a do-nothing morning, before the office as it was now constructed and I myself disappeared into the dry annals of Senate history.

I reached Russell 248, which had been my office's main reception room. My heavy brass nameplate was still bolted face-high onto the wall outside the door, just where it had been posted in the Russell Building for the past six years:

SENATOR

Jim Webb

Virginia

Three flags had always stood next to my door: the American flag, the flag of the Commonwealth of Virginia, and the flag of remembrance for those still missing or unaccounted for on our nation's battlefields. They were gone now, wrapped up and shipped away. Senate maintenance personnel would soon unbolt my nameplate from the wall and have it hand-delivered to my home. The high-ceilinged marble hallway was lined with large trash bins piled to the top with mounds of memories—discarded papers, binders, and odd pieces of cardboard, all the refuse and political detritus from six years of intense staff functioning. Until a few days ago the office spaces were occupied by more than two dozen energetic staff members of all ages and backgrounds, united by their desire to serve our country and to carry out the goals that I had laid before them.

I had put a lot of energy into the selection and development of my staff. I had personally interviewed every person who served on it, from receptionist to chief of staff, including those who worked in the distant regional offices in Richmond, Virginia Beach, Roanoke, Danville, and in the far southwest heartland of the Appalachian Mountains, whose struggling coal mines and disappearing tobacco fields are nearer to Detroit than they are to Washington. I personally invested myself in each of their futures, in the same spirit that I once took pride in the career evolution of what I termed "Webb-trained Marines." More than any memorial highway or bridge or piece of legislation, these people and the principles of leadership and political philosophy that hopefully I imbued in them will remain the most important legacy of my time in the Senate.

They were gone, off to other things. The desks and tables they had occupied were empty and bare, as were the now nail-bitten walls. Their computers had been scanned, stripped of all data, and removed. The "landline" phones had been taken out. Personal cell phones had been returned, the numbers rendered inoperable. And on January 2, like a surrendering army, every staff member had formally turned in all room keys to the Senate sergeant at arms.

I left the corridor, walking inside the main reception room. The walls of the room had been filled with my personal memorabilia: photographs dating to my time in Vietnam, including one in which I stood shirtless in front of an enemy bunker, hard-eyed, gaunt, and bearded, a reminder that we should always respect military sacrifice but never glamorize its toll; a dozen framed newspaper and magazine articles; the *Publishers Weekly* cover from July 10, 1978, announcing my novel *Fields of Fire* as "the most powerful war novel in a generation"; the tally card from the final roll-call vote when we passed the historic Post-9/11 GI Bill in 2008; and some classic eighty-year-old black-and-white photos taken in the coal fields of southwest Virginia.

I stuck my head into the conference room next door. The room was dark, made darker still by the high wooden cabinet on one wall and the long table that filled the center of the room. Nineteen stiff-backed chairs lined the conference table, eight on each side, two on the far end, and another just inside the door, where I sat during our meetings. A shaft of grey light from a courtyard window illuminated the tabletop as if it were a dull mirror. I could see faint smudges on the table from the hands of people who had once sat in its chairs. These walls also had been filled with dozens of plaques, photos, and memorabilia, all of which had now been taken down, bubble-wrapped, boxed up, and sent away.

I had spent uncountable hours at this table, meeting with schoolkids, religious leaders, business executives, community organizers, union members, university presidents, military commanders, advocates of prison reform, law enforcement officials, judges, political figures, ambassadors and foreign ministers, and, of course, the story-seeking members of the media. Not even counting unscheduled meetings with members of my staff, which numbered in the hundreds in a typical week, during my time in the Senate I had taken 5,005 official meetings in my office, as well as 2,300 personal meetings and 675 interviews with the media. Almost all of them had taken place inside this now-shadowed room. Since we're counting, I also attended 1,078 committee hearings, appeared at 264 formal speaking engagements, and spoke at 358 political events. And on the Senate floor I had taken more than 1,800 roll-call votes.

I crossed the hallway into Room 247, for another hour or so still my personal office. Three desks inside the narrow anteroom had housed the immediate nerve center of my staff: the press secretary, my scheduler, and my executive assistant. Across from the desks a small closet held a microwave oven, a small fridge, and room for storage. Curious, I looked inside the closet and confirmed that it was still a crumby, noodle-infested mess. The latest human occupants were gone, but the Senate roaches soldiered on.

At the back of the room I turned into a short breezeway, walking

7

past a small closet and my private bathroom before entering my personal office. There I was suddenly overwhelmed by a wave of memories and emotion.

Now stripped bare of all my personal memorabilia, the contrast with the intimacy of the years I had spent in this room gave a hard edge to the reality of my departure. My desk was just inside the door. The age-old fireplace marked the middle of the far wall, a gigantic, gold-framed mirror above it. The shelves, credenzas, chairs, and circular working table remained in place. And yet everything had become sterile and depersonalized.

This sudden emotion was a surprise, since my wife Hong and I had decided nearly two years before that six years in the Senate was enough, and that once we made the final decision to leave we would not second-guess it. The tangible effects that had warmed this room were gone, but I could see them still: the hundreds of books on the shelves, the underlined and earmarked papers that had been piled upon my desk, the personal computer, the phone with its intercom connections to personal staff, the TV set against the wall by my desk, the notepads and ever-revolving stacks of memos from my staff, and the dozens of family photos that had surrounded the walls and tables around my chair, nestling me into my daily routine.

I reached my desk and ran my hand along its right-hand corner. The desk was beautiful, huge and ornate, a piece of history, as are so many objects in the Senate. My fingers traversed more than a dozen small gashes in the wood. I smiled to myself, for this was another private remembrance: in those gashes in that desktop corner was an unforgettable, defining memory.

For the past six years I had kept two objects on this corner of my desk, unspoken reminders for everyone to see and for those who were intuitive enough to contemplate. The first was a beautiful gold-embossed Bible inscribed with my name on the cover, a gift to me from my friend Barry Black, the chaplain of the Senate. The long cloth ribbon inside its pages had been permanently kept at the paragraphs of the second chapter of the book of James, verses 14–18, which defined for me the overriding reasons that I had decided to run for the Senate. Part of those verses reads, "And what good is faith without works? Show me your faith apart from your works, and I by my works will show you my faith."

The second object was a traditional black-bladed, leather-handled Marine Corps combat knife, which I had jammed into the time-hardened wood of the desk itself, just behind the Bible.

At some moment during just about every day, the Bible and the bayonet would catch my eye, both reminding me of why I was sitting at the desk in the first place. I have led a sometimes hard and complicated life, but I am strong in my faith. I also know what it's like to fight in a philosophically controversial war and to have shed my blood on a faraway battlefield. I came to understand at a very young age that moral complexities are an inseparable part of hard face-to-face combat. These twin realities deepened not only my faith but my respect for the burden of military service, irrespective of the political decisions that impel it.

Some would look at the Bible and wonder about the bayonet. Some would look at the bayonet and wonder about the Bible. For me, they go together. And all I have asked, as the ancient philosopher intoned, is not to be understood too quickly.

From the window behind my desk I looked out at the expansive park that stretched across the street, up to Constitution Avenue. My office window was a great vantage point from which to watch the frequent political rallies that were held in the park. I have always taken comfort in these rallies, no matter their political viewpoint, for they represent the greatness of an America where at least most of the time we can vent our ideas and even our anger with bullhorns rather than bullets. The park was quiet today, on the morning when new senators would be sworn in and others would say good-bye.

I turned away from the window and sat in the thick, high-backed leather chair that for years had been my private senatorial throne.

Without deciding, I swiveled the chair around toward my desk. Like a modern-day Ozymandias, I surveyed my empty empire, knowing this would be the last time I would sit at this desk and probably the last time I would ever even be in this room. I looked at the clock on the far wall. It was fifteen minutes before eleven, when the swearing-in proceedings for the newly elected senators would begin. I needed to make my way to the Senate floor.

A thought from my childhood struck me: I began wondering if after all of this preparation I had left anything behind. It was the last thought my father would always raise whenever we moved, or even if we simply vacated the latest ten-bucks-a-night motel room—both of which we often did. *You always forget something.* That was my pa's mantra, and he was almost always right: a favorite baseball cap in one remote closet, a dollar bill on the floor, or maybe a bar of store-bought soap in the shower. Such a final search had become a longtime family game.

I pulled out all the drawers in my desk, finding each of them empty— nothing in there, not even a paper clip. I searched the two wide drawers underneath the end tables that flanked the window behind my desk; once filled with personal files, they too were empty. My staff had done a thorough job, shipping more than sixty large crates and smaller boxes to my home and to my writing office in Virginia. Walking across the carpeted room, I reached the wide credenza that stood along the far wall. Empty. Then I opened up the minifridge inside its left-hand cabinet door.

Bingo. Four beers and a plastic container of rice had been left inside. I laughed aloud, delighted at this discovery, for here were the truth-tellers of my Senate tenure. The rice box had been prepared months ago by my wife. It brought back memories not of gala banquets, grand speeches, or my frequent trips abroad but of the usual lunches at my desk, spent staring at a computer screen, catching up on emails and time-sensitive news. Hong had prepared the rice box because I had grown sick of the gut-roiling daily specials from the Senate cafeteria. And the beers made me remember all the frustrating, ridiculous late nights sitting bored and restless in the office, waiting for the majority and minority leaders to schedule usually meaningless votes on the Senate floor so that we might finally go home.

My first thought as I pulled the objects from the fridge was that Hong, who had escaped South Vietnam on a fishing boat following the communist takeover in 1975 and spent time in two refugee camps after her family was saved at sea by our Navy, would insist that I bring the container home. The thought struck a suddenly fragile nerve. The very normality of thinking to bring a container home reminded me that this was the last time I ever would actually be going home from the Senate.

I picked up the rice container and dismissed the thought as quickly as I had entertained it, for again I heard my father's voice: *If you're going to miss it, then maybe you should have stayed, Sonny Boy.*

No. It was definitely time to go.

I now had ten minutes to stash the container in my car and then make my way to the Senate floor. My private visit was over. I would never again return to this room. But I was leaving the Senate with what, for me, was the ultimate satisfaction. I had lived up to every promise I had made when I had asked people to elect me a little more than six years before. I had never backed down. I had never said a word that I did not mean. And I had never cut a political deal.

Good-bye was over. I walked out the door, heading for the Senate floor. I would bring the rice container home. But I left the beer for the cleanup crew.

Chapter Two

THE GOOD OF THE SERVICE

My life has aligned chronologically and in spirit with the Baby Boom generation that followed in the wake of World War II. I was born on February 9, 1946, almost exactly nine months to the day following Germany's surrender in that war, which in America we remember as V-E Day. I have often thought about the serendipitous coincidence that might have played into the moment of my conception. Since I never worked up the gumption (or lack of propriety) that it would have taken to put the question directly to my now-departed parents, these kinds of secrets will never be answered. But the poet in me can contemplate its possibility.

May 8, 1945, was a glorious day. Much of the world was rocked with a fantastic celebration. The war was over in Europe, and soon it would be over in Asia. Most Americans seemed sure that a generation of peace would follow. What an emotional day it must have been for my dad, who at that time was an Army Air Corps bomber pilot, and my mom, who, although only nineteen, was already nursing a nine-month-old child, the first of four that would be born by the time she was twenty-four. Nine months later, in the tree-lined tranquility of the beautiful old town of St. Joseph, Missouri, lo and behold I was born.

I like to think that it must have been a pretty good party.

America's historic Baby Boom generation, spawned by the return of millions of veterans from World War II, grew up not in an era of world peace, as had been expected, but in a nation living under the constant threat of nuclear war, even though our country had undeniably grown more prosperous. The tensions brought on by what was termed the cold war also had a couple of so-called flash points that resulted in 100,000 American military deaths, in Korea from 1950 to 1953, where even now a full peace settlement has not been agreed upon, and in Vietnam from 1964 to 1972, with the final communist victory over our South Vietnamese allies coming in 1975. Debates about our nation's foreign policy would sunder the Baby Boomers during Vietnam, when 9 million among their age group were called upon to serve in the military and 2.7 million of them shipped out to war, while others took to the streets in frequent and sometimes violent protest.

Another, less-noted reality took place as a result of the cold war and the very hot "conflicts" that flared up during the same decades: America's new place in world affairs brought about a dramatic, historic change to the size, structure, and so-called peacetime deployments of its military forces. For those of us who grew up inside the military, these changes shaped every element of our daily lives.

The present size of our military and the enduring worldwide commitments that followed in the wake of World War II were never contemplated by our Founding Fathers. Normal to us now, they are unique to the post–World War II environment. Article 1, Section 8 of the U.S. Constitution affirms the belief of our Founding Fathers that America should not keep a standing army during peacetime. Congress would have the power to "raise and support Armies," while limiting any appropriations toward that end to no more than two years—a deliberate check against limitless military campaigns. At the same time, Congress was empowered to "provide and maintain a Navy," with the understanding that securing our sea lanes was a deterrent to war, a protection of national commerce, and thus a vital interest during war or peace.

Until the aftermath of World War II, the United States closely adhered to these objectives, keeping a very small peacetime military. In times of peril the country would follow tradition, its citizens laying aside the plow and picking up their rifles to serve until the crisis passed. Amid the unspeakable carnage of the Civil War the tradition of citizen-soldiering during wartime was expanded to include federal conscription. This planning model was built around a small peacetime military, which could be expanded by conscription in times of war, and was repeated in World Wars I and II. But after a brief and largely unremembered drawdown in the aftermath of World War II, it was abandoned in the face of continuous international obligations. Conscription at some level was considered necessary to fill the ranks of our Army not only for the Korean and Vietnam wars but also during the cold war interludes in between.

In sum, during peacetime America has traditionally fielded a volunteer military, which would grow rapidly during a period of war and then shrink just as quickly once the war was ended. All that changed after World War II. Except for a two-year interval between 1945 and 1947 our military has been sized and deployed as if on a permanent wartime footing, even though war has never been formally declared during this entire period. Given the necessity to continually field a sizable military, the challenge for our political system has been to balance a moral argument against a fiscal debate. Should these requirements be met through a cheaper (and, some would argue, a fairer) system of conscription, with the attendant concerns about forcing our citizens into uniform, or should we continue to spend an ever-growing portion of our defense budget on compensation and family support programs in order to maintain an all-volunteer military force? From the final days of the Vietnam War through the end of the cold war and during the continuous deployments of the wars in Iraq and Afghanistan, we have opted to pay the financial costs of an all-volunteer military rather than endure the uncertainties and unending moral debates over forced conscription.

What, you may ask, does this have to do with family support programs and the childhood experiences of the military brats among the Baby Boomers? The answer is: a lot.

It was easy for the military to reduce its size in 1945; our service members were largely young, most had been drafted, and particularly among the enlisted ranks few wanted to stay anyway. It was the same with the weapons of war that our nation had so capably and prodigiously produced during wartime. We took blowtorches to many combat aircraft and weapon systems, often right there on former battlefields, leaving them to be hauled away as scrap metal rather than shipping them back to the United States, where it would have been a challenge to house all of them anyway. We cut up, gave away, civilianized, or mothballed our ships. Except for necessary occupation forces in key countries, we brought our soldiers back to America as fast as the troopships could carry them, rewarding our "Greatest Generation" veterans with a generous GI Bill and sending them home to pursue civilian aspirations. And we ended conscription, seeking to reestablish the concept of a smaller, all-volunteer military that had preceded the war.

But the entire face of the international order had changed during that horrific war, as had America's role in guaranteeing worldwide stability. With the back-to-back maelstroms of two world wars fought within the space of only thirty-one years, former dominant powers such as Great Britain, France, Germany, and Japan had bled themselves white and spent their economies to the edge of oblivion. Tens of millions of people were dead—more than 40 million in Europe alone. Their home countries had been devastated. Colonial empires were being dissolved, leaving unprecedented political and economic vacuums all over the map. The European powers and Japan were receding rapidly from their former holdings throughout Asia. Europe and Japan themselves were largely in ashes. In the aftermath of such horrific slaughter, governing philosophies throughout the world were being questioned. The Soviet Union, itself devastated in every sense by the war, nonetheless was seeking to expand incessantly into the creases and vacuums left over from the carnage. China, torn apart by decades of internal strife and a fourteen-year Japanese occupation, was steadily consolidating under a communist system that would take control of the country in 1949 and was antipathetic to our own view of stability in East Asia.

In economic terms America gladly accepted its place at the top of the new international order. But we did not claim ownership in any lands that we had taken through military force during the war, nor did we seek the military burdens of the postwar world. In fact, we did not want either. The uncomfortable reality was that in terms of guaranteeing international stability, no other country was capable of carrying the responsibility that had now fallen onto America's shoulders. And so despite our effort to demobilize and to bring most of our military forces home from foreign places, beginning in 1947 and accentuated with the 1948 Berlin Airlift, the formation of NATO in 1949, and the 1950 invasion of South Korea, it became clear that the United States had no other alternative but to accept these worldwide obligations.

World War II was over, but the cold war had begun. Our military would again have to grow, and in 1947 conscription was reinstated. For the first time in its history the United States would be required to field a standing army during what could arguably be called peacetime. From this rather reluctant decision came the "draftee army" that eventually would be replaced by today's all-volunteer force.

Even then, however, American defense planners did what they could to preserve the historical concept of citizen-soldiering. The most important benchmark was not the reinstatement of the draft but rather that the military would be required to become permanently larger. The

Army would rely on conscription to fill its enlistment quotas, but except for rare occasions the Air Force, Navy, and Marine Corps remained all-volunteer, even in the days of the draft and even during bitterly debated conflicts such as Vietnam. Ironically, the truest draftee army in our history was not the one that eventually fought in Vietnam, but rather the one that had just finished fighting in World War II. Two-thirds of those who had served in our military during World War II were draftees. By contrast, two-thirds of those who served during the war in Vietnam, the so-called Draftees' War—as well as 73 percent of those who died in Vietnam—were volunteers.

Along with this decision the military would be required to adjust, not just with respect to its operational objectives but most important in terms of family support programs and the actual physical structure of its facilities. With a first-ever standing army came the necessity to build a different kind of military basing system that included infrastructure capable of meeting the demands for family-assistance programs on a scale that the American military had never before faced, either with previous peacetime armies or during wartime, since draftees and enlistees alike were usually required to leave their families behind.

Thus began an enormous and historic journey.

Today's leaders in the Department of Defense rightly pride themselves on the vast array of programs designed not only to protect the well-being of military family members but also to include them as integral parts of the military community itself. Our military families receive full, comprehensive medical care, and those who stay until retirement are covered by a generous postcareer insurance program called TRICARE. Military housing on bases throughout the world is first-class. The Department of Defense school system is ranked among the top public school systems in America. Almost every military base of any size is able to provide day care centers for children, recreational facilities for everyone, grocery stores known as base commissaries, retail stores known as base exchanges, gas stations, golf courses, jogging tracks, fast-food franchises, and advisory offices dedicated to a wide range of counseling and legal protection and advice for family members. Indeed, a few years ago, during a windshield tour of an Air Force facility on Okinawa, the base commander boasted to me that Americans stationed at Kadena could spend three years on that populous Japanese island and never have to leave the base.

Many commentators like to point out that the overriding emphasis on family support programs had its roots in the creation of the all-volunteer military after the Vietnam War. The challenge of sustaining such a sizable all-volunteer military has indeed been something of a grand experiment. But it would be wrong to assume that the concept of an all-volunteer military was unique to post-Vietnam America, and it would be just as wrong to argue that the programs now in place are simply a manifestation of the need to pay off our military in order to recruit and retain them. Some may view such support programs as extravagant or too costly when budgets come under scrutiny, especially if one is far removed from the operational military or after a national crisis has passed. But our military members earned these benefits the hard way, as did their families. Anyone who wishes to dispute this should begin by putting himself into the shoes of those who have stepped forward to serve.

And there is another point to be made. In the days when our wars were fought largely by young, unmarried men these programs took on a different meaning than they do in a military that is largely married and continually deployed for years on end. So let's just say that when it comes to family support programs the military, like the international position of the country itself, has evolved dramatically since the end of World War II.

Watching and participating in this evolution has been one of the most satisfying parts of my professional life. I am proud of my family's service during this era, including that of my brother and the husbands of both of my sisters, as well as my son and three of my seven nephews. I have covered the military as a journalist, including the fighting in Beirut in 1983 and in Afghanistan in 2004. I worked on veterans' issues for four years as a committee counsel in Congress just after the Vietnam War, at a time when groundbreaking research was being done on such issues as post-traumatic stress, and Agent Orange. I spent five years in the Pentagon, four as an assistant secretary of defense and Secretary of the Navy during the mid-1980s, at a time when family-assistance programs were becoming a top priority. And in the Senate I had the privilege of chairing the Armed Services Subcommittee on Personnel, directly responsible for the authorization and oversight of all Department of Defense programs in that area.

These vast changes are rarely understood by most Americans and seldom discussed by commentators and policymakers, but they are central to budget issues as well as philosophical arguments about military service. Our post–World War II military became a completely new phenomenon, different in size and family makeup from any military that preceded it. As it evolved, new bases were being built at home and overseas, while others were being expanded in order to address the strategic challenges of the cold war. And many existing bases were undergoing extensive infrastructure shifts from the old models that had dominated the peacetime militaries of the past.

Even today a visit to military bases whose roots reach back to the years before World War II offers a glimpse of the simpler life that once dominated America's peacetime military. A nostalgic drive through the central areas of Fort Myer, Virginia; Offutt Air Force Base, Nebraska; Fort Lewis, Washington; and Schofield Barracks, Hawaii; just to pick a few, still provides reminders of the elegant officers' quarters and the cramped but orderly barracks where hundreds of enlisted personnel lived in long rows of bunk beds, sharing common toilet areas, all built around a wide parade field where the officers and troops once met for morning musters as the bugles played and the flag was raised, then marched off to their daily regimens.

The size and demographic makeup of our military after World

War II and during the cold war also provided an institutional shock to the country's budget makers and to the age-old military culture itself. It took years for our bean counters and leaders to catch up, and thus to build the housing, schools, and other support structures that would accommodate this new approach.

I spent my childhood inside this reality. Its bottom line was that for several years a whole lot of kids were going to be growing up without the frequent presence of their fathers (for then it was almost always the father) and that a whole lot of mothers would be left to struggle on their own while their husbands were away.

It is difficult for many Americans to fully comprehend the impact of what it means to take the oath to defend our country and then put on a military uniform. From the moment you enter the military until the day you leave it, every aspect of your life is under the control of others. You can argue, hope, and try to persuade, but every decision about your military career is subject to what the higher-ups of leadership call "the good of the service." During the time you are serving in uniform your individual needs and desires are not only subordinated to the good of the service, but they are irrelevant if the service decides it needs you elsewhere. You can sign up for a particular occupational specialty, but there is no firm guarantee you will be chosen for it if the good of the service intervenes. Even if you are given the occupational specialty of your choice you cannot decide what your actual job will be or, in most cases, even ask to interview for a specific job. You cannot decide to quit if you don't like your job. You cannot look for another place to work if you don't like your boss. And here is the biggest rub: if your boss does not like you, you may be totally screwed, not only for the moment but for your longer career. Several times a year this boss will evaluate your "proficiency and conduct," which, whether fair or not, has the potential to affect your reputation and your potential for any future assignment.

You cannot decide where you will be stationed or for how long. You cannot tell your commanding officer that thanks very much, but you really don't want to be deployed overseas right now, much less to a combat zone. In an operating environment you might be required to carry far more gear than you need or than your body can absorb, in the process permanently wearing down your orthopedic structure at an early age. It could become normal to operate for long months in the scorching heat or under torrents of rain, with little sleep, bad food, and only sporadic news from home. You might be billeted near hateful, menacing neighbors or downwind from health hazards such as toxic burn pits. And all the while you will be legally obligated to carry out the orders of those in charge of you, whether or not you agree with the wisdom of those orders. This includes the distinct possibility that even against your own better judgment you might be placed in a situation in which you will get injured, blown up, or shot.

Not incidentally, if you are in the operating forces of any of the military services you will probably spend a lot of time away from your family—a lot of time. My mother had four children, and due to his military assignments my father was unable to be present for three of those four births.

My father, a World War II veteran, was discharged from the military during the demobilization of 1945, returning home to his prewar job as an electrician, but he was invited to rejoin the Air Force in 1947 due to the realities of the cold war. Immediately upon reentering the military my father all but disappeared from our daily lives; it would be more than three years before our family was able to live together full-time again. He spent a long deployment flying B-29s from a frigid strategic outpost in a remote area of Alaska, their missions designed to deter or respond to activities by the Soviet Union from just across the Bering Strait. He was sent to England for similar reasons, while we stayed behind. He did a stint at Biggs Air Force Base in Texas, where there was no available family housing. He was deployed to Germany, flying C-47 and C-54 cargo planes during the Berlin Airlift. Finally returning to our general geographic area, he was assigned to Scott Air Force Base, Illinois.

For his first year at Scott Air Force Base my dad "commuted," more or less. In those days before interstate highways, almost every Friday night he would climb into his old Kaiser and drive 380 miles one way along narrow two-lane roads, arriving just before dawn to be with us at our home in St. Joseph, Missouri. He would then drive back again on Sunday afternoons in order to be at work on Monday morning.

For all of the family support programs in place today, it is hard to imagine that in those days just after World War II, "quality of life" for a military family was defined not by the availability of a day care center or a good school or a commissary but by whether you were able to live in the same house as your dad. And adequate family assistance did not consist of counseling or support groups, which at the time were unheard of. For our family it was whether my grandmother and Aunt Carolyn would be able to move to St. Joseph to live with us and help my mother during those long years while my father was either deployed or assigned to bases where there was no housing.

And so, as my father deployed again and again, the Webb family support program became my granny, Aunt Carolyn, and the kindness of our neighbors.

My dad, one of the most innovative thinkers I have ever met, was the first known Webb in many generations harkening back to the Appalachian Mountains of Southwest Virginia and Eastern Kentucky to finish high school. When the Japanese attacked Pearl Harbor on December 7, 1941, he was living in a two-man room at the YMCA in St. Joseph, and working at Townsend and Wall, the city's largest department store. An excellent if unpolished athlete, he was a phenomenal swimmer. When I was a young child it was nothing for him to swim laps at the local pool with me and my older sister, Pat, clinging onto his back. In the days before World War II his frequent regimen was to swim across the swirling, eddy-filled

Missouri River from St. Joseph to the hamlet of Elwood, Kansas, where he had lived during his teenage years, and then back again.

Like so many others in his generation, the day after the Pearl Harbor attacks my father walked down to the local recruiter's office and enlisted in the Army. Accepted into the aviation cadet program of the Army Air Corps, he became a pilot and was commissioned as a second lieutenant. Flying B-17 and B-29 bomber aircraft, by war's end he had been promoted to the rank of captain. As it turned out, my dad loved the military and he loved to fly. But when the war ended, he, like many other officers without a college education, was RIFFED—an acronym for a mandatory reduction in force—and sent back to the civilian world.

In the halcyon days just after the defeat of Germany and Japan, people with my father's reserve commission and lack of education were basically cut from the team, deemed expendable as the military's force structure shrank. It was one thing that thanks to their intellect and basic skills these uneducated, so-called ninety-day wonders could qualify to become pilots and officers during the rigors of wartime. It was quite another that they and their ever-expanding families could join the class-conscious officers' club milieu and fit into the historical peacetime model.

But then the cold war came. The old peacetime model was broken. The military was once again expanding. The draft was begun again. People with wartime experience, and particularly pilots who like my father had logged thousands of hours of flying time, were being sought out and brought back to active duty as the country faced new and unexpected geostrategic challenges. But these veterans were now a few years older. While the skills they had learned and honed during World War II were immediately valuable, thus saving the military the cost and time that it took to train and mature younger pilots, the families that they so frequently brought along with them carried their own challenges.

My dad and his non-college-educated peers were something of a quick-fix solution. On the other hand, his wife and kids and other families like us were something of a problem. What would the age-old hierarchy do with us—not rhetorically but physically? Where would they put us? How much would it cost to house, educate, and medically take care of us? And how long would it take to put such systems in place?

My mother did not quite fit the Officers' Wives Club model either, at least in those early days. Vera Lorraine Hodges grew up in the steamy, poverty-stricken cotton fields and strawberry patches of rural East Arkansas, the sixth of eight children. And as so often is the case with those who have really had it hard, my mother did not like to talk about how hard she really had it. She had grown up without indoor plumbing or electricity. She usually went barefoot. She brushed her teeth with twigs. She started working in the fields as a child, chopping cotton, picking strawberries, cutting and "ricking" wood in the middle of the night. She never had the chance to finish grade school.

Her father and three of her seven siblings died of now-curable or preventable illnesses. In the space of only a few months just after she turned ten, her father, Birch Hays Hodges; her closest younger sister, eight-year-old Eunice; and her grandfather, Francis Adolphus Doyle; all died suddenly, a trilogy of unanticipated tragedies that she never fully overcame. When she was sixteen her mother, my granny Georgia Frankie Doyle, was forced to make something of a Sophie's choice, leaving my mom behind and alone in Arkansas as she took her youngest child, my aunt Carolyn, to California, having saved enough money for only two one-way tickets in search of work as Rosie the Riveter in a factory that made American bombers.

My mother met my dad in Monahans, Texas. She was seventeen years old. She had been sent by her aunt Minnie from Kensett, Arkansas, to live in Monahans with her next older sister, my aunt Zara, whose nickname was Dot. Dot's husband Calvin, also of Kensett, had escaped the cotton fields by finding work in Monahans as a fireman. My dad was stationed at nearby Pyote Air Force Base, an outpost that had sprouted up in the Texas desert like a cactus weed just after the war began. One afternoon, completely by chance, he met my mother on a crowded bus and offered her his seat. They began to talk. Immediately smitten, he got off at her bus stop and walked her home.

When they neared her house my aunt Dot saw them approaching. Rightfully leery of any potential rascal wearing a military uniform in this remote region of Texas, she blanched. It was Dot's worst nightmare to look out a window and see my brash, talkative dad with his military cap pushed jauntily to one side, walking her seventeen-year-old sister home from the bus stop. Springing into action, Aunt Dot raced to the front door, pulled my mom inside, and quickly slammed it in my dad's face.

Somehow my dad persisted, he and my mother finding a way to work past Dot. Eleven days after meeting my mom, he asked her to marry him.

However he managed to keep in contact with my mom, neither of them were fooling my aunt Dot. Dot was an uncannily shrewd and knowing woman. She did not exactly drip with sentimentality. You did not want to be across the table from her in a gambling casino or facing her down in a barroom brawl. The brutal, draining travails of East Arkansas and her own personal scars had hardened Dot like tempered steel. This was not necessarily a bad thing, because on the other hand if you were in a fight you could do no better than having Aunt Dot on your side. Dot never backed down and she always thought ahead. She was already saving her dollars in hopes of escaping from the parched vistas of the Texas desert in favor of the postcard-pretty orange groves and palm-lined beaches of California. She would soon do exactly that, working her way up from cocktail waitress to managing a casino in Lake Tahoe before settling in as a real estate agent and tax preparer in a town just north of San Diego.

And so as my dad became ever more obsessed with my mom, Aunt Dot wisely reached into her piggy bank and bought her little sister Vera a one-way bus ticket to Santa Monica to stay with my grandmother. Aunt

Dot had a double motive in sending my mom to California in those early days of 1943. First, my granny's letters back to Texas indicated that she had grown tired of her job as a riveter. California may have looked pretty on a postcard, but Granny was spending her days on all fours, pooled in sweat, crawling inside the nose cones of bomber aircraft, prized by her employers for her tiny size and her muscled arms. But she was thinking of moving back to Arkansas. If she was going to work in a factory, she reasoned, she could always return to the Army munitions plant in North Little Rock, where she had worked long shifts making artillery shells while saving money to head out to California.

By sending my mom to California, Aunt Dot was slowing my granny down, upping her financial ante for a return ticket home by another one-third. Second, and more obviously, Aunt Dot did not want this moon-struck military man who was almost eight years older than her younger sister to mess up Vera's nubile mind. In her seasoned view this braggart of a pilot might simply defile her little sister and then escape, unannounced and unscathed, as he moved off to his next military assignment and a brand-new girlfriend.

But my dad was equally persistent. He was impossibly in love. He wired my mother enough money for a return ticket from Santa Monica to Monahans. And there in the Texas desert, less than three months after she turned eighteen, to the utter chagrin and doomsday predictions of my aunt Dot, he convinced my mom to marry him.

My dad's strongest memory of my mother at that age was not just her violet eyes and dark-haired beauty but his amazement that her years of working in the cotton fields and chopping wood on absentee farms in the middle of the night had given her the arms and shoulders of a boxer and hands whose palms were as rough as the bark of a tree. Throughout her life my mother was a soft-spoken deal maker, inclined to teach and argue through the use of biblical parables, just as she had learned from her beloved father, whose early death had forever scarred her, and just as she would teach her children. But she was also infused with a legendary stubbornness that she inherited from my departed grandfather, that doomed, lame Kentuckian who could quote Shakespeare, argue politics, and dream of diamonds as he broke the clods and tilled the soil of his backyard truck farm.

In my father's eyes this odd combination, along with a physical beauty that was honed and, in his mind, even accentuated by the struggles she had only recently left behind, was fresh and magnetic and overwhelming. Like a real-life Daisy Mae she had stepped out of the cotton fields and strawberry patches of a much harsher world whose tragedies and daily burdens had blunted her temperament and quelled her emotions. But its most immediate impact on this teenage girl was not the lack of a demure coquettishness that otherwise might have defined her had she grown up in better circumstances; it was the visible evidence of the hardship of her journey. This was not a pom-pom-waving homecoming queen or a varsity athlete who had toned her body in a local gym. My mother never complained, but it was her struggles that had visibly shaped her shoulders, grown her biceps, and crusted her palms—while in a less visible way narrowing her view of her own long-term horizons.

Decades later, when I was in my forties, I suppressed a defensive anger as I watched my mother sit quietly in an expansive waterfront Florida living room while a well-bred woman her age described the supposedly difficult impact of the Great Depression on her family. As the woman told it, the crash on Wall Street and the failed economy had made it necessary for them to ship their car by rail from New York to Florida when they headed south for the winter. Who could predict, she reasoned, whether there would be food or gasoline if their driver had to refuel and dine in the remote and hostile environs of small-town Georgia?

My mother merely smiled and nodded, as if in agreement. I myself squinted unbelievingly, waiting for the punch line, unsure if the woman was serious. How could Vera Hodges, child of despair, whose favorite retort to any of her children who complained was "I felt so bad that I had no shoes, 'til I met a man who had no feet," even begin to explain

27

the grinding reality of true poverty? I recognized the smoke that momentarily glazed my mother's eyes, and I watched her file that comment away behind the enigma of her little Mona Lisa smile. She would not respond, but I knew that she would never again trust this woman with a private thought. The Great Depression, what was that? In family conversations my mother would often quip that in East Arkansas they did not even know there had been a Depression. As the old country song put it, when you've got nothing, you've got nothing left to lose, so how could you tell if things went bad?

And here was my dad, sending her a return ticket from Santa Monica to Monahans, swearing his eternal devotion. High school, that hadn't happened. College, what was that? A job in a factory, riveting bolts into the nose cones of bombers? Granny hated every minute of it. A future in a Lake Tahoe casino, or maybe running a penny arcade on the pier at Santa Monica? Aunt Dot hadn't yet pulled that off, and anyway how did you go about chasing those kinds of seemingly impossible dreams? How could she sort her way through their implications, and what was she supposed to trade to get there?

What my mother did know was that in a world where her father and grandfather and closest sister had suddenly died, and where her mother had been forced to leave her behind, this bragging, frustrating, but intrinsically good man really loved her.

I am not sure if there is really anything such as a truly smooth marriage. If there is, my parents did not have one. Their fifty-three years together were an unstoppable, hold-your-hands-over-your-face rollercoaster ride, for them and for us. But from my early childhood to his final days on earth, every time I heard my father tell the story of how immediately he had fallen for my mother when he gave her his seat on a bus in Monahans, Texas, and how he so achingly pursued her, I understood clearly that no matter the battles you may fight along the way, there is truly such a thing as the mystery and power of love.

●   ●   ●

My parents were married in September 1943. Eleven months later, in August 1944, my sister Pat was born. In February 1946 I became their second child. My mother was then twenty. By the time she was twenty-four she had also given birth to my sister Tama Sue and my brother, Gary Lee. My dad was not present for either birth. I was the only child born while he was at home, during the two-year interval when, against his wishes, he had left the military and returned to civilian life.

St. Joseph, Missouri, was a beautiful old town whose population had peaked at 100,000 just after the turn of the century. The launching point for the famed Pony Express, at one time it had been a hub for Conestoga caravans heading westward into Colorado and beyond. It had also been a railroad center where the packinghouses along the river had shipped beef and pork that had been brought in from the nearby farmlands. St. Joe was smaller and quieter in the days following World War II, filled with gentle hills, well-kept parks, and narrow, tree-lined streets. We had warm, thoughtful neighbors who were constantly helpful. One of my daily routines as a small child was to walk unannounced into the house of the Colestocks, who lived next door, and, without even asking, take my nap on their living-room couch. Through much of this time my very young mother was largely alone, in a town she had never even visited until after the war, with a husband who was constantly deployed.

My mom had a rare touch with babies and young children that would continue throughout her life, including when she first became a grandmother at the age of thirty-nine. Loving and filled with song, she was infused with the teaching points that had come from her father's proverbs and parables. And yet in those early years she was really just a kid raising a bunch of kids. In many ways my mom and I grew up together. There were times, even during my childhood, when I would be scolding and didactic with her. Before I turned thirteen she had already nicknamed me "Grandpa." In retrospect, given my mother's own childhood, the postwar life in St. Joe was probably a walk in the park for her. Although my dad was gone, she knew he loved her and that he was coming back. In the meantime we lived in a nice if small house on a quiet street in a well-kept city. We had food, and the rent was paid.

But in retrospect, I'm not sure how we would have survived those years if it had not been for my grandmother. Granny probably needed us as much as we needed her, but if there is such a thing on earth, Georgia Frankie Doyle became our savior.

There is no way to explain how much I loved my grandmother and what an impact she had on my young life. Some evenings in our house at St. Joseph as a very little boy I would simply lie next to her on the hard-wood floor as if I were a puppy, hugging her ankles and kissing her feet while she ironed clothes. Granny's favorite passage from the Bible in fact defined her. As Paul wrote in his letter to the Romans, "We rejoice in our sufferings, knowing that suffering produces endurance, and endurance produces character, and character produces hope, and hope does not disappoint us, because God's love has been poured into our hearts."

Just short of five feet tall, with bulging arms like Popeye's from her own years in the cotton fields and then in the military factories, Granny was the embodiment of sheer toughness. If Aunt Dot was shrewd and knowing, Granny was imbued with a steady, quiet invincibility. If she was angry she could scare your socks off without even raising her voice. But if you were scared, she would nestle you up against her and calm you down, talking away the demons in her slow, slow Arkansas drawl. Granny's bright blue eyes held a magic power, at least for me, as she stared out toward a dark unknown into a place where you somehow knew she had already been and where she would not let them take you. I could always sense with certainty that she had fought those demons before, and had beaten them, and that if I only had the courage to be unafraid, I could beat them too.

In the southern oral tradition, Granny was a natural storyteller. Every night before we went to sleep she laid our family history out before us, one long-remembered tale at a time. Listening every night, constantly asking questions, I learned about the great Scots-Irish migration down the Appalachian Mountains from Pennsylvania through Southwest Virginia and into the midlands of North Carolina, Kentucky, and Tennessee. The covered-wagon journeys, the marriages and births and deaths, the wartime enlistments and the historic battles fought, all came alive from the recesses of her memory, just as they had come from her mother and her mother's mother before her, with precise dates and specific places that I would later verify in writing to have been exact.

Her stories about her childhood made me feel as if I myself had lived it. Her mother had been the only person in the family other than my great-great-grandfather Samuel Jasper Marsh to survive a cholera epidemic that hit the Memphis area in 1873, just after the Civil War. As a small child Granny had journeyed along with nearly a dozen siblings in a covered wagon from Tipton County, Tennessee, down into Tippah County, Mississippi, then crossed the Mississippi River on a barge into the swamplands of East Arkansas. She had walked in the muddy ruts behind the wagon as the men dropped small trees and saplings in order to make "corduroy roads" that would hold the weight of the wagons as they pitched and yawed through the snake-infested swamplands. At the end of those wanderings she had grown up in the remote, panther-ridden farmlands of White County.

Granny's later journey from Arkansas to California had been driven by more than the family tragedy of poverty and widowhood. Indeed the decades before and during World War II saw a migratory explosion of a scarred but stubborn people. The United States prides itself on being a nation of immigrants, but sometimes we forget that there are many ways to become an immigrant, and in that respect the internal migration out of the severe hardship and regional isolation of the South is perhaps the most misunderstood movement of people in American history. The novelist John Steinbeck brought the world a microcosm of this journey in his masterpiece, *The Grapes of Wrath*, following the Joads, an "Okie" family, out of Dust Bowl Oklahoma to the discrimination that faced them in some areas of postcard-pretty California. Even today, when people

think about this migration—which is seldom—many tend to character-
ize it as simply the Dust Bowl journey, brought on by a drought that hit
some areas of the mid-South particularly hard. But make no mistake,
it was not just the dust that set so many people into motion during the
early decades of the twentieth century, some of them up north to places
like Chicago and Detroit and others out west to the Promised Land of
California. There was no dust in East Arkansas; there was only Mississippi Delta mud. Nor, by the way, was it the dust that caused the people
of my father's family to pour westward out of the hollows and the un-
tamed ridges of the Appalachian Mountains.

Even today, driving west from Memphis up toward White County,
Arkansas, where Granny's family settled and where my mother was born,
one can see the mud and remember its long-ago seduction and what had
once been its economic power. Black gold, at least for the people who
owned the thousand-acre farms and at one time the slaves, a rich soil
that lured settlers from across Big Muddy, the mighty Mississippi River,
and in time produced wide, unending fields filled with thick stands of
cotton. On some summer mornings as you drive past or walk along the
fields the Mississippi Delta's mud seems almost to boil from the heat, the
humid soil and lush undergrowth cooking up into the air until a low, thin
mist lies like smoke above the land as far as the eye can see. And every
now and then, where the thick stands of trees rise up at the edges of the
swamps and meet the wide, rich fields, the boiling earth spits out a long,
fat rattlesnake or maybe an irritated water moccasin.

No, it was not just the dust that put these people into motion, black
and white alike, as they pushed northward and westward from the
hamlets and the mountains and the cotton fields. Nor was it simply the
economics of the Great Depression, whose impact had actually been felt
much more strongly in the northern factory regions than in the already
struggling small farms of the South. It was the painful, life-squelching
poverty that had choked off the South and punished its people for more
than seven decades since the end of the Civil War.

Yes, the South had fought and lost the Civil War. And for that fight and because of that loss, the entire region had richly paid, in a way that modern America no longer understands or even dares to teach in its hypersensitive, politically correct academic classrooms. Slavery had ended, although its pervasiveness among the white population of the antebellum South is now wildly exaggerated in our classrooms and films. John Hope Franklin, perhaps our country's most eminent African American historian, wrote pointedly many years ago that only 5 percent of the whites in the South had actually owned slaves, and less than 25 percent had benefited economically from the slave system. The Union had been preserved, but in the war almost one of every three adult white males in the South had died, including two of my own ancestors. In its aftermath the region had become destitute, angry, and alienated from the rest of the United States.

This observation is not a political rant or a fantasy dreamed up in order to advance fictional theories based on the supposed grandeur of the antebellum, *Gone With the Wind* years of plantations and slavery. Nor does it seek to minimize the cruel, vindictive Jim Crow society that grew out of the Union's military occupation just after the Civil War and the Reconstruction era that followed. The retaliatory Jim Crow policies of segregation lasted for decades, into my own childhood. I saw their denigrations and humiliations with my own young eyes. But what we have forgotten over the years is that the South was, and always had been, not simply white against black but a three-tiered system. In many ways that system was consciously designed to pit poor white against poor black, while the false aristocracy of the plantation owners, and later the country-club elites, preserved their social and economic dominance.

Behind those policies was always a simple, though often delicately ignored truth, even among struggling whites who were always mindful that the elites at the very top could in a heartbeat shut down their little tenant farms and send them spiraling down even further into abject and humiliating poverty. The truth was this: when it came to poverty, the average white farm worker in the South had it little better than his black counterpart. And in the end the only true option of either was often to accept this reality or leave the region.

Nowhere has the stark hopelessness of the conditions that caused the mass migration out of the South during those years been so carefully and concisely documented as in a thorough and largely forgotten report issued by President Franklin D. Roosevelt during the very period that saw the tragic destruction of my mother's nuclear family and my widowed granny's decision to try her luck in California. I cannot summarize this report or the situation that spawned it any more accurately than I did in my 2004 book *Born Fighting*:

> The years since 1865 had brought such deep and enduring fault lines that the entire South had become the North American equivalent of a Banana Republic, replete with colonialism from the outside and abuse by a thin patrician class from within. This disparity became ever clearer during Franklin Roosevelt's presidency, and as the innovative Democrat reached the midpoint of his second term he asked the National Emergency Council to report to him on the economic conditions of the South. In his letter of transmission Roosevelt stated his conviction that "the South presents right now the Nation's No. 1 economic problem—the Nation's problem, not merely the South's," and wrote bluntly of "the long and ironic history of the despoiling of this truly American section of the country's population."
>
> On July 25, 1938, the National Emergency Council reported its findings to the President. The document issued by the Council is one of the most telling—and damning—pieces of evidence ever assembled in illustrating the impact of the long decades of rapacious abuse of the region following the Civil War. Chapter by chapter, issue by issue, the Report to the President unmasked the long-term damage caused by the policies of exploitation and retribution that had begun during Reconstruction, coupled with the failure of the South's old aristocracy

to adapt to modern ways. But the heaviest blame clearly lay with the outside forces that had bought up and effectively colonized the region during the turbulent years after the War.

The Report's factual conclusions, while stunning, were no surprise to any thinking Southerner, and in some measure validated much of the resentment expressed toward the Yankee and his minions. On the evidence, the South had clearly become an owned place. As the report mentioned, "The public utilities in the South are almost completely controlled by outside interests. All the major railroad systems are owned and controlled elsewhere. Most of the great electric holding company systems . . . are directed, managed and owned by outside interests. Likewise, the transmission and distribution of natural gas, one of the South's great assets, is almost completely in the hands of remote financial institutions. The richest deposits of the iron ore, coal, and limestone . . . are owned or controlled outside the region. . . . Most of the rich deposits of bauxite, from which aluminum is made, are owned or controlled outside the region. Practically all important deposits of zinc ore in the South are owned elsewhere. . . . Over 99 percent of the sulphur produced in the United States comes from Texas and Louisiana. Two extraction companies control the entire output. Both are owned and controlled outside the South."

And there was more. "For mining its mineral wealth and shipping it away . . . the South frequently receives nothing but the low wages of unskilled and semiskilled labor. . . . On the one hand, it is possible for a monopolistic corporation in another region of the country to purchase and leave unused resources in the South which otherwise might be developed in competition with the monopoly. On the other hand, the large absentee ownership of the South's natural resources and the South's industry makes it possible to influence greatly the manner in which the South is developed and to subordinate that development to other interests outside the South."

Additionally, in policies reminiscent of issues that John C.

Calhoun had so vigorously debated a century before, both tariff rates and domestic charges for the use of railroad freight blatantly discriminated against the South, impeding its ability to grow and compete. The rates charged for shipping goods along the nation's railways had for decades been rigged to protect northern markets from southern goods. . . .

In short, as John C. Calhoun had warned during the debate over tariffs in 1832—a prediction that was lost in the larger debate over slavery—the South had become an economic colony of the North. Further, the years since the Civil War had in many ways legitimized this colonization, tinting it with an odd morality that flowed from the Republican Party's "rescue" of the region from slavery. As historian Arthur M. Schlesinger pointed out, "the technique of 'waving the bloody shirt'—that is, of freeing the slaves again every fourth year—enabled the Republicans long to submerge the fact that they were becoming the party of monopoly and wealth." The South's resources were being plundered and shipped north. Its citizens were reduced to the status of wage laborers. The profits from these enterprises accrued to northern corporations, where the infrastructure continued to improve both through the direct advantages of individual wealth that went into such things as luxury spending and bank deposits, and indirectly through the larger tax base that allowed better roads, schools, libraries and social services.

How bad was this drain?

In 1937 the thirteen Southern states had 36 million people, of whom 97.8 percent were native born—an important statistic, meaning both that the Scots-Irish culture remained predominant among average whites and that none of the South's economic deficiencies were due to assimilating new immigrants from poorer nations. With 28 percent of the country's population, it had, in the words of the Report, "only 16 percent of the tangible assets, including factories, machines, and the tools with which people make a living. With more than half

the country's farmers, the South has less than a fifth of the farm imple-
ments. . . . In 1930 there were nearly twice as many southern farms
less than 20 acres in size as in 1880."

Of vital importance, the educational base of the South had been
decimated. Illiteracy in the South was almost five times as high as in
the North Central states and more than double the rate in New England and the Middle Atlantic states, despite the recent European
immigration into those areas. In addition—and tellingly—"The total
endowments of [all] the colleges and universities of the South are less
than the combined endowments of Harvard and Yale [alone]. . . . The
South must educate one-third of the Nation's children with one-sixth
of the Nation's school revenues. . . . In 1936 the Southern States spent
an average of $25.11 per child in schools, or about half the average for
the country as a whole. . . . At the same time the average school child
enrolled in New York State had $141.43 spent on his education."

If there was little money for public education there was none for
much else beyond subsistence, either, and in some cases money had
actually disappeared as a medium of exchange. The richest State in
the South ranked lower in per capita income than the poorest State
outside the region. In 1937 the average income in the South was
only $314, while the rest of the country averaged $604, nearly twice
as much, even in the middle of a Depression. An actual majority of
the farmers in the South did not own their own land, instead having
to operate as tenant farmers or sharecroppers. Tenant farmers averaged $73 for a year's work; sharecroppers varied from $38—a dime a
day—to $87, depending on the State. While few black families were
on the high end of the economic scale, it would be wrong to assume,
as so many social scientists of today immediately do, that they alone
dominated the low end. As the Report mentioned, "Whites and
Negroes have suffered alike. Of the 1,831,000 tenant families in the
region, about 66 percent are white [the South's population at this time
was 71 percent white]. Approximately half of the sharecroppers are

white, living under conditions almost identical with those of Negro sharecroppers."

Tenant farming and sharecropping had evolved from two post–Civil War realities. The first was that many large plantation owners were left with "plenty of land but no capital or labor to work it. Hundreds of thousands of former slaves and impoverished whites were willing to work but had no land. The result was the crop-sharing system, under which the land was worked by men who paid for the privilege with a share of their harvest." The second was the prevalence throughout the South of large tracts of land owned by absentee landlords, some of them from wealthier families that had moved away and others owned by speculators from outside the region. Farmers who lacked the capital to buy their own land "leased" these properties, again usually paying with a percentage of their harvest.

These practices fell even harder on tenant farmers and sharecroppers due to the fragility of the Southern banking system. As the Report indicated, "the majority of Southern tenant farmers must depend for credit on their landlords or the 'furnish merchant' who supplies seed, food, and fertilizer. Their advances have largely replaced currency for a considerable part of the rural population. For security the landlord or merchant takes a lien on the entire crop, which is turned over to him immediately after harvest in settlement of the debt. Usually he keeps the books and fixes the interest rate. Even if he is fair and does not charge excessive interest, the tenants often find themselves in debt at the end of the year."

"Even if he is fair" was a very delicate phrase to be put into a report to the President of the United States. And those words were no doubt carefully chosen, for fairness was not a hallmark of this system.

In a nutshell, over the decades the national policies of the Republicans had raped the region, while the actions of many state and local Democrats too often were designed to preserve the assets of a select few at the expense of just about everyone else. Thus, tenant farmers and sharecroppers, white and black alike—and this means the majority of the farmers in the South at that time—found themselves to be manipulated and powerless, living under a form of "double colonialism." First, the entire region had been colonized from the outside, impoverishing basic infrastructure such as schools and roads while the banking system and corporate ownership sent revenues from Southern labor to the communities of the north. And second, in many local areas they and their fellow farmers had become little better than serfs, laboring without hard cash inside a myriad of petty fiefdoms where the local banker or general store owner would supply "seed, food and fertilizer" so that they could grow a crop, harvest it, and turn it over to the man who had given them seed and food, in order to live in debt for yet another year.

And so the working people and the small-scale farmers, white and black alike, had in droves left their homes and their accumulated history behind. They were even poorer and less educated than their counterparts who had been pouring in from Europe over the past few decades to settle in the urban slums and factory towns of the North. Lacking other choices in the region of their birth, they had abandoned the small farms and the haphazard communities that their ancestors had so agonizingly carved out of the wilderness at the end of the rut-filled roads left by their Conestoga wagons, in many cases leaving only untended graveyards behind. They went north, to the factories that made the cars and tempered the steel. They went west, to the assembly plants and shipyards and orchards near the palm-lined dreamy beaches of the California coast. And some of them, like my granny, later circled back, ending up in places like 3137 Felix Street, St. Joseph, Missouri, if for no other reason than to take care of a daughter who had borne four children by the age of twenty-four and whose husband was deployed overseas again and again, separated from his family as he sought to do his part in defending the security of the United States of America.

• • •

My granny was the epitome of a pioneer woman, her skills shaped mother to daughter by generations in the wilderness. She knew how to save things and how to make them last. When cooking dumplings she could measure out *exactly* a cup of flour using just a spoon. She was an expert at cutting pieces from a worn set of clothes in order to keep them for a quilt or to make knee patches for an almost-worn pair of pants that had been passed down from an older cousin, and that still fit you. An excellent seamstress, she measured, cut, and hand-sewed my very first suit—a thin-striped brown seersucker for Easter when I was five years old. I have no doubt that if I had given her a rifle, at least during my childhood, she could immediately have outshot me and then taught me how to get a better sight picture while I was aiming at my target. And she could get more enjoyment and utility out of one cigarette—indeed a half-cigarette—than anyone I have ever met.

On special days in St. Joseph she and my mother and my aunt Carolyn would take us downtown on the bus to walk among the shops and to get a cherry Coke at the counter of the Katz Drug Store. It was poetry or at least clockwork to watch Granny fuss with her purse as the bus slowly made its way back toward our house. At the top of a hill where Noyes Boulevard intersected with Felix Street, Granny would reach above her head to pull the lanyard, buzzing the driver to let him know she wanted to get off at the next stop. Then as she rose from her seat she would reach inside her purse and pull out her ever-present pack of unfiltered Lucky Strikes. As the bus came to a halt she would already have expertly broken one of her precious smokes into a half that couldn't have been more exact if she had measured it on a cutting board. And then making her way down the narrow aisle, Granny would mechanically put the smooth end of the cigarette between her lips, slipping the other half back into the pack, and inserting the pack itself back inside her purse.

The bus would stop. The accordion-like door would unfold. And by the time her tiny, leathered feet had stepped down from the bus onto the sidewalk, Granny would have struck a match and lit her smoke.

This was all done with deliberate precision. It was only a block or so from the bus stop down the hill to our little house at 3137 Felix Street, but Granny had measured every step and had figured out how much tobacco she could inhale along the way. In my little boy's mind, whether I was traipsing behind her from the bus or watching her approach while waiting on the front-door step, this counted up to be about four deep drags on half of a Lucky Strike, with three or four steps left over for her to flick the half-inch cigarette butt past the honeysuckle vines near the curb, all the way into the street itself.

In these modern times we all appreciate or at least understand the evils of tobacco use, but in those long-ago days a cigarette was something of a luxury. For my granny this pre-rolled bit of Lucky Strike nicotine (and it was always Lucky Strikes, never a Camel or a Chesterfield) was far removed from the hot Arkansas evenings when she and my grandfather would sit on their front porch and dip snuff from the same tin as they watched the sun go down in the western sky. Perhaps that magical half-smoke even reminded her of the lost horizons they had stared at during those cricket-loud swampy evenings, toward a yet unseen place where she would someday journey in order to work in the aircraft factories of California.

Waste not, want not. Despite overwhelming challenges my granny lived a life measured by the very definition of frugality and precision. We needed that certainty and her quiet strength during the long years when my dad was continually deployed and so intermittently at home. I missed him all the time, and even when he was at home I knew that he would soon be leaving again.

I was three years old during one of these cycles, when my father came home for a brief leave and then was ordered to return overseas. He had been flying in the Berlin Airlift and was going back to Germany. By then he had already been deployed for more than half my life. After he left this time, Granny tried to reassure me that he would return home again in the fall, at least for a while. I did not understand what the fall was. She told me that it would probably be seven months or so. But I did not know what a month was.

Finally Granny took me into the narrow, leafy backyard and marked a spot in the grass. "When the weather gets warmer, we are going to dig up the grass and plant four rows of corn right here," she said. "Every day we are going to come out and check it and water it and take care of it. First you are going to see little shoots, like blades of grass. Then the blades of grass are going to grow their way into cornstalks. When the cornstalks grow higher than your head, they are going to sprout tassels at the top. And along those stalks there are going to be ears of corn. When the corn grows ripe, the tassels are going to go brown and the ears of corn are going to swell up. Pretty soon after that we're going to pick those ears, and we're going to eat that corn. And after we eat the corn, your daddy is going to come home."

Granny was a child-rearing genius. How else could she have so clearly understood and translated such a complex intermingling of emotions and definitions of time to a scared and anguished little kid?

I couldn't wait to grow that corn and eat it. Every morning we would have our breakfast in the tiny makeshift porch just off our kitchen that overlooked the backyard, and after that Granny and I would climb down the rickety wooden steps and go out back to check the corn. We watered it religiously as the little shoots broke through the soil. We urged it on during the long hot months of summer as the stalks thickened and grew far higher than my head. We pulled the corn ears in the early fall, shucking them and boiling them and eating them, just before my baby brother was born, a month premature due to an accident that almost killed my mother.

And after the corn was eaten my baby brother, Gary Lee Webb, was born. My mother went into and came out of the hospital. And finally my father did come home.

In the long nights between his latest leaving and his return I went to bed clutching a picture that had been sent from Germany, an official Air Force photo that showed my dad standing at attention in his military uniform on a runway next to his top sergeant as they answered questions from a visiting two-star general. When the picture arrived in the mail my mother excitedly explained it to me, although my first reaction was to wonder why my father's hands were balled into fists. Was he going to hit this man? My mother reassured me that Dad was not angry, that this was what soldiers called the position of attention, and when they met with senior officers, this was how they stood. And from that point on, I did so as well, every chance I got.

I still keep that picture of my dad framed above my desk, along with one of my grandfather Birch Hays Hodges, gaunt and sun-blistered in his work boots in East Arkansas just before he died. In years past, whenever I began to question the tedium and frustrations of public service, the calm stare of my dad in uniform on the tarmac in Germany and the bitter, abandoned grimace of my grandpa Hodges kept my motivations firmly in check.

Excitement in our little women-filled house grew daily as the time for my father to return drew near. My sister Pat and I discussed how we were going to welcome him. Aunt Carolyn and my mother suggested that we might entertain him with an improvised stage play. I would ride on my sister's back as if she were a bucking bronco. We would say some comical lines, which I have long forgotten. Then, seeing my dad, I would fall off the horse in mock surprise. And we would all run together and embrace, as if it were Christmas and my father were a suddenly discovered Santa Claus.

The day came. The hour approached. Somehow my mother knew the approximate time; I do not remember how or why. We waited in our small living room next to the hallway that went to the front door. Finally the doorbell rang. Mom, Pat, and I rushed forward joyously, Granny and Aunt Carolyn behind us, my younger sister Tama somewhere in the background, not yet two, and my just-born brother probably in a crib.

The door opened. My father filled it, dressed in his uniform and his garrison cap, a bulging B-4 military suitcase at his side.

Through the mists and memories of all the years I can still see him standing there in the doorway like a giant cardboard silhouette, the bright light of the afternoon sun at his back, making his image even more powerful and boldly mysterious. He called my name, his voice as always loud, brash, and tough. But under the force of his sudden presence and his booming baritone I could not respond.

I choked.

Looking back, I guess I simply could not bear the happiness. I had missed him so achingly and for so long that I could not process the reality that he had returned, even to run forward and embrace him or to speak. I do not know precisely why, but perhaps it was because I had already learned even at that young age that these moments of exuberance were always temporary, coupled as they were with the reality that he would soon go away yet again. And so his coming, in my little boy's mind, served as an instant reminder that before long he was going to leave.

I ran away, into the dining room, and hid underneath the table. He dropped his suitcase, walking toward me and calling my name again. As he approached I found myself sobbing uncontrollably, unable to speak or move. Finally he crawled underneath the table, grabbing me and holding me. He was a giant to a little kid, both figuratively and literally. The man who flew the cargo planes to help people in a faraway place as we waited in our little house on Felix Street; the man whose picture I had carried with me as I went to bed, practicing how to clench my fists and stand at attention; the man for whom Granny and I had planted and grown and eaten the corn.

"You can't go away again," I finally managed to say.

He gave me a reassuring hug. "Any time that phone rings, you and I are just going to hide underneath this table so they won't find us," he said.

And so from that point forward, whenever the phone rang my dad and I would run together, laughing and scrambling, and hide underneath the dining room table while my mother took the call.

This approach was fun. And it worked fine, for about three weeks.

The months moved forward. The basing structure of the cold war military was catching up with its new, permanent size and its family-heavy makeup. Military housing was being built across the country. Old barracks and wartime hospitals were being transformed into schools. Finally it was we who made the 380-mile journey down the narrow two-lane roads from St. Joseph, Missouri, to Scott Air Force Base in Illinois. We were leaving St. Joe behind and would finally live full-time with my father.

Chapter Three

LIFE WITH FATHER

"Are you tough?"

"Yes, Daddy, I'm tough."

"Then hit my fist."

Sitting comfortably on the couch, my dad held his huge fist in front of me. I wound up my arms like a baseball pitcher and hit the fist, knuckle to knuckle, as hard as I could. But, as Sancho Panza so memorably put it during a monologue in *Man of La Mancha*, whether the stone hits the jar or the jar hits the stone, it's always bad news for the jar.

My hand crumpled. I winced, holding it against my chest.

"Did it hurt?"

"No, it didn't hurt."

"Then hit it again."

I wound up and hit it again. Same result, although now I was fighting back tears.

"Did it hurt?"

"Yeah, Daddy. It hurt."

"Then you're not tough."

"I am tough."

"Then hit it again."

He laughed as I wound up and whacked his fist one more time. I was now moaning uncontrollably. I nursed my hand, grimacing and shaking my head, secretly wishing that he would just go back to Germany and save some more of those people with another airlift.

"Come on, hit it!"

"I don't need to hit it again."

"Don't talk back to me. Hit it again."

I looked at him, my fist throbbing and my lips growing tight, delivering a judgment that he would tease me about for decades to come.

"I don't need to hit it. And I just don't like you anymore."

"Well, I didn't ask you if you liked me. Hit it!"

So began my sessions with The Fist. Whenever he demanded it, I would hit it. And it would hurt. And he would laugh some more. And some days I would wish that whatever he was doing here in Illinois or anywhere else, maybe I could just go back to St. Joe. And to hell with Granny's corn.

But in my heart I knew that my dad loved me. He took me fishing and taught me how to bait-cast. He took me deep into the woods to pick walnuts for my mother. In the woods he taught me how to make a small "Indian campfire" and how to lay and follow a pioneer trail. He took me hunting when he shot red squirrels, calling on me to be his retriever, running among the trees and putting the dead squirrels into a bag so that we could bring them home, where he would skin them and have my mother cook them. He bought me two sets of boxing gloves when I turned six, teaching me how to keep my hands just underneath my chin and how to throw a straight, hard punch.

And he was frequently funny, in his impetuous and taunting way. One day he bought us a fishbowl full of guppies. A week later I

47

accidentally poured the guppies down the drain while changing their water. He immediately poured a measure of their food into the sink, saying that wherever the drain might take them, at least they needed to have a meal along the way.

In fact, there was even a bittersweet irony in the story of the Fist. When my dad reached the far side of sixty, on the annual fishing trips that we would take to remote cabins in the lake country of Minnesota, I would greet him in the morning with a smile and a balled-up hand, now thicker than his own: "Come on, Old Man. Hit my fist!"

"I don't need to do that." He'd grin. "Just remember, I was hard, but I was never cruel."

But in those early days in Illinois, my dad was in a hurry. He was making up for the time we'd lost to his deployments, and he was teaching me his version of what it took to be a man. When he would leave the house to go to the airfield and fly the cargo planes to wherever they flew in that day and age, he always left me with an order: "You are the man of the house. Take care of your mother." His worries and the way he went about my early training might sound harsh or sexist in these kinder and gentler days, but his own life had taught him that as I grew older I would be measured by the timeless standards of whether or not I could meet the demands of manhood.

So somewhere in the middle of all this fist-hitting and butt-spanking and despite my periodic resentment, there was a teaching lesson, although I'm not sure that Dr. Spock would have approved of the methodology. Nor at the ages of five or six or seven did I appreciate having to face The Fist or to endure the sometimes taunting laughs. As the *I'm OK, You're OK* self-help books might put it, there was a relational transition going on here. To put it delicately, after years of knowing my dad mainly as a mythical, iconic figure whose intermittent presence in our home was filled with the intense emotion of always preparing ourselves to say good-bye, we were now, as the psychologists like to say, having ourselves a journey. And as we got to know each other on a daily basis, sometimes the challenge of living with my dad, particularly at the beginning, was a lot harder than it had been to miss him when he was gone.

Typical of my father, during our three years at Scott Air Force Base we lived in three different houses, although most of our time was spent in a new military apartment complex known as Paeglow Housing. Typical of my mother, Granny lived with us for much of that time, and Aunt Carolyn for an early part of it, before we deployed to England in 1954.

Upon arriving at Scott Air Force Base we first lived in a small rented home in the nearby town of Belleville. After a brief waiting period we moved into one of the first units that had become available in Paeglow. Hapless and unembellished, Paeglow was nonetheless one of the first attempts by the postwar military leadership to provide the infrastructure necessary to support the new concept of a large, peacetime standing army. The drab complex of white-fronted apartment units was built on a flat, treeless expanse of former farmland. There were no shops or malls around it, save for a small gas station nestled into the corner of a cornfield.

But few families who lived there complained of its starkness or its lack of amenities. For the wives and children who had endured long separations, Paeglow was a hopeful signal of things to come. Indeed Paeglow would be followed nationwide by a series of more modern and attractive apartments called Wherry Housing. A few years after that came the unimagined luxury of Capehart Housing, whole neighborhoods of single- or dual-unit structures that boasted their own yards, driveways, dishwashers, and often their own garages. We knew very little of this at the time, of course, nor did it matter. After years of separation Paeglow was a blessing.

The Paeglow project was still under construction when we moved into our unit. Eventually it would consist of ten identical eight-unit tenements, separated by small fields and connected by narrow roads, all of them constructed just outside the main gate of the base. Paeglow, carved out of farmland, was surrounded by endless acres of cornfields. Our unit, the fifth apartment in the building, was officially designated Quarters 1404-E. Since there were four children in our family, under military regulations my father was allotted three bedrooms. For us that meant one bedroom for my parents, one for Granny and Aunt Carolyn until she departed for California at age seventeen, and one for the four children: my two sisters, my brother, and me.

Our small bedroom was just that: a room full of beds with a couple of chests of drawers along one wall. Pat slept on an army cot in the middle of the room. Tama Sue slept on a small single bed along one wall, underneath the window. Gary and I shared a thin mattress on a trundle bed just inside the door. At night, even in the dead of winter, Granny opened up the window when she told us our bedtime story. No matter how hot or cold it got, she explained, we needed to breathe the clean air from the nearby farmland or risk being sent to live inside oxygen tents in the deserts of Arizona in order to purge tuberculosis or mildew from our lungs. She kept us from leaving our beds at night by warning us that huge nests of poisonous snakes magically appeared underneath them as soon as she left the room, only to be chased away by the first grey slivers of dawn.

I began kindergarten in a makeshift school at the center of the base that had been converted from an old building called the Fourth District Barracks. As he would do with almost every school until I reached the sixth grade—which would be a lot of schools—my dad escorted me to my first day of class. I can still remember the soft fabric of his blue woolen Air Force overcoat as it brushed against my face and how tightly I clutched his hand—yes, the same hand whose fist I had so repeatedly crumpled my own fist against as he sought to teach me some unexplainable lesson or another—while we walked the hallways toward the classroom. The wide spaces of the old troop barracks had been sectioned off by room dividers, turning them into multiple classrooms. As we walked I could see the lights above and below the makeshift walls and could hear the noise of schoolkids on the other side. I was scared. How ironic it is, in retrospect, that my young years were filled with continuous family dislocation but that in my entire life I had never spent any time away from the warm cocoon of someone in my family—my mother, Aunt Carolyn, Granny, or my father—for any long period of time.

Inside the classroom my father walked me to the teacher's desk, then turned to me to say good-bye. I held tightly to his hand, not wanting him to leave. He pointed to a little girl in a wheelchair, sitting alone in one corner of the room. It was my friend Mary Ellen, a polio victim who lived in the next unit over from us in Paeglow. I ran happily to play with her and forgot about my father, who quickly disappeared. He had done his fatherly duty; now there was a country that he had to save. And for me, school was no longer a frightening unknown. Throughout my adult life, I have always made a point of taking every one of my children to their very first day of school.

At home, daily life in Paeglow had a special drama all its own. Dad and Granny, both strong, authoritative figures, engaged in a continuous battle over who was Top Dog. Over the years when my father had so frequently been away they had tolerated each other, but now they were like two scorpions in a jar. Granny had her way of doing things, and Dad had his. My mom, like us kids, tended to get out of the way, usually finding a dish to clean or a floor to mop when their stingers came out.

Whatever the meal, my dad would demand that we kids eat everything on our plates. Refusal brought reprisal and sometimes physical intimidation, to the loud objections of Granny. This running battle between the two sometimes reached an unintended, comedic extreme. My sister Pat simply did not like squash or mashed potatoes, two of our daily staples. With a wink from Granny, Pat would secretly scoop her portions from her plate and smash them onto the underside of the table when my father's attention was distracted. And after he excused himself from the dinner table, Granny would scrape those globs onto a plate and quickly dump them into the trash can.

In a way, Granny was protecting Pat from my dad's unnecessary wrath. At the same time she was also encouraging our continuing rebellions. But I knew that it did not pay to rebel against my dad on something as irrelevant as a plate of food. He had the size, the intellectual power, the belt if he needed it, and the final word at home.

I did not like tomato juice, especially the flat, metallic taste that came from canned fruit juice. One Saturday afternoon as we stood at the kitchen counter, Dad poured a glassful of it from a half-gallon can and ordered me to drink it. When I declined he then repeated the order—*seriously*. At that point, whether or not I liked tomato juice had ceased to be the issue; the prospect of disobedience had suddenly overwhelmed the epicurean merits of canned tomato juice. Knowing the consequences of refusing an order from the man whose life revolved around such things as immediate obedience, I picked up my glass and quickly drank it down.

"Did you like it?"

This of course brought back visions of my never-ending bouts with The Fist. "Yeah, Dad. I liked it."

"Then have another one."

Six glasses later, the half-gallon can was empty. Not incidentally, the Old Man had come upon a parable that he would use to teach a sort of *Green Eggs and Ham* lesson about children overcoming their unfounded predispositions after they had been encouraged to experiment. "I once knew a little boy who didn't like tomato juice," he would begin time after time. "And then when he tried a glass, he liked it so much that he drank seven glasses in a row."

"No." I finally convinced him many years later. "Dad, I never liked tomato juice. But drinking it was less of a hassle than getting my ass whipped."

On Saturday mornings we would have military-style room inspections, standing at parade rest in front of our chests of drawers, our bedroom so filled with beds that it was difficult to maneuver around them, much less create a semblance of military order. When my dad walked into the room we were supposed to snap into the position of attention and report the room ready for inspection. Sometimes, not ready for the drill, my socks not yet rolled or my underwear not yet folded in the drawer, I would begin to argue as he walked into the room.

"Dad—"

"Come to attention when you talk to me," he would say officiously, checking out the arrangement of socks and underwear in my dresser drawer. "And don't call me Dad. I'm Captain Webb. And you're a corporal."

Kids were everywhere at Paeglow. You could not walk out of your front door or into the open spaces of the playing areas out back between our eight-unit building and the next one over without bumping into a crowd. The Baby Boom had struck, especially among the returning veterans, many of whom had lost years of family life to World War II and subsequent deployments.

My dad was an electronics whiz, having been a ham radio operator in his youth and spending his nonmilitary years as a trained electrician. Our cluttered living room was constantly filled with the latest versions of Hallicrafters radio sets, short-wave radios, telegraph keyboards for sending messages in Morse code, and decades-old 78 rpm phonograph records. Ever the innovator, my dad bought, assembled, and installed a tiny television set, making us the first unit in our Paeglow area to have one.

Almost every afternoon after that my mother would open up the back door and yell into the area behind our tenement, "Hey, kids, what time is it?" In minutes our living room was crowded with neighborhood kids who came to watch that day's action on the famed and emblematic *Howdy Doody Show*.

It's Howdy Doody Time . . .

One of our favorite characters on *Howdy Doody* was a lovely American Indian girl named Princess Summerfall Winterspring. My dad pointed out that she was a TV version of my mother, since we four kids were each born in a different season: Pat was born in summer; Gary was born in fall; I was born in winter; and Tama Sue was born in spring. And so as we watched Buffalo Bob, Howdy Doody, and Clarabell the Clown, our mother was also represented on the screen, a more beautiful, real-life version of Princess Summerfall Winterspring.

To state the obvious, beyond these family jokes and tribulations my father was engaged in a very serious profession, and our country was now involved in yet another war. In June 1950, when I was four years old, the North Korean army attacked across the 38th parallel, vowing to unify a divided Korea. Thus, completely unexpectedly, began the carnage of the Korean War. Our peace-softened troops in Korea as well as the reinforcements shipped in from comfortable occupation duty in Japan were brutally routed in the initial invasion. Whole units crumbled from North Korean assaults. Fighting was intense, and medical care was scarce. During the first month of the Korean War as many American soldiers died as were wounded, the highest killed-to-wounded ratio in our military since the Civil War. (Eventually the ratio was four wounded for every one killed.) The Americans retreated in confusion and panic, pushed by the North Korean offensive all the way to the southern tip of Korea in what became known as the Pusan Perimeter.

In September of that year General Douglas MacArthur had taken the breathtaking risk of landing the First Marine Division halfway up the Korean Peninsula at Inchon, well behind North Korean lines. The Marines, many of them battle-hardened veterans of World War II called up on short notice after their return to civilian life, had responded brilliantly, crossing an almost impossible, tide-driven beachhead and pushing inland. Within days they had cut off the North Korean Army's logistical lines in the north from its combat units in the south, completely stopping the momentum of their invasion. Joined on their western flank by reinforcements from the Army, they then turned north in a counterinvasion of North Korea. By December, as the American military's pivot northward approached the Chinese border, the Chinese Army had crossed the Yalu River and expanded both the scope and the international consequences of the conflict.

The war would continue to ebb and flow until the middle of 1953, its impact never far away from the lives that we and the other families were leading at Scott Air Force Base.

Aside from its other strategic and tactical dimensions, for the Air Force and for people such as my father and our friends and neighbors in the Paeglow Housing project, the Korean War introduced a totally new concept: never before in history had piloted jet aircraft been deployed to a battlefield. The bombers that my father had flown during World War II and in places such as the remote borderland regions in Alaska would continue to be important, but they were not game-changers in the tactical challenges of limited warfare such as in Korea. The cargo planes that he had flown in the Berlin Airlift and now from the airfields of Scott Air Force Base would remain a key element of logistical operations throughout the world but would not play a dominant role in the day-to-day encounters on the fluctuating, ground-centered battlefield. Helicopter doctrine also was evolving, although its greatest impact would come later, in the rice paddies, jungles, and mountains of Vietnam.

In Korea the greatest challenge for the most highly skilled pilots in the Air Force was to fly the jet. Unlike in World War II, when the bomber pilots took the highest casualties and received the most admiring adulation, during Korea flying the jet represented the technology-driven, video-game-like future of air warfare. Quick decisions had to be made while flying hundreds of miles an hour as pilots resisted the roller-coaster effects of gravity. Jet pilots were esteemed as a modern version of the slow-talking, cool-handed gunslingers in the old American West. And yet even a highly skilled pilot could do only so much. The technology involved in the aerodynamics of our early jets was still unproven. The sudden need to send these aircraft into the battle space of an unanticipated war sometimes pushed the ever-developing technology beyond its proven boundaries, to the detriment of our pilots.

To borrow an observation I have often made about the danger of booby traps in the war I would fight in Vietnam less than twenty years later, a pilot could be 100 percent right when flying one of these evolutionary jet aircraft and still end up 100 percent dead. In the Air Force during the Korean War, there was no greater risk than that involved in attempting to master the intricate life-or-death decisions that were required in the high-tech jets that now were being sent into harm's way against Soviet-made MiG fighters. The slow-moving, vulnerable F-84 was cynically nicknamed "the ground-loving whore" by its own disillusioned pilots. The better-performing F-86 Saber Jet was nonetheless an imperfect and temperamental aircraft.

Death did stalk the pilots of these newfangled jet aircraft, not only in the airspace over Korea but also back at home, even at Scott Air Force Base. Our pilots were constantly pushing against the envelope of evolving technology and the limits of human endurance. In our housing project just beyond the boundaries of Scott's airfields it became routine for our daily activities to be interrupted by a sudden sonic boom, as one aircraft after another broke the sound barrier, each one sending a shock wave through the neighborhood.

Mishaps were a part of our daily lives. The father of one of my first-grade classmates was killed in a midair collision while we were at school. Not long after that an F-86 Saber Jet flew too low over our heads as I was standing with my mother in the backyard while she was pinning the day's wash on a clothesline. The pilot was attempting to land on the airstrip inside the base, whose outer fence was just across the street from our housing project. It narrowly missed the roof of our tenement, falling far short of the runway and crashing on the other side of the street, near the gas station that had been carved out of a cornfield. The jet roared over our heads and exploded before our eyes, killing the pilot. Although the crash scene was quickly sealed off by Air Police trucks and other vehicles from the base, like little kids everywhere my friends and I searched and played in the debris of the wreckage for days.

As the war went on, my dad was sent on temporary duty orders to Keesler Air Force Base in Mississippi, where he would transition from propeller-driven planes into jets in preparation for combat service in Korea. While on a high-altitude solo flight in an F-86 Saber Jet during his training regimen a technical malfunction caused the air pressure in his cockpit to suddenly drop, blowing out both of his eardrums and causing middle-ear damage and vertigo. Cross-eyed with dizziness, he vomited into his oxygen mask, clogging up his airflow. Heading back to the airfield, he saw two identical versions of the same landing strip, one from each eye. In a "you bet your life" moment, he picked one and descended toward it. Partly due to his skills as a pilot and partly out of luck, he had picked the right landing strip. He managed to land the aircraft, although they had to carry him out of the plane once he taxied onto the runway. For the rest of his life he was affected with middle-ear damage and periodic bouts of vertigo. And he was grounded from flying.

Back at Paeglow, a foreboding filled the air when we heard the news. Long days passed following his cockpit accident, and we had no way of knowing how serious it was. Finally my mother gathered us together and told us that my father, whose greatest joy was in flying, had been taken off of flight status. "They took his wings away," she solemnly announced, with the same tone she might have used if he had lost both of his legs or suffered a paralyzing heart attack. He was coming home, to be sent to a desk job at the training command. And she warned us that when he came home, we were never to mention that he no longer had his wings.

A few days later my father walked solemnly through the doorway of our home, dressed in his Air Force blues and carrying his B-4 suitcase. This was nothing like the joyous reunion that had so overwhelmed us when he had returned from the Berlin Airlift. For a long moment we all stood uncertainly in the living room, kids and Mom on one side of the room and my dad on the other, staring at each other wordlessly.

Then I noticed something that I thought was odd and possibly encouraging. My father was still wearing his pilot's wings on the left side of his uniform jacket, above his rows of ribbons. "Dad, they let you keep your wings!"

My mother groaned. Dad shook his head stoically, embarrassed. He exhaled, visibly deflating before our eyes. My mother gave me an exasperated look.

"In the military they don't take things away that you've already earned," he finally said, visibly humiliated. He pointed at his pilot's wings, which had been earned years ago for flying propeller-driven planes. "But these don't count. If I were going to fly jets, I would be a 'master pilot' with a star on the wings, above the shield."

I was pulling for him, but I didn't quite understand that the middle-ear damage was irreversible. In fact it could have qualified him for a medical discharge, and it did preclude him from ever flying again. "But, Dad, if they don't take those wings away, then you can still fly the planes that they gave you the wings for, even if it's not jets, right?"

"*I can't fly anymore, okay?*" He closed the front door behind him and started upstairs, carrying his bag toward their bedroom. "I don't want to talk about it. Don't you ever mention it to me again."

Learning the details of my father's near death in the cockpit and then watching him go through the depressing transition after being told he would never fly again gave me a strong, early dose of reality. We all love Horatio Alger stories, but in life there is not always a happy ending, despite one's determination, courage, and persistence. As the Greek tragedies remind us, even our greatest heroes are fallible. Achilles was felled by one small spot on his heel, where his mother had held him while dipping him into the waters of the River Styx in order to ensure his invincibility. Even Superman could be rendered helpless by a little piece of kryptonite.

Few people ever live out their dreams. The question for my father became, and for all of us still remains, What do you do when your young dreams die? A severely wounded Marine friend from Vietnam would later concisely answer this way: "Life is not in drawing a good hand, but in learning to play a poor hand well." Having lost forever the professional pursuit that he loved the most, and still nowhere near a college degree, my dad pushed forward in search of a new obsession.

In addition to being one of the main transportation hubs of the Air Force, Scott housed a number of technical schools, serving as a principal communications training center. Now completely grounded from flying, my father was assigned as an instructor at the schools. To his own surprise, but in retrospect not to mine, the Old Man thrived in this new role. Garrulous, smart, and given his extroversion naturally entertaining, my dad was a born lecturer. It did not hurt that he was also deeply versed in electronics and communications media. After less than a year as an instructor and despite his lack of formal education, my dad, already respected as a leader, had proven his ability as a teacher and was handselected for a prestigious assignment in Bedfordshire, England, as the sole American exchange officer at the Royal Air Force Technical College in Henlow.

As my mother would say, there are forty-two ways to skin a cat. As a kid, all I knew was that our lives were about to dramatically expand.

From the tenements of Paeglow and the small-town vistas of St. Joe and the frequent family visits to the poverty-racked hamlets of rural East Arkansas, we would soon be driving along freshly constructed turnpikes in Pennsylvania—a new concept in the transportation systems of America—and staring up at the skyscrapers of New York City. Not long after that we would be crossing the Atlantic Ocean on a military troop transport. Upon landing we would be transplanted into a wondrous new world, loading up on a bus that would take us past sprawling tulip fields in full bloom and old neighborhoods with thatched-roof homes as it made its way along the narrow two-lane roads that ran from the busy seaport of Southampton to the historic streets and parks of London. For two years our lives would be immersed not only in the British Isles, from which our ancestors had migrated to America nearly two centuries before, but also within the boundaries and the culture of the British people.

We were going with my father, but unlike many Americans who lived overseas in Europe during that postwar period, we would not be living on an American base that happened to be in England. As he carefully reminded us, we would be the only Americans living on a British military base, going to school inside the English state school system, almost completely removed from other Americans for the next two years. Each one of us would have a special responsibility. In the eyes of every British person we met, and whether we intended it or not, we would be America. Barely two months after my eighth birthday my father convinced me that everything I did or said would have an impact not only on me personally and not only on our family but also on the reputation of our country. I began to understand what was meant by the word *leadership*, as well as the concept of long-term accountability.

Chapter Four

AMBASSADORS

The USS *General H. W. Butner*, known in Navy terminology as troop transport AP-113, departed for Europe from Brooklyn in late April 1954, just after the Easter weekend. The old-style grey two-stacker with its crew of 477 sailors was as long as two football fields. Underneath the water line its turbine engines pushed twin propeller shafts with 17,000 horsepower of energy apiece. Bulky and slow, she steamed at a steady rate of twenty knots. With a seventy-five-foot beam amidships, in proportional terms the *Butner* was much wider than a traditional warship such as a destroyer or a cruiser. But the *Butner* was not a fighting ship. Built in the early days of World War II, she had been designed to carry thousands of troops overseas inside the protection of large convoy formations. Since 1944 she had ferried American troops to battlefields and bases across the world, from Morocco to Guam and from South Africa to Australia. Most recently she had earned two Battle Stars in Korea.

The *Butner* was capable of transporting more than five thousand troops inside its cramped, belowdecks quarters. Even now, following World War II and Korea, American soldiers and airmen were constantly being deployed to and from the bases that we maintained in Europe and Asia. Down inside the *Butner*'s gloomy, dim-lit hold, this latest complement of fresh soldiers heading for duty in England and Germany often slept four-high on rigid canvas bunks that lined the narrow passageways. On its first leg the *Butner* was heading for Southampton, England, where many passengers, including our family, would disembark. Stopping next at Bremerhaven, Germany, the ship would drop off a second load of soldiers. It would then complete its regular shuttle run by reversing its journey, picking up a new group returning home from tours of duty in Europe and taking them back to Brooklyn.

The *Butner*'s eight-day voyage across the Atlantic was as routine for its crew as a modern-day seven-hour flight from Dulles to Heathrow on United Airlines. But it was a new, eye-opening transit for most of its passengers. A roller-coaster of emotions surged through me as I walked with my family up the forward brow. All around us sailors were making their final preparations before unleashing the giant ship from the cleats and bollards of pier-side Brooklyn. Movie-picture moments filled the pier and the main decks of the ship, of a sort that could easily have been witnessed three hundred years ago or tomorrow.

The size, design, and capabilities of naval ships have changed over the history of our country, from the wooden hulls of sailing vessels, with their haphazard, short-range iron cannonballs, to sleek metal warships boasting laser weapons that can vaporize a missile as it descends from its remote arc hundreds of miles above the sky. But human emotions remain a constant. The ambience and palpable energy at pier-side as a ship goes through its final moments before setting out into the open sea are timeless.

The harbor's chalky brown water lapped up against the grey walls of the ship as we stepped from the pier onto its brow, greeting us with a fecund odor, a mix of fuel and rot that held its own promises and whispered to us of untold mysteries. Along the pier and on the ship's main deck tattooed sailors in their Dixie Cup white hats, dungarees, and boondocker boots expertly worked the lines around the moorings and the cleats and bollards. Serious with the business of getting a ship under way, they barked pointedly to one another, quickly responding to whistles and hand signals that only they could understand. The crisp nonchalance with which the cocky boatswains carried out their finely honed skills spoke to me of the same expertise my father had described when explaining the intricacies of flying the bombers and cargo planes that he so loved. Watching them work, I understood that love more fully.

Aboard the ship a collection of loudspeakers blared ubiquitously and yet anonymously while the ship's boatswain whistle blew: "All aboard that's going aboard. All ashore that's going ashore. I say again, all ashore that's going ashore."

The ship hummed and purred, almost a living thing as it prepared to get under way. Clusters of people crowded the pier and the *Butner*'s main deck, saying their often emotional good-byes. Everywhere around us were the unfamiliar and enchanting sounds of horns blaring and engines idling. The odors of the harbor and the gentle groundswell waves that rocked the small skiffs that flitted to and fro hinted to us of what soon would become the open sea.

On a second brow toward the stern of the ship, a long line of same-looking, uniformed soldiers laboriously made their way up the narrow planks. They struggled one after another on the wooden ramp, now and then steadying their ascent by grasping the metal-posted ropes that served as fragile railings. Their chins were down and their sea bags were slung tightly over their shoulders. They were quiet and purposeful, each one strangely alone although their column seemed never-ending. They reminded me of the pictures I had so often seen in newspapers and magazines that recalled the days just before my birth, when our young citizen-soldiers had headed off to the far-flung battlefields of World War II.

Finally the *Butner* was fully loaded. Soon after that it began, ever so slowly, to move away from the pier. We stood behind the railings on the main deck along with dozens of other families as the ship inched into the channel that would take us seaward, taking it all in like the naive tourists we were. Gliding past Ellis Island and the haunting majesty of the Statue of Liberty, we lifted our faces as we stared in awe at the imposing sky-scrapers of New York City that rose steeply behind them. These iconic national symbols were, to us and to the world, reminders of the promise of America. They had served as a welcoming embrace to waves of immi-grants who generations before had come to our country from the conti-nent to which we now were headed. And they were a proud reminder of our national spirit as we left them in our wake.

Within a matter of hours we had exited New York Harbor. The foghorn of the Ambrose Lightship uttered its famous signal to the ships entering and leaving the channel just off Sandy Hook. Finally the Light-ship's forlorn *Beeee-Yoooo* came from behind us, telling us that we had cleared the Ambrose Channel and would soon be churning through the open sea. The ship's engines kicked into full throttle. The flat brown wa-ters of the harbor seamlessly gave way to darker, higher waves and after that to the charcoal blackness of the sea. And in our steady, froth-filled wake, the coastline of America finally disappeared.

Family by family the passengers left the decks, climbing inside the hatches and heading toward their cabins. As we walked along a narrow passageway toward our living spaces a small knot of uncertainty grew in my stomach. It would be two years—one-quarter of the time I had already lived—before we would see our homeland again.

Since my father was traveling on "accompanied" orders, our six family members were assigned to a two-room compartment in Officers' Country, just above the main deck. As soon as we entered the compart-ment I grabbed an upper bunk. My mother set to work, busily unscrew-ing a circular porthole near my bunk. A cool, salty sea wind immediately washed over me, mixed with a tinge of fumes from the ship's decks and the smokestacks just above us. Inhaling deeply, I thought of my granny and all the stories she had told us as she cracked open the bedroom windows at Paeglow.

We were on a different kind of boat than the flat barge that had taken Granny and her family across the Big Muddy of the Mississippi when she was just my age. And we were moving in a different direction. Granny's family had been heading inward, just as their parents and grandparents had before them, toward the little-known swamps and cotton fields of a raw, new land. We were heading the other way, in the direction of England, Scotland, Wales, and Ireland, a collection of countries that had nurtured our own cultural and family history. Those memories had been kept inside a special little jewel box, like a different kind of family Bible, a set of remembered moments passed down from generation to generation in front of the fireplaces and on the front porches of the cabins that had been built out in the wilderness. We would now have the opportunity to open it up and reexamine our heritage.

I liked this ship, and I was coming to more fully understand my father's passion for military service. To be more precise, the DNA that had impelled two thousand years of Celtic wanderlust had flared up like a light switched on from the moment I had first seen New York Harbor. The Webbs, it seemed, were born on the run, and there was nothing more natural than to be heading off into yet another unknown. For the next eight days, come storm or sunshine, I would be rocked in the cradle of my swaying bunk bed as we crossed the big old Atlantic, the same deep ocean that our ancestors had traversed in the small sailing vessels that had brought them to America.

A fierce storm hit the Atlantic as we crossed. The horizons all around us disappeared, the sea and sky blurring indiscernibly together in ugly grey swirls of foamy ocean water and vicious rain. Black squares of waves larger than our house in Paeglow roared toward us and smacked repeatedly into the ship. The bow shuddered as it climbed huge waves and then settled back into the sea. The ship yawed like a pendulum, side to side, even as it plowed forward. For two days many passengers re-mained in their beds. Seasickness was rampant and contagious on deck and in the cabins. The dank troop spaces where, as an officer, my dad was required to make daily inspections reeked of vomit near the bunks and in the toilets. Those of us who spent our days in the recreation rooms just off the main decks could look out of the portholes on one side and see only the white-foamed, roiling ocean, while on the other side we could see only the bleak grey sky. Then as the ship rolled and swayed from the storm, the views would be reversed, the ocean where the sky had been and the sky where just before we could see only the ocean.

Finally the storm cleared. Still, all around us was only the grey sky and the bleak darkness of the sea. My younger sister, Tama, now six, worried repeatedly to my father that the ship's captain had gotten lost in the storm and that we would never find England. We journeyed past pods of whales, pointing and staring at them from the railings of the main deck as if we were Captain Cook's exploring sailors. We were required to attend daily lifeboat drills, where we reported to our assigned lifeboat and put on our life preservers, ready to go overboard if the massive ship were to go down. The ship's bells rang every half-hour through their cycle of eight bells every four hours. The orders to the crew and some-times to the passengers came from the speakers placed throughout the ship, bleating out odd, esoteric messages like "Now, sweepers, man your brooms. I say again, now, sweepers, man your brooms."

These unfamiliar practices and sounds quickly developed a rhythm and even a melody, until I felt as though I had been given a peek into another, more exciting world. After a day or so at sea I felt like a prac-ticed hand. I understood the bell system on the ship's clock. I properly minded my manners as our family sat for meals in the wardroom. I found myself looking out at the vast and empty seascape as if its very bleakness held a thrill that astronomy nerds might find only in outer space. I got my sea legs, growing used to walking along the narrow, dim-lit passage-ways as the ship shuddered and rolled, pushing into the rising bow as it ascended giant waves and then walking downhill as it topped the crest and then settled back toward the sea.

I found myself watching with acute interest as the sailors did their jobs on the decks and in the ship's compartments. The ship was a small city, almost a living thing. I was eight years old, but with the instinctive nose of a bird dog born for the hunt I knew that God had put me on this earth to be a soldier or a sailor. I loved the swagger and the certainty of this can-do life of motion and adventure, where the whole world might change on the far side of the very next gigantic wave. I did not know what or how, but I knew that someday I would be a part of it. And I understood better why my dad so loved the military life.

This was a hell of a lot more fun than sitting at home waiting for the corn to grow in St. Joe or playing in the open fields next to Paeglow while the jets banged their sonic booms and screamed anonymously overhead.

★　★　★

With his fascination for history and his previous tour in England, my father had prepared us well for the stop in London. We entered a world of cluttered roads, antiquated cars, double-decker red buses, and boxy black taxis. Justified by written military orders and paid through government funds, we stayed at the beautiful, ornate Kensington Palace Hotel, just across from the splendid majesty and ponds of Kensington Gardens. There could not have been a better place to be introduced to the history and traditions of England. The area around Kensington Gardens is dead-center in the heart of old London. Today it is known as "Billionaire's Row," holding some of the priciest real estate in the world. In the years following World War II the neighborhoods that bordered the lush gardens and the tranquil ponds in the center of the city were somewhat tattered around the edges, but they still held the charm of Victorian England.

The American embassy was nearby, which was why we were staying at the hotel. For several days my father met with officials at the American embassy there for in-country briefings as we prepared to go north to Bedfordshire, where he would report for duty at the Royal Air Force Base at Henlow. While he was locked inside his meetings, and sometimes when he was free to join us, our family roamed about the city from this envious starting point with a greedy, insatiable curiosity.

In my young imagination this must have been the neighborhood where Peter Pan had stolen Wendy and her brothers away to Never-Never Land, all of them sprinkled with Tinker Bell's pixie dust and flying above the glowing evening skyline as their dog Nana howled at them from the window of their apartment, still chained to her leash. In the real world it was near the neighborhoods where Winston Churchill had marched along blood-spattered streets during the worst nights of the German Blitz in the middle of the Battle of Britain, railing against Hitler with a cigar clenched between his teeth and a glass of Scotch waiting for him in the car. Churchill was an oversized melodramatic giant at a time when his country needed a leader whose fierce rhetoric could reach Shakespearean heights. Here on the very pavement where we walked were the places where he had done his greatest work, rallying a battered but defiant population and warning Hitler—accurately—that the British people would never be persuaded to compromise their heritage by yielding to the threats of an invasion or by crumbling under the bombs and the booted heel of an outside invader.

Always in the back of my mind there was a rhetorical but serious question: How in God's name had we earned the honor of walking these streets and visiting the incredible history of downtown London? To paraphrase Dorothy after a Dust Bowl Kansas tornado unexpectedly dropped her and her dog Toto onto the Yellow Brick Road in the middle of the Land of Oz, this definitely wasn't Paeglow anymore.

We quickly mastered the intricate connections on the underground subway called the Tube and learned the difference between a farthing and a ha'penny and between a thruppence and a shilling. We walked

endlessly along the fog-dampened sidewalks, adapting to our new surroundings. We made the obligatory stops at such landmarks as Big Ben,
Winchester Cathedral, Buckingham Palace, London Bridge, the Houses
of Parliament, Trafalgar Square, and the infamous Tower of London. But
for me our wanderings became something larger. In his love of history
and culture my father had found not only a willing student but also an
eventual intellectual partner. Encouraged by our long discussions over
the past several months, I had never experienced such a thrill as seeing
before my eyes the monuments and buildings that paid tribute to Great
Britain's remarkable journey, both at home and abroad. As we walked
and rode through London, every street corner seemed to hold a lesson
and a celebration of individual grit, societal determination, and governmental genius.

The landmarks of London did not seek to overpower a visitor with
garishness or artificial, hyperpolitical messages. Rather they spoke
almost bluntly of centuries of accomplishment, the evolution of democracy, and, uniquely, not a small measure of self-criticism from the lessons
that had been learned at the hands of frequently insensitive monarchs.
The most difficult conflicts in British history seemed always to have been
among their own strong-willed people, whether it was the bloodbaths
between royal families to determine which of them would become dominant as the centuries rolled forward, or the unending battles with popu-
list Scottish and Irish dissenters who for thousands of years—and to this
very day—have refused to accept full English dominance.

As it muddled through history, this relatively small island nation had
become not only a democracy but also the unquestioned Queen of the
Seas, a truly great military power whose Navy set the standard throughout
the world. Great Britain had built an overseas empire that extended to
every single continent. The British Empire, and later the British Commonwealth, was a dominion on which, as they rightly boasted, the sun
never set. Undeniably brilliant though not necessarily kind colonial
administrators, their reach and influence through the economic and

governmental concepts that the British introduced in these widely varying locations are more long-lasting—and one may daresay more permanent—than anything the world has ever seen, at least in modern times.

Unlike other imperialist nations, wherever the British formed a colony they quickly established trading companies and a judicial system that, for all the flaws of imperialism, brought with it a tradition of individual rights under the rule of law. True, the British economy benefited greatly from the economic systems that they put into place. The colonial concept, euphemistically justified under the rubric of the "White Man's Burden," brought immense, tangible rewards to the average British citizen. It is more difficult to explain, but nonetheless inarguable, that in the long run most of these colonies also benefited greatly from the economic and legal traditions that were implanted by British colonial rule. My family remains proud that a half-dozen of my direct ancestors, the progeny of immigrants who came to America mostly from Scotland and Ireland, fought the British during the Revolutionary War. But once the dust finally settled on the Age of Imperialism in the years following World War II, there was no doubt that the political and economic systems of the countries that had been colonized by Great Britain fared far better than those that had been under the control of any other nation.

At the Kensington Palace Hotel we ate breakfast in our room. One morning as I spooned out my porridge and nibbled at an unfamiliar biscuit called a scone we were surrounded by the almost magical beauty of a single violin playing a sad and haunting melody. The entrancing song was coming from the street below. I went to the bay window, opening it outward and standing at the edge of the small railed balcony. On a sidewalk just underneath the balcony an elfin, greying man was playing a complex piece of classical music. His sad, ruddy face and his distant eyes told me that he was remembering something powerful but no longer within his grasp. There was an artist's knowing firmness in the way his bow so gracefully stroked the strings of the violin. This earnest little man had performed in better places; his music clearly belonged with a symphony rather than on a side street in London.

His fedora was at his feet, turned upside down. Lost inside his music at this early morning hour, this accomplished musician was begging for coins that might be tossed from the windows of our hotel. I ran to my mother's purse, grabbing a handful of this strange new money. Over her loud objections I raced back to the window and tossed the coins down toward his hat. Two years earlier I had given all my Christmas money to a legless man outside a department store in St. Louis who was upholding his dignity through the fiction of selling pencils. At that time my mother and Granny had been moved to tears by my little-boy negotiations with the legless man, whereupon I finally accepted one pencil in exchange for all of my money in order to allow him to maintain his pride. But on that morning in London my mother exploded, for in my naiveté I had tossed the violinist a fistful of serious British money.

In the ponds of Kensington Gardens and Hyde Park, boys my age dressed in woolen shorts and knee-high socks spent their days racing homemade wooden boats equipped with pencil masts and paper sails. Nearby, under blankets in the grass and on the benches of the parks, teenage lovers curled together openly, even as proper Britishers turned their eyes away from such public displays. The openness of their lovemaking was a tacit recognition that almost everyone's privacy had in some manner been blasted away during the war by German bombs that had devastated nearby homes.

London in 1954 still prided itself on being the financial capital of the world. But beyond the top-hat façade of its international elites, in the neighborhoods and among the factories that had absorbed the Blitz, the city was a wounded place. More than 750,000 homes had been damaged or destroyed by German bombs. Even though nearly a decade had passed since war's end, the fragility of the British economy was such that wartime food rations continued throughout the country, and many homes had yet to be rebuilt.

We had grown up singing English nursery rhymes. As we traversed the city, we verified that despite the verses of the song, London Bridge was not really falling down. One morning we decided that we would try to find the "Muffin Man who lived on Drury Lane." Searching earnestly along the Lane, we discovered that he was gone. There may have been other reasons that the Muffin Man had moved on, especially since the song had been written so many years before, but Drury Lane in 1954 was a crumbling shambles. If the Muffin Man had still been selling his wares on Drury Lane in the early 1940s, he probably was dead, and there was no doubt that his shop would have been obliterated by German bombs.

It may have been true, as the boast went, that the sun never set on the British Empire, but by 1954 the sun was indeed setting on the empire itself. A generation earlier, Great Britain had been shaken to its roots by the unexpected battlefield carnage of World War I. More than 700,000 British soldiers had perished in that unexplainable war, which, through what can only be called the self-immolation of its participants, forever shifted the dominance of Europe in world affairs. By comparison, the United States, whose population at 99 million was more than double that of the British Isles, lost 55,000 dead in combat and that many again at the very end of the war from an epidemic of the Asian flu. Even factoring in the flu epidemic, this meant that the British casualty rate in World War I was more than ten times that of the Americans.

Twenty years later World War II had seen another 290,000 battle deaths among British forces, as well as the deaths of nearly 70,000 civilians due to German bombings. The United States, whose population was now three times that of Britain's, had lost 416,180 military members due to combat or disease and 1,700 civilians, most of them in the bombing of Pearl Harbor. Thus in World War II the British military casualty rate was still more than twice that of American military forces, while their civilian casualties were more than 120 times our own. On top of the carnage, financing these two wars had brought the British economic system to the brink of collapse, from which it would never fully recover.

The ever-stolid, stiff-upper-lipped British would never lower themselves by outwardly complaining, especially since the military and civilian casualties in Germany, Japan, and Russia were several orders of magnitude greater than Britain's. From Winston Churchill to the shopkeepers in the little stores along Hitchin Road, where we would soon be living, they all knew that American involvement in both wars had eventually saved the day. But the irritating, self-important braggadocio of postwar America did not sit well with the Brits. Across the world in the aftermath of World War II, many overseas Yanks displayed an unthinking attitude that often earned them the sobriquet of "the Ugly American." The British who had endured the hardships of the back-to-back world wars and the rationing that attended the recent peace knew something from hard experience that most Americans, for all of their good intentions and contributions, did not.

Britain was bled out and spent out. Americans had inarguably paid a price, often on behalf of the beleaguered British and other allies. But they also had emerged from the war as the world's foremost economic and military power, while for many British this unavoidable war had resulted in a Pyrrhic victory. The British had watched their empire contract as the casualties from both world wars grew ever larger and as their homes and neighborhoods were blown apart. They understood the great price of the recent wars in a much more sobering way than did most Americans. The Brits were not prone to lecturing, but they could dismiss a boastful American with a knowing scowl and the quick flecking of their eyes that had no need for words.

Sometimes a single moment can illuminate, if not completely clarify, such distinctions. I recall a taxi ride along the George Washington National Parkway in October 1983. I was returning home to Virginia after serving a stint as a journalist in the war-ravaged city of Beirut, which was marked by the constant violence of a half-dozen different factions in a civil war that by then had gone on for more than eight years. I was exhausted. Unable to fly out from the Beirut Airport because it was constantly being shelled by Druze artillery, I got out of Lebanon on a Russian hovercraft that took us to Larnaca, Cyprus, from where we caught a flight to Athens. Within a matter of days after my return home, a suicide bombing would destroy the Marine Corps headquarters at the Beirut Airport, killing more than 220 American Marines.

I had just left a country where senseless, unpredictable violence was as normal as a traffic jam in Washington, returning home to a sterile debate that raged daily in Congress and the media as to whether American forces should have been injected into the middle of the chaos. A perplexing irritation that I could not articulate was bothering me as the taxi made its way in the early morning drive along the sleepy, tree-lined Parkway. It nagged at me further as I stared out across the Potomac River at the beautiful monuments in Washington on the other side.

I finally realized that the source of my agitation was simply the overwhelming silence. This reflective peace was, thankfully, the emblem of America. But it also represented the protective vacuum that surrounds our understanding when it comes to the viciousness that war brings to so many innocent noncombatants in other lands.

We have since then had our moment of stark terror and loss in the bombings of the World Trade Center and the Pentagon. We also live inside what a journalist friend of mine once called the "CNN Syndrome." In our society if you see something on TV, whether it is a tsunami or a kidnapping or a war, you somehow begin to think that by viewing pictures of it you yourself have actually experienced it. But the plain truth is that very few Americans have heard the explosion of a single artillery round, much less witnessed the destruction of their neighborhood as a deliberate act from a hostile force.

This was the message that I could read in the eyes of many British as we walked the streets of London in 1954, and even as we lived among them for two years afterward. The British, by and large, loved us. They welcomed us. They intermarried with us. They jovially treated us as their long-lost colonial progeny, now embarrassingly grown up and having come back to bolster their energies as if they were the doting parents and we were the children who someday might understand the inevitable travails of middle age. The look in their eyes as the Yanks swaggered and bragged about winning The Great World War II was that of a people who have been through a journey that could never be actually explained, and whose understanding of the truth was unconsciously being derided. Their unspoken signal was that they hoped we could somehow come to understand their hard-earned truths through our own experiences, and that once we did come to understand, perhaps there would be no need for a conversation that just now would be too complicated for them to undertake anyway.

In their knowing eyes we were the well-intentioned, naive do-gooders that Graham Greene loved to place at the center of his slyly moralist dramas such as *The Quiet American*. For two years as we lived among them they would welcome us with respect while at the same time hinting of the reality that they knew, and that they hoped from their own long history we might someday understand, bringing us to a sobering but hopefully more reflective maturity.

What do you know about the Blitz, mate? And how do you think it feels to be one of the greatest military and economic powers in the world, only to lose the empire abroad and be reduced to rations at home while our former enemy rebuilds its cities and its economy with the financial assistance of your own bloody Marshall Plan?

★　　★　　★

Mr. Clem Hanley was standing on my toes.

He had seated me in the middle of the classroom, just in front of his desk. Just now he was deliberately looking past me, lecturing the class as if he were totally unaware that his large leather shoes were mashing the tops of my feet. As always, over his patterned shirt Mr. Hanley wore a sleeveless yellow woolen vest. His frumpy red hair shot out in all directions from his wide pink forehead, which, along with his piercing eyes and stentorian voice, made an imposing presence on the ten- and eleven-year-olds in the class.

If that were not sufficient to gain our full attention, a very large and smooth-soled tennis shoe sat on his desk for all to see. Mr. Hanley referred to the long white rubber shoe as his good friend Mister Benjamin. Those who spoke out of turn or were otherwise unruly were called to the front of the class for a visit with Mister Benjamin. The boys would hold out a hand, palm up, for a painful smack. The girls would touch their toes and take one on their bum. A second offense during any given week required two smacks, and so on, up to the maximum of six. Mercifully, every Monday Mr. Hanley wiped the slate clean again, and the count would start back at one.

As painful as that was, Mister Benjamin was a walk in the park compared to a swat from Mr. Bunny's slender bamboo cane. The diminutive, grey-suited headmaster would frequently visit the classroom while Mr. Hanley lectured or as we wrote out our daily lessons using quill-tipped pens that resided in the inkwells at the corner of our wooden desks. Ever-scowling, hands folded behind his back, his bespectacled head tilted to one side, Mr. Bunny would silently walk the rows between the desks, examining the attentiveness and the penmanship of the students. Sloppy writing or a moment of perceived disrespect could cause a student suddenly to be yanked from a chair and brought into the corridor outside the classroom. In the hallway, he (and it seemed always to be a boy) would be required to hold out his hands, palms down, and receive a bash on his fingernails or knuckles from the whip-like bamboo of Mr. Bunny's cane.

Mr. Hanley was giving us a geography lesson. A large world map hung in the blackboard space at the front of the starkly furnished classroom, on which the countries of the British Commonwealth were marked with a special pink. So many countries were lit up with

British Pink, especially in Africa, South Asia, and the Middle East, that it seemed as though the little guppy of the British Isles had swallowed several worldwide whales. Sometimes as we studied the colonies we took out our music books and sang martial melodies from the wars and conquests that had put the pink upon the maps. Among Mr. Hanley's favorites were "Marching to Pretoria," a song from the Boer War, and "The British Grenadiers," which I had come to suspect was a paean to the Army regiment in which he had served during World War II.

Some talk of Alexander and some of Hercules
Of Hector and Lysander and such great names as these
But of all the world's great peoples there's none that can compare
With a Tow-Row-Row-Row-Row-Row, to the British Grenadiers.

We were required to memorize the names and locations of such esoteric British Commonwealth domains as Tanganyika and Yemen, Belize and Burma. We learned of famous British explorers such as Sir Francis Drake, Dr. David Livingstone, and Captain James Cook. We studied Britain's seemingly never-ending conflicts with other colonial powers such as France, Spain, the Netherlands, and Portugal. We learned about the battle alignment, the strategy, and the ultimate victory of the outnumbered British fleet over the Spanish Armada in 1588. And it goes without saying that we committed to memory the Duke of Wellington's attack plan and defeat of Napoleon at Waterloo.

Along the way, as was the tradition among many British schoolkids, I had become an avid stamp collector. On the weekends my friends and I would visit the musty bookstore next to the RAF Henlow barbershop, in its dim light sifting eagerly through boxes of old stamps and envelopes, calling gleefully to each other when we found stamps that matched the countries on Mr. Hanley's map. "Hey, wot? Here's a three-penny Victoria Red from India!"

Mr. Hanley had big feet. I knew that by stepping on my toes he was being fiendishly clever. He was overtly and yet subtly testing the only Yankee boy, indeed the only foreigner, in his class, to see if I could match the stoic mettle of the English. I stared straight into my desk, suppressing a rather pained grin as his shoes deliberately rocked on top of my toes. Firm disciplinarian that he was, Mr. Hanley was secretly hoping that I might outwardly complain or suddenly emit an anguished noise, which then would allow him to invite me to the front of the class for a visit with Mister Benjamin.

Over the past year I had made a few of those trips for such crimes as laughing or holding my ears when his chalk screeched across the black-board. But I knew what he was doing, and I kept my cool, aware that this was a personal test. The pain in my toes was nothing compared to a whack from Mister Benjamin, and especially compared to the familiar feeling of my knuckles smashing up against my father's unconquerable fist. Now Mr. Hanley was testing my pride. I finally won. Giving up, and never missing a beat in his lecture, he strolled back toward his desk.

Mr. Hanley was devilishly sarcastic and impossible to please. My older sister, Pat, who had preceded me in his class, had nicknamed him The Mean Old Man in the Yellow Vest. But secretly I liked and admired him. Despite his veneer of harshness he gave all of us measurable challenges, urging us to meet them and thus to learn how to perform under pressure. He would never openly acknowledge it, but I usually met those challenges. Along with other teachers in our school he had quickly promoted me to higher academic levels. The year-round British school system advanced students individually rather than by class. In less than two years I had been promoted through four grades.

Most memorably, Mr. Hanley was a remarkably effective teacher. He made odd moments of history and complex analytical issues come alive. At the ages of nine and ten I learned more about Greek mythology, me-dieval and Renaissance history, the mechanics of drawing and painting a picture, and the proper construction of a sentence than at any time until I went to college. And although he was extroverted and demanding, in the

British spirit Mr. Hanley was at the same time painfully modest. He had
served in the Army for six hard years during the war, from 1939 to 1945,
fighting in Europe and North Africa. Three troopships on which he was
sailing had been torpedoed by German U-boats. He never spoke of these
experiences, other than in factual terms. What would be the point of ex-
posing one's emotions to a room full of obstreperous students?

In the mornings before we left for school and in the afternoons after
our return Mr. Hanley often passed in front of our house, although he
never looked our way. His chin held high and his eyes firmly focused on
the road, he puttered along atop a green bicycle that had a small motor
attached to its rear wheel. Bicycles and motorcycles were more common
than cars on the narrow, winding Hitchin Road. Small farms and cottages
were the only real landmarks between the Royal Air Force Base a mile to
our south and Mr. Hanley's home village of Henlow a mile farther to our
north. A proper Englishman, Mr. Hanley never so much as acknowl-
edged any of us as his motorized bicycle whined along the road. He was
the teacher. We were the students. And that was that. Why wave to a yard
full of kids when that afternoon or tomorrow you might be bringing them
up for a visit with Mister Benjamin? Indeed, if you waved today, what
would stop you from waving tomorrow? And if you waved every day,
what would come next—friendship with a bunch of little brats?

Characteristically for my father, in England we lived in three different
homes in less than two years. But this time my father's innate restlessness paid off. With the third house we hit the jackpot. The Cedars, a
historic 125-year-old brick farmhouse normally reserved for officers of
much higher rank, had suddenly become available. Group Captain Reed,
the rotund, mustachioed senior officer in charge of the RAF Technical
College and the other military units at Henlow, liked and respected my
father. When the house became vacant he personally intervened in order
to assign us to the quarters, telling my father that he wanted our family
to have warm memories of our time in England. In this desire the group

captain certainly succeeded. As the Brits would have put it, given my father's mundane rank and position, by being assigned to The Cedars the entire Webb family was happily overmounted.

In my father's nomadic fashion our family would live in more than a dozen other houses before I left for college eight years later, but we would never stay in a more elegant and memorable home. You know you have won the military-family lottery when your house has a name instead of an address. All the locals knew our house by name. We lived, simply, at The Cedars, although our return address on the envelopes we sent home to America formally referred to our home as Number 7 Hitchin Road, Bedfordshire, England.

Whenever I crossed the shallow little stream at the edge of Hitchin Road and entered the narrow driveway of The Cedars I felt as though I were falling through a time warp to the days before electricity and automobiles. Lush grass, thick shrubs, and sturdy brick structures welcomed me. As I passed the outer buildings and looked inside the lead-pane windows of the house I could imagine long-ago workhorses and busy servants. I could almost feel what it had been like in the age of Queen Victoria and in the golden era before the tragedies of the two world wars. It took only a day or so at The Cedars not only to comprehend Great Britain's rich history but also to understand how its technological edge had been so disrupted by the wars and their aftermath. The best of England's daily life was now reflected longingly through the mirror of a past that would never be recaptured rather than an optimistic vision of a cutting-edge future. Indeed, the most memorable aspect of The Cedars was its echoing reminder of the time when there could have been no better lot in life than to have been a member of upper-scale English society.

Ivy-covered, thick brick walls marked much of The Cedars's boundaries. Hedges, beautifully flowered gardens, a small orchard of pear and apple trees, and a flourishing greenhouse were in the outer yard. An old carriage house, a remnant from the Victorian era, sat just to the left as one entered the driveway. An equally old stable, companion to the carriage house, sat beyond another brick wall on the far side of a swallow-thronged patio which led to the side entrance to the house. Beyond our backyard, just across the fence, was a stand of trees and a musky, frog-filled pond. Owls and eagles flew above the pastures and the streams, making their homes in the nearby woods.

Our family always used the side entrance to the house rather than the formal front doorway that overlooked Hitchin Road. Opening to a small breezeway, the side door led directly into the kitchen on the left and a recreation room on the right, both of which were the centers of our family activities. A few steps farther in, a stairway descended into a shadowed basement, which my mother firmly believed was haunted by dead servants from the distant past. Down the hallway beyond the stairs was a warm, small sitting room whose double doors opened to the flower-filled gardens and the greenhouse on the other side. Finally, at the end of the hallway, was the front door, with a formal living room to its left and a dining room on the right. A stairway descended from the four upstairs bedrooms, ending at the landing in front of the door.

The Cedars was a veritable mansion.

Our wooden-fenced front yard bordered the stream that paralleled Hitchin Road, and in the middle of the thickly grassed yard stood a giant elm tree. A tree house big enough for three or four kids at a time sat half-way up the tree, covered by a piece of curved metal and plastic that had once been the cockpit roof of a World War II bomber. The tree house was a great place from which to watch the somnolent traffic on the road below. It was also an excellent vantage point where we could secretly observe the chin-high, prideful Mr. Hanley as he puttered by on his little motorbike.

Antiquated though elegant and, like so much of Britain, frozen into an almost regressive technological time warp brought on by the economic realities of World Wars I and II, The Cedars was a constant reminder of the days of British dominance. The house and its grounds were themselves a microcosm of an era when world power was defined by the coal-fired furnaces of the Industrial Revolution and by the steam-driven warships that had replaced the days of wooden hulls and canvas sails. The house was warmed by water-heated radiators, whose piping system was fueled from a coke stove just inside our kitchen. My mother cooked our meals without electricity or gas on an anthracite-fueled Aga stove. The Victorian fireplaces in the living room and sitting room burned not wood but bituminous coal. Thus my first job every day when I came home from school was to refill eight to ten buckets of coal, coke, and anthracite from the three different bins out back in the ancient stables and to empty the ashes from the previous day's burnings.

The patterns of daily life in the small-town agricultural surroundings of Bedfordshire were similarly reminiscent of an earlier time, at least as measured through American eyes. As in Victorian novels and children's nursery rhymes, we had a milkman, who appeared twice a week at our side door in his little truck, taking our empty glass bottles and delivering fresh bottles according to my mother's written requests. The tin foil that covered the top of the bottles was color-coded to indicate the richness of the milk. The cream itself gathered at the very top of the bottles, requiring us to shake them before drinking. Similarly the local greengrocer delivered vegetables to our door from the back of a panel van.

Henlow Village and its environs was a quiet and pastoral place. Wide acres of potato farms and occasional fermenting haystacks sat along Hitchin Road between our house and the base at RAF Henlow. The wire fences of the farms that bordered the road were intertwined with lush weeds, patches of stinger-nettles, and vast tangles of wild roses. On the other side of the road, the grass runway of the Royal Air Force base hosted small hangars and outdated aircraft. In those modern days of jet aircraft and bombers that could take out entire cities it was like a view into a more innocent past to stare over at those grass runways. Silent unarmed gliders seemed oddly at peace with the old-style grass airstrip, as did the famed canvas-and-wood Mosquitoes and old Moth trainers that one otherwise saw only in movies featuring biplanes and wing-walkers, before the brutal era of bombings and air warfare brought on by World War II.

During harvest season the gypsies appeared from nowhere, dark and mysterious in their creaking caravans, suddenly upon us as if called to our small section of rural England by the same inner radar as a flock of wild geese heading south for winter. Once the potatoes were picked, the gypsies disappeared, their wagons heading north along the narrow Hitchin Road to their next destination, somewhere beyond the horizon.

Such were the ancient rhythms of small-town England in the days that followed World War II. Neither wars nor the strains of peacetime food rationing could affect these rhythms, other than perhaps to stiffen spines and to more permanently entrench them. The pink-colored countries on Mr. Hanley's maps that showed the reach and power of the British Empire might come and go; Rolls-Royce engines and Canberra aircraft and Jaguar luxury automobiles might become ever more profitable in the international marketplace or might fail completely and go out of business. It did not matter. The British people, having seen it all, and determined to remember it all from one generation into the next, would endure.

Great Britain was a land of memorable contrasts living almost complacently side by side. At the same moment it offered up world-renowned poets and grotesquely vulgar soccer fans; eighteenth-century minuets mixed among the most creative innovations of a new era of rock and roll; arrogant, born-to-be-rich millionaires and uncomplaining, early-dying coal miners; and a curiously enduring affection for royalty countermanded by a contagious resistance to any edict from above.

Our front yard, large as it was, became the weekend gathering place for dozens of our fellow schoolkids. They came on foot or on their bikes, often with their dogs following behind. They brought soccer balls, cricket bats, slingshots, and pellet guns, for all the obvious reasons. None of them had ever heard of playing cowboys and Indians, the favorite pastime of American kids my age. Sometimes we picked sides and reenacted the battles that had taken place two thousand years before between the Picts and the Romans after—as we were constantly reminded—Julius Caesar first invaded Britain, fifty-five years before the birth of Christ. Sometimes we played Robin Hood and his Merry Men. Sometimes we were King Arthur and the Knights of the Round Table. Sometimes we made rough swords and linoleum shields and refought the battles between King Charles's Cavaliers and Oliver Cromwell's Roundheads. Often we simply pulled out the boxing gloves that my father always kept nearby, gathering in twenty-kid circles and matching up different kids by size, age, and talent as the rest cheered and jeered.

On other days we walked through the woods and along the nearby streams, carrying slingshots or pellet guns or, in my case, the Daisy BB gun that my father had bought me when I was seven. We spent hours playing in the ubiquitous air-raid shelters and pillboxes left over from the war, which still dotted the air base and the countryside with the same normality as bus stops in urban America. *Howdy Doody* had not gone international; there was really no such thing as watching TV. Radio was sporadic. News from America, even for our family, was rare.

In rural England the past and the traditions impelled by its experiences reigned supreme. This was not on the whole a bad thing. It gave continuity and perspective to our daily lives, although it did have its occasional oddities. World War II had ended a decade before, but the local authorities still periodically conducted air-raid drills, requiring us to close the wooden shutters over every window of our house and to turn down the lights so that we could not be seen by night bombers from the air. We read books, constantly and with intense discussions, at the ages of nine and ten becoming conversant with such great writers as Robert Louis Stevenson, Jane Austen, Rudyard Kipling, and Charles Dickens. We collected birds' eggs, raiding nearby nests and blowing out the yolks so that the eggs could be carefully labeled and displayed in glass cases, eggs from robins, meadowlarks, sparrows, swallows, wood pigeons, and the highly prized golden eagle, each one an environmental intrusion but at the same time a lesson in revering wildlife. On the weekends my father and I would sometimes go book hunting, often finding precious, centuries-old treasures in the attics or back rooms of estate sales or in used-book stores, the rare volumes so numerous and common that each one could be bought for a pittance.

I still keep one of those books on a shelf in my writing office, *Christmas Entertainments, 1740,* printed in that year and sold at that time for the price of one shilling. My father and I found it at a book sale in the front room of an old home in Henlow Village, 215 years later. We probably paid no more for it in 1955 than its original purchaser paid when it was new.

Over the course of two years I had adapted well to the English way of life. I had an English schoolboy's haircut. I had learned to curse proficiently in British slang and to use British rather than American hand gestures that were themselves an expression of profanity. I played cricket and soccer regularly, while at the age of ten I had never thrown a baseball or a football. I had learned enough history to take sides in the age-old British debates. In my mind I was a Pict or certainly a Celt, not a Roman. I was a Breton, not a Norman. I was Robin Hood, not the Sheriff. I learned to celebrate Guy Fawkes's Night rather than the Fourth of July and Halloween (for it was a combination of both), a tradition that, as with so many other British festivities, carried with it a subtle political message: *Remember, Remember, the Fifth of November.* Feel free to complain all you want, the tradition intoned. Make all of the radical speeches in Hyde Park that you desire. But if you ever try to overthrow the system, no matter how sympathetic your cause might seem, you will be chased down, drawn and quartered, and your carcass thrown onto a burning bonfire. *A penny for the Old Guy . . .*

I did pretty well as a smart-ass, quasi-authentic version of a state-school British schoolboy. And yet there was no other place in my childhood that taught me greater lessons about what it meant to be an American.

A few months before we were scheduled to return home I suddenly became violently ill. I had a high fever and a raging migraine headache. My system could not absorb any food or liquid. I had become so sensitive to light that if one removed the towel over my eyes during the daytime I would vomit. A kindly old English doctor visited me at our home, swabbing my throat for indications of strep bacteria and conducting a thorough examination. The doctor found no strep, but he grew deeply concerned when my symptoms had not changed by the next day. His worry was that I had come down with meningitis, which in bacterial form was frequently and quickly fatal. He did not have the facilities in Henlow to treat me, so he recommended that my father take me immediately to the American military hospital at a base called Wimpole Park in Cambridgeshire, more than twenty miles away.

This journey was not as simple as it might sound in these days of interstate highways and instant communications, particularly in a foreign land. Driving twenty miles along the narrow, winding, fog-ridden roads of postwar England was the equivalent of perhaps one hundred miles in today's America. Arrangements needed to be made with the American military at Wimpole Park. There was no direct-dial on any phone, and out-of-town connections required being passed through a chain of voice communications with several different operators.

In due course my father bundled me into a grey woolen robe and threw me into the backseat of our car. The big American car lurched clumsily as my father drove along the left side of the narrow British roads. The car was as wide as a British delivery truck. The steering wheel was mismatched against the road, since the car was designed for American right-lane traffic. The fog was so thick that it seemed to be evening, even though it was the middle of the afternoon. My nausea intensified as the car made turn after turn.

Finally we reached the main gate of Wimpole Park. An American military policeman checked my father's identification and waved us onto the base. Suddenly we were inside a little piece of America. Uniformed

Americans walked the streets of the small base. An air of tranquility seemed to wash over my father, which I immediately absorbed. In an odd sense, we were home.

On the base's parade ground, to our front as my father drove toward the hospital, a cadre of airmen was standing at the bottom of a tall flagpole, readying to lower the American flag. It was five o'clock in the afternoon. As would happen every day at this time in bases in America and all around the world, American soldiers, sailors, airmen, and Marines would stop whatever they were doing, come to attention, and pay respect to our flag. From somewhere a bugle started playing "To the Colors." The cadre began lowering the flag, two of them working the lanyard and the other two solemnly saluting.

My father immediately stopped the car, climbing out of it and coming to attention, facing the flag ceremony. As the bugle played, the flag slowly descended, its colors flapping gently in the chilly, fog-saturated air. Forgetting me for the moment, his mind perhaps lost in the memory of other places where he had so proudly served, my father stiffly saluted. Emergency or not, sick and maybe dying kid in the backseat or not, my father was not going to disrespect our flag.

But he was not alone in that insistent pride. Sick or not, and puking or not, I was not going to languish like a self-pitying puppy while the bugle played "To the Colors" and my father stood rigidly in the foggy evening air and saluted. Wearing only my bathrobe, I crawled out of the car and stood next to him, my hand over my heart. The bugle finally finished playing. The cadre gathered the flag in their arms, flattening it and carefully folding it in a time-honored sequence that left only the blue background and the white stars exposed, in a perfect triangle.

Finally recognizing my presence, the Old Man patted me on the back, uttering a rare but welcome encouragement. "Are you okay?"

"Yeah, Dad, I'm okay."

He gave me a more discerning look. "You look like you're going to puke."

"Yeah." I leaned over into the road and dry-heaved.

"Are you all right?"

"I'm okay."

"Well, that bugle was playing 'To the Colors,' " he said, as if it had been his own idea that I join him on the damp road. "That's our flag. Don't you ever let our flag touch the ground."

"I won't, Dad."

"If it touches the ground we have to burn it. The doctors are going to take care of you. Now, get back in the car."

I climbed back into the car. We neared the collection of Quonset huts that made up the hospital. I was nervous about what the doctors were going to do. But I decided that it didn't really matter that much if I was sick, because I was going into a good hospital and had no doubt that I would eventually get well.

But Wimpole Park had made me homesick.

"I want to go home, Dad. I want to play baseball. I want to shoot a squirrel. And I want to catch a bass."

"You get better, you hear? Listen to the doctor. And then we'll go home."

"I know I'm going to get better."

My dad left me at the hospital. I stayed for a week. The doctors took care of me. I got better.

And in a few months we did go home.

Chapter Five

MILITARY BRATS

My father had now served four overseas deployments, although our time at RAF Henlow was the first one on which we had been able to join him. At the end of every one of these tours the faceless officials in charge of military assignments somewhere in the bowels of the Pentagon had told my dad that he would be given either his first or second choice of locations once he returned home. Following their guidance, as he finished every overseas assignment he sent an official request that he be posted to an Air Force base in either Florida or California. And all four times, as he later took cynical pleasure in pointing out, they had split the difference and decided to send him to Texas.

This time he was posted to Amarillo, a small base located in the far north of the Texas Panhandle. There was no family housing at Amarillo Air Force Base, nor was there any way of predicting whether rental homes would be available in the relatively remote city of Amarillo itself. And so, after making the return voyage across the Atlantic from England on a military troop transport, my mother and siblings and I proceeded to St. Joseph, Missouri, while my father reported to Texas and looked for a place where we might live.

Sending us to St. Joseph as we awaited further news was more a matter of arcane military protocol than practical logic. The city was listed in my father's personnel file as his official "home of record." It had now been six years since we had regularly lived there, but this was the military, and orders were orders, so my father dropped us off in St. Joe and then reported to his duty station some seven hundred miles away. The home at 3137 Felix Street where we had waited during his earlier deployments now belonged to someone else. We stayed in a house at the outskirts of the city, just above a section of railroad tracks that led into St. Joe's ever-diminishing packinghouses and stockyards. True, we were back in the city where Tama, Gary, and I were born, but we were in a different neighborhood, surrounded by people we did not know. And most important, what we did know was that we would soon be leaving St. Joe again, perhaps never to return.

No longer really our home, St. Joe was instead a way station before we headed out to a completely new place, and after that another new place, and after that another one. Years before, my father's family had viewed St. Joe as little more than a transitional spot in a journey designed by fate to put all of them elsewhere, and this seemed also to be the town's fateful role for us. Thousands of pioneers had passed through St. Joe on their way west. Its greatest claim to historical remembrance occurred in 1860, and for eighteen months thereafter, when the town had served as the launching point for the short-lived but romantically remembered Pony Express.

The Pony Express was a far less successful but equally imaginative prototype for today's Federal Express, although its dreams died early with the coming of the Civil War and the invention of the telegraph. At the height of the California Gold Rush, for the then-stunning price of $5 for a half-ounce letter, the Pony Express guaranteed that each satchel full of mail would be delivered from St. Joseph across the Great Plains and over the Rocky Mountains to Sacramento, California, within an undreamed-of delivery time of ten days. The Pony Express used 120 riders and 400 galloping horses, connecting like relay racers through a series of 184 stations and changing horses every ten miles.

It might be beef or hogs. It might be grain or mail. And especially it might be people. But St. Joseph was more than anything else a gathering place and a launching point to other places.

The Webbs had come upon the city during my dad's teenage years. All of them had long since departed, one carload or train ride at a time, most of them migrating to the storied land of Southern California. Years later, when people asked me if I was from St. Joe, I would shrug and say that my parents had shared a few cups of coffee there, in between my dad's deployments.

But to be fair to the Air Force, there really was no other place to send us as we awaited the rental house that my father might find in Amarillo. The other option was East Arkansas, but even there the outward migration from the poverty-stricken South had changed our family dynamics; only one of my mother's surviving siblings still remained in her home village of Kensett.

Inured to the unpredictability of military life, we had no thoughts of complaining. The Air Force bureaucrats had their forms to fill out and their decisions to make. We were, in truth, just one more piece of paper to be pushed across their desks, a family name to be filled out in the giant puzzle of how to allocate the human resources of the cold war American military. If St. Joe was not our home, it was still the closest box for them to check on this latest set of travel orders. Besides, we loved the Air Force and felt a part of it. The military had been a blessing for my father, whose greatest pride was in serving his country and who otherwise might have remained half-fulfilled in a nontenured job as an electrician or maintenance engineer, or perhaps chasing his vague prewar goal of running a gravel pit with his best friend, Bud Colwell.

The realities inherent in this intermediate stop at St. Joe firmly clarified for all of us not only who we were but what our future entailed, for here was the ultimate, defining question: If we were not from St. Joe, then where indeed did we belong?

The romantic notion of a hometown that we might someday return to had firmly disappeared. The umbilical cord that connected us to our civilian past was finally cut. In Kipling's words, my father was, above every other pursuit in his life, a "service man, henceforward, evermore." Major James H. Webb Sr., U.S. Air Force, was a consummate military professional, and in America a military professional's home could be as large as the country's international obligations or as small as whatever bleak corner of the world the military told him to go to. My dad's love of serving in uniform had permanently trumped every geographic tie, including our long-term connections to our extended family and even to our cultural community.

If nothing else, by returning for these few months to St. Joe we were at least in a town that we once had known. We had warm memories in St. Joe. My parents still had friends there. My dad's close childhood friend, Carl Goatcher, and his wife, Norma, looked in on us from time to time. We frequently shopped at Sidney Naidorf's grocery store on Mary Street, behind which my parents had lived in a basement apartment when I was born. Sidney was like an uncle to us. Bighearted, flame-haired, and missing the ends of a few fingers from more than one miscalculation on his meat-slicing machine, he would frequently bring our groceries to the house in his old green panel truck. On lazy weekend afternoons we could still go downtown and sit at the counter of the Katz Drug Store, where I would nostalgically order a cherry Coke and remember the special bus trips from Felix Street with Granny and Aunt Carolyn, both of whom were now living in California.

But because I had been away from this town for more than half my life, the thought of permanently leaving St. Joe did not disturb me. The

Webbs had always been a restless lot. As the Southern gentry like to put it, they were "born smart but un-landed" and thus of little local consequence. Their lineage was scattered like random apple seeds throughout the mountain and border South. We counted cousins from eastern Missouri all the way to Tennessee, Kentucky, and the mountain regions of the far southwest corners of Virginia. On my mother's side the Hodgeses and the Doyles, who had pioneered and settled just a bit farther to the south, were a little better educated and a little calmer but otherwise not that different. The Hodgeses could trace their lineage to well before the American Revolution, and the Doyles at least to the years before the War of 1812. Their family journeys also began in Virginia, then dipped into the Carolinas and all across Kentucky and Tennessee before spilling across the Mississippi River into Arkansas.

I knew my ancestry and my family roots. Due mostly to my father's sense of history and to Granny's bedtime stories, I understood my place in our culture's larger journey, which had never been defined by any particular state or town. And yet we were oddly adrift here in the city of my birth, even though we had just returned from a foreign country where we might have expected to feel alone and even though, according to my father's military personnel file, we were technically at home. It was not the past or the present that had unanchored us but rather that we had no way to predict the future. As we waited in St. Joe for my father's summons to join him in Amarillo, we had no idea where we would be living in even a year or two, or where my father would want to finally settle when his time in the military was over.

In England I had felt a sense of purpose and national pride, made stronger by my father's guidance that we were, in our own small way, American ambassadors while living among the British at the Royal Air Force Base in Henlow. But upon our return to America a new reality set in, and it was permanent. We literally belonged to, and inside of, the military. In a larger sense we had become disconnected from traditional definitions of local loyalties. Whether we liked it or not, we would always be different from the local population near any base where my father was assigned.

The good news was that we were learning that we could live and survive anywhere. But the bad news was that no matter where we lived, it would never really be our home. This subtle distinction would not change; in fact it defined us. Sometimes it sustained us. More often than not, it was used against us. But the reality of our separateness would dominate the remainder of a highly chaotic and geographically turbulent childhood. The military itself was the moral equivalent of our hometown. No matter where we lived, we were always peering from the outside into a separate world, which usually appreciated what our father was doing even if it seldom fully understood us, but whose faces would constantly change, almost on a yearly basis. As my dad liked to say with a laugh as we hit the road yet again, "Here we come, going yonder."

To borrow a phrase from the sociologists, we had irreversibly joined the ranks of America's military brats, a social caste spawned by the postwar concept of a large peacetime military. No matter the starting points of our parents, all of our hometowns had faded into disconnected memories, replaced by one military base after another, each new location chosen not by our parents but by box-checking bureaucrats in an assignment office somewhere inside the Pentagon. No matter our personal interests, be they ballet or biology or baseball, our common bond was that our fathers (for in that era it was always our fathers) had been offered up to serve the nation whenever and wherever called and were subject to being sent to a new location, with us or without us, on a moment's notice.

We military brats grew up with the understanding that everything around us was temporary, even though it was defined by the greatness and the permanence of the country that our fathers were defending. We knew full well that every single facet of our daily lives could be quickly altered by the needs of the service. And thus our own future was tangled up in uncontrollable outside forces, incapable of firm prediction or even definitive family discussion, depending instead on the roulette wheel of a seemingly unending national peril called the cold war.

In St. Joe the months slowly passed. We had arrived from England in May, allowing us to skip the end of the school year but also making it difficult for our family to link into the community itself. Seeking closer ties in St. Joe, as the public school system began its summer break my mother put us into daily Bible school at a local Baptist church. As the philosophers might have opined, her idea was logically admirable, but I failed utterly in its implementation. After a few days of hymns and prayers and lectures, I decided that the morning cookies and Kool-Aid were a good way to start the day but that it was not in my nature to sit for hours endlessly coloring pictures from books that recounted the parables or to sing hymns in a room filled with people I did not know.

Life often imitates art. During our last months in England my father had fortuitously introduced me to Mark Twain's stories about a couple of other wild Missouri boys, who went by the names of Tom Sawyer and Huckleberry Finn. Luckily for me, despite the discipline-minded nature of the Baptists, there was no real order in the school. In the mornings my mother would drop us off at the front door of the church. I would wave good-bye to her, walking dutifully through the entrance, and head for the cookies and Kool-Aid. Within minutes I would then slink out the back door, where I would climb over a wall and head off to explore the nearby neighborhoods and parks. Later I would climb back over the wall, some-times sitting in on one class or another or making my way through the building to the school's entrance, just in time to greet my mother as she pulled up in the car.

As the summer months neared an end, my father returned to St. Joe to take us to Amarillo. In August we packed our car and loaded up a U-Haul trailer, heading south from Missouri to Texas. My fa-ther made two half-joking predictions as we made our way through Kansas and Oklahoma, then turned west in Texas along the storied east-west highway called Route 66. The first prediction was that due to the parched flatness of the prairie and the ever-burning smokestacks from Amarillo's numerous gas and oil refineries, we would be able to see the city on the far horizon for several hours before we reached it. Coming into Amarillo late at night as we drove through the Texas Panhandle, he proved to be correct. The prairie roads were empty and the wide glow on the horizon seemed unreachable, even though the fume-filled, odorous reality upon our arrival was hardly worth the anticipation of the journey.

The second prediction was that if we were to squirt a hose up into the air in an Amarillo backyard, the Texas Panhandle was so dry that only half of the water would come back down. This was only partially a joke. Amarillo's vegetation was brown and brittle, its air skin-cracking dry. Water locales made up less than one-half of 1 percent of the landmass of the entire city.

The city of Amarillo had sprung up among all this dust, cactus, and tumbleweed in the late 1800s as a cattle town where a few main roads intersected in the dry environs of the Texas prairie. Decades later it became known as an oil town and one of the largest helium producers in the world. But the most memorable aspect of Amarillo was its weather. Local citizens may have been moved to defend the city's dubious loveliness, and their urgent, Texas-size sense of patriotism was palpable. But at bottom this was a desolate place of wild temperature fluctuations, frequent tornadoes, and late-winter blizzards, all of which we experienced in the one year that we lived there. The summer heat was scorching, and the stories about sudden late-winter blizzards were real. On March 25, 1957, the day after Tama's ninth birthday, a snowstorm hit the city with such intensity that local radio and TV announcers warned us to stay off the streets for fear of being swept away and buried inside a snowdrift. The snow did pile up, the wind pushing it so fiercely that the drifts rose like ocean waves, higher than one side of our house.

The wind never seemed to stop blowing. Scientists and meteorologists might debate the accuracy of such calculations, but Amarillo has long been ranked as the third-windiest place in the United States. This was great if you were a curveball pitcher for the local minor league baseball team or if you wanted to fly a kite. But it was terrible for everyone else, especially the Elvis-crazed, bobby-socks-wearing high school girls who had just spent an hour ratting their hair while getting ready for the sock hop in the new era of rock and roll.

For a ten-year-old kid who had just spent two years immersed in the rich and intricate history of Great Britain, life in the Texas Panhandle was a study in marked contrasts. Merely mowing the yard, one of my weekly chores, or pitching a tent while camping with my father in the nearby wilderness of Palo Duro Canyon offered up all the textbook oddities of an episode on today's National Geographic channel. Furry, jumpy tarantulas congregated frequently inside the relatively cool dankness of the outer shed behind the first home in which we lived, where I often went to fetch our electricity-driven mower or to secretly smoke a cigarette. As I pushed the mower over the brittle grass of our backyard it was common to hear the whirring blades suddenly slur and thwack and then expel a prehistoric-looking horned toad, which, although numbingly confused, usually survived the experience with the mere loss of a few moving pieces. Shaggy buffalo gathered dumbly in the dusty arroyos of Palo Duro Canyon, so slow-moving that they seemed half alive, descendants of the vast herds that had been reduced almost to extinction by unregulated slaughter decades earlier as the railroads were being built across the Southwest. One had to be careful when pitching a tent or piling rocks in order to make a campfire, for rattlesnakes were as common in the Texas Panhandle as church mice were in the urban tenements of London.

When my mother enrolled me at the Margaret Wills Elementary School, the administrators did not know where to place me. At age ten

I would have been expected to enter the fifth grade, but due to the individual promotion policies in the British school system I had already finished the Texas equivalent of the sixth grade. No one wanted to advance me to the seventh grade, but my mother insisted that it would be a waste of time to put me back into the fifth. She and the school counselors finally compromised, agreeing that I would enter the sixth grade, which academically would be a repeat performance but where I still would be the youngest student in the class. The oldest, a child of tenant farmers who had just moved to Amarillo from the swamplands of eastern Texas, was just about to turn sixteen. His younger brother, also in the class, was thirteen.

Thus began my unpredictable and sometimes paradoxical post-England journey. My father outdid himself in Amarillo, eventually finding us three different rental homes during our one-year stay. In those years before the enactment of equitable landlord-tenant laws, after four months in our first home we were forced to move when the owner returned early and sent us packing. Our family of six was then squeezed into a cramped two-bedroom house, where my brother and I shared a trundle bed on the small, breezy back porch. Then, just after we found a decent third home, my father received orders to report in August to Maxwell Air Force Base in Alabama, where he would attend the Air Command and Staff College.

If you believe in karma, you might say that these moves were nature's little way of bringing us back into balance after our spectacular luck at The Cedars. But there was always an upside if you looked hard enough for it. We became very good at unpacking and packing our things on short notice. And despite the logistical turmoil, we took some small pride in the fact that my father had just broken an all-time family record: we had moved into and out of four different houses within the space of one year. But Amarillo was merely a harbinger of things to come. In the five years from Mr. Hanley's class at Henlow to the second school I would attend in Nebraska during my sophomore year of high school,

I would be the new guy in nine different schools, from England to Missouri, then to Texas, Alabama, California, and finally Nebraska. As we constantly relocated across the country, widely varying curriculums in different public school systems created gaps and overlaps in my education. Most tellingly, the next four years would be a time of constant dislocation and frenetic movement, causing me and my siblings to hit the "reset" button of our cultural and personal interactions again and again. With our constant moves we were spread wide across the country, but like ivy or mistletoe, our roots never penetrated deeply into the soil of any one location.

This was not a challenge exclusive to my family. It was the defining characteristic of the post–World War II generation of military brats. Our educational experiences were often negative and frequently filled with havoc. But there was a trade-off for those of us who adapted well enough to manage the turbulence. Our personal and cultural education had a depth and reach that could not be paralleled by any other journey. Ever the new guy and frequently under scrutiny, I learned quickly how to read a room and to know instantly where the worst threats might come from. Constantly on the move, I had a front-row seat to observe almost every societal change that was occurring in postwar America. And in the urgent creation of America's missile program, I was able to watch history being made, partly at the hands of my own father, during the beginnings of the Space Age, in an evolving near-wilderness along the central coast of California.

The famed World War II novelist James Jones observed in his book *The Thin Red Line* that American soldiers might be characterized as "the fighting tourists" for their propensity to observe and in a perverse way almost enjoy being able to visit obscure foreign places, despite their obligation to kill enemy soldiers and blow things up once they got there. Here at home, we, the children of these fighting tourists, underwent similar rituals and challenges. Inside our own country, with every new assignment for our fathers, we remained outsiders. For some, a measure of personal charisma, academic performance, or athletic excellence allowed at least marginal entry inside closed and even xenophobic circles. For others, the feeling of blatant exclusion caused unnecessary failures and emotional scars. But we came to accept being viewed as potentially disruptive threats to an established social order and to be treated with curiosity and less than full acceptance. At one time or another almost all of us knew what it felt like to be the awkward stepchild at someone else's family dinner.

I not only learned how to read a room but by necessity became an acute observer of the subtle body language of each new tribal circle. In the 1920s and 1930s the anthropologist Margaret Mead made history by traveling to Samoa to examine and write about such distinctions in the Pacific islands. She might have found it just as fascinating to study our generation of military brats as we skimmed the surface of a dozen different places in the America of the 1950s and early 1960s. I became survival-shrewd as we bounced from town to town, learning how to pick up on each new social dynamic and the ebbs and flows of everyday courtesies and nonverbal signals among cultures that were not my own. Each place and indeed each grouping was different, even though this was all, at least on the surface, America.

In each place I learned valuable distinctions that helped me to develop skills and insights that carried over into leadership challenges during my later life. In order to lead people, you must first motivate them. In order to motivate them, you must understand them. And in order to understand them, you must be able to grasp not simply their words but the emotions behind their words. The same words and gestures can have vastly different intentions in Alabama and Southern California and Nebraska, and sometimes even within the same town.

I learned to be a receiver of information as well as a rather careful broadcaster. I learned to keep my cards close to my chest. I learned when to talk and, just as important, when to shut up. I learned that sometimes you had to fight, but that if you were the new guy, arriving without friends or backup, fights once begun might never end, and when possible it was better to listen intently and think carefully before speaking. In short, I learned—sometimes the hard way—that before I ever put my mouth in motion I should always try to put my brain firmly into gear.

★   ★   ★

Not dissimilar to our short stay in St. Joe, Amarillo became not so much a place where we lived as a launching point for wherever my father's curiosities—and the orders of the Air Force—might take us. On the one hand, having been away in England for two years my father was again trying to compensate for his most recent absence. He was intent on finding a future home, a place where he and my mother might belong once he finished his twenty-year obligation to the military and would be eligible to retire. Unsurprisingly, as with so many members of his generation, his mind was fixed on Florida.

On the other hand, because of his intellectual brilliance and in spite of his lack of formal education, my father had been quietly selected to work on the highly classified development of America's embryonic missile program. From our first months in Amarillo, in ways that he could never fully discuss with us, he had begun to play a part in our country's military response to the vast strategic challenges of our national security policy as a result of the expansionist aims of the Soviet Union and the evolution of America's nuclear policy during the cold war.

For us as a family, these two realities meant that we would be seemingly forever on the road. And each trip got a little harder to endure. The backseat of our car did not grow any wider, but all four of us were definitely getting bigger. Life in the years after England meant a whole lot of time sitting in the ever-more-cramped backseat of a non-air-conditioned car as we burned rubber and bought 24-cents-a-gallon gasoline along the highways that stretched from Texas to Florida to California and back again, with visits to just about every point in between.

This was not a wholly bad thing. Half grudgingly, as the legendary singer Merle Haggard would later write in a country classic, I was becoming seduced and swept away by the "white line fever":

I wonder just what makes a man keep pushing on
I wonder just what makes me sing this highway song

I hated the backseat of the car, but, like my father, I loved to be on the road. In various ways, that wandering spirit became deeply—and permanently—embedded in my own makeup. Driving home along a Virginia road not long ago I saw a bumper sticker on a beat-up old car in the traffic next to me that made me laugh, thinking of those long-ago days: JUST BECAUSE YOU'RE WANDERING DOESN'T MEAN YOU'RE LOST.

During Christmas break in 1956 we piled into our 1952 Cadillac, my dad's most prized possession, and drove more than 1,600 miles in each direction to Sarasota, Florida, to stay with Dad's best friend, Bud Colwell. Uncle Bud was one of the great influences in my life. He and my dad had been roommates at the YMCA in St. Joseph when Pearl Harbor was attacked. Walking with my dad to the military recruiting offices the next day, Bud had been rejected by the Army, Navy, Air Corps, and Marines due to bad eyesight, but within a few months he was drafted into the Army. He spent nearly three years overseas in the campaigns of North Africa, Sicily, and the mainland of Italy, gaining a battlefield commission and rising from private to the rank of captain. Just after the war his eyesight suddenly worsened from macular degeneration that left him legally blind, causing him to be involuntarily retired from a longtime job with the Otis Elevator Company.

This had set Bud back, but because of his amazing resilience that throughout my life has motivated me, it had not knocked him down, much less out. On a small pension, he was spending his days rebuilding a run-down house just across the street from Sarasota Bay, one nail and one saw blade at a time, learning to use his hands through a sense of touch rather than sight. And however inadvertently, Bud was now living where my dad wanted to be, having preceded my dad to his own dream retirement in Florida.

We left Amarillo at dawn, just a few days before Christmas. As always, my dad and mom sat in the front seat, a cooler filled with sandwiches in the space between them. We four kids were jammed tightly against the musty fabric of the backseat. My brother's pet turtle Churchy LaFemme rode on a rock above a puddle inside a metal cookie can in the trunk, along with the luggage. Crossing all of Texas, then traversing Louisiana, Mississippi, a corner of Alabama, and half of Florida, we reached Sarasota in just under two days. Unnecessary complaining from the backseat was forbidden. Pit stops, as on all family journeys, were infrequent. And on New Year's Day we reversed the journey, losing Churchy when the car bounced over a Louisiana railroad track at forty miles an hour and flipped him upside-down into the puddle below his rock.

The following May, when school let out in Amarillo, we drove to Southern California, where my father was assigned to temporary duty at a Department of Defense installation in Inglewood, just southwest of Los Angeles. He could not discuss his assignment with us, other than saying that it was related to the Air Force's involvement in America's emerging missile programs. This reticence was not unusual; in fact, due to his security clearances, it was mandatory. I will never fully know what my father did in the crucial years that preceded and followed this assignment or during his many years as a quiet trailblazer in the Air Force missile programs. Indeed I was well into adulthood before I learned that during the summer my father was on duty at Inglewood, the Air Force was putting together the structure and missions of what would become the Strategic Air Command's First Missile Division.

The First Missile Division would soon be relocated from Inglewood to Cooke Air Force Base, later to be named Vandenberg Air Force Base. My father would be among the first people assigned to it. And like the family pioneers who had preceded us into the mountains of southwest Virginia and beyond, we would be among the first families to move onto the base at Vandenberg. My father would spend a total of four years on the launching pads and in the sea-swept wilderness of Vandenberg, bracketed by a three-year assignment at Strategic Air Command headquarters at Offutt Air Force Base in Nebraska. In that seven-year period, from 1958 to 1965, Vandenberg and the towns around it would transition from a remote region of scrub brush along the central California coast into relatively vibrant and thriving communities. More important, during those years the United States would firmly regain its position as the world's leader in nuclear and missile technology.

Much is owed to those magnificent officers and airmen, and to the scientists and engineers who frequently worked alongside them. Our country was at serious risk. The technology they were putting into place was unproven, and if it did not work our country would be, without exaggeration, in existential danger. They spent unbelievable hours that stretched into unending months out on the launching pads that were being erected in this coastal wilderness. My father took no leave or vacations. He was usually gone from the house when we awoke in the mornings and did not return until after we had gone to bed. Our only family trips were built around his intermittent periods of temporary duty back at Inglewood. During breaks from school we sometimes drove down with him and visited our many aunts and uncles from both sides of the family who in the war years had migrated to Southern California. By then my granny was living in Riverside, a few blocks from my recently remarried Aunt Carolyn.

But during that summer of 1957, as we drove out to California from Amarillo, we knew none of this.

We reunited with Aunt Carolyn, who at the age of twenty-four was married with two children and living in the town of Oceanside, north of San Diego. We spent a couple of months there while my father attended to his Top Secret tasks in Inglewood. Granny was nearby, as was

Aunt Dot and all three of my dad's brothers, Tommy, Charlie, and Art, as well as a legion of cousins. In midsummer we drove back to Texas, picked up our things, and headed again to Florida for a visit to Uncle Bud before reporting to Montgomery, Alabama. Following a year in Alabama, during which we spent our second consecutive Christmas with Uncle Bud and his family, we vacationed in Florida once again and then headed back out to California.

Thus in the space of one year we had not only lived in four different homes; with six people jammed inside our increasingly confining car we had also driven from New York to Missouri to Texas to Florida, back to Texas, on to California, back to Texas, off to Florida, up to Alabama (where we moved into and out of a fifth home), from there to Florida and back twice, and then all the way across the country back to to California.

Traveling thousands of miles through the desert and swamplands with four growing kids jammed into the backseat was not, shall we say, the equivalent of summer camp in the Poconos. The most exciting part of the day was not canoe lessons or learning how to dance but whether we might consolidate our persuasive powers and convince my father to stop at a $10-a-night motel along the highway before the neon "No Vacancy" signs began to flash, keeping us on the road all night for lack of a place to sleep. Crammed together, thirsty and sweating, we grew irritable, bored, and stiff. But with respect to the inevitable noise that came at least hourly from the backseat, in all such journeys my father kept an inalterable "three shut-ups rule." The miles would tick by on the car's odometer. The boredom was pervasive. There were no computer games to play, because there was not yet any such thing as a personal computer. There were no friends to call on the cell phone, because there was no such thing as a cell phone. Books were out of the question since reading in the stuffy, smoke-stale air made me carsick. There were only so many times you could play tic-tac-toe or verbal games such as Box Car. The irritation in the backseat would grow. The bickering would begin. And the noise among the four of us would increase.

"Shut up," my dad would warn whenever the cacophony threatened either his patience or his ability to concentrate. A quiet moment would pass, but like restless puppies we would not be able to contain ourselves.

"*Shut up*," he would warn again, never taking his eyes off the road. This would buy us, maybe, another thirty seconds before one of us would smack another, trying to get in the final blow in a long-simmering argument.

As he uttered the third "SHUT UP!!!" my father would swing his right arm wildly toward the backseat, again never taking his eyes off the road, hitting whoever happened to be just behind him.

The blow most frequently landed on Gary. We, the lowly occupants of the backseat, were not fools. Although the space just behind my dad had the advantage of being next to a window, replete with an armrest and a view, we had all learned the three shut-ups rule. Thus on the long trips, particularly late in the day after a few hundred miles on the road, since my brother was the youngest he got fourth choice. As soon as my dad uttered his second warning, Gary, who sat just behind my dad, understandably became very quiet. His eyes would widen and he would begin to frantically bob and weave. As the third "shut up" was uttered, Gary demonstrated valuable skills in the sacrificial seat, particularly the ability to duck quickly and to use his forearms and elbows to divert the blow.

My dad loved to drive, but more than that he hated to stop. This made him at best a questionable tour guide. The hours would drone on as we crisscrossed the country in the dank and ever more malodorous car. The four of us would grow restless and cramped in the backseat, perennially arguing with each other and inventing games to fight off the monotony. My dad would press forward relentlessly, trying to make six hundred miles a day, every now and then invoking the three shut-ups rule and lashing out into the noise and cramped restlessness of the backseat. In the front seat my mom would patiently act as his navigator, reading the map, periodically making Wonder Bread and lunchmeat sandwiches, and now and then twisting the dial on the radio to try to find some music and local news.

I finally figured it out. My dad's mind had been shaped by flying a B-29 bomber on long-range missions. As he drove, my mother became the navigator, and we were the crew, although it wasn't clear whom he wanted to bomb. You could see the business in his eyes. He smoked constantly, the strong odors of his Camel or self-rolled cigarettes or of his weird metal-stemmed pipe piercing our nostrils and often bringing the rear windows down, even in the most brutal heat of the day. His eyes were intent, never leaving the road in front of us.

But every now and then an alert for a coming historical marker would pop up along the side of the road, causing my dad to suddenly snap out of his trance and remember that this was not actually his air crew sitting in the backseat. A teachable moment had arrived, giving him a quick opportunity to exercise his parenting skills and a chance to shower us with some much-needed cultural immersion. "Okay, guys, historical marker coming up on the right. I'm going to slow down to forty-five miles an hour. There it is, here it comes! *Jim, read the SIGN!*"

I would squint, trying to speed-read as we whizzed past our latest lesson in American history: "Uh—let me see. Blue Star Memorial Highway, something about a Trail, I don't know, something, eighteen hundred, something . . ."

"Blue Star Memorial Highway, what do you know, did you hear that?" Dad would say, biting into his pipe. "Just remember all the history you're being exposed to."

We saw the Painted Desert, too, stopping for a few camera shots just off the highway, and the Grand Canyon, kind of, while taking a restroom break on at least one of our cross-desert journeys. We passed the time by counting how many different states we could identify on the license plates of passing cars, or playing the alphabet game of seeing who could find objects along the road that began with each letter, in sequence, or trying to estimate the distance before we reached a hill or a radio tower on the distant horizon.

When we complained of thirst or boredom my dad would remind us that the pioneer kids who went before us would control their thirst by keeping a piece of metal on their tongue in order to salivate and would conquer boredom by walking next to the wagons holding a string tied to one wheel, counting the revolutions of the wheel and multiplying that by the wheel's circumference in order to calibrate the number of miles the family had journeyed along the dirt paths on that particular day. "How can any of you complain, sitting there in the backseat of a car zooming along a highway and sleeping in a motel room at night? Do you know how many weeks it would take us to make this trip if we were traveling in a covered wagon? How tired would you get walking next to this car? Shut up and count your blessings."

Like so many other bored travelers of that era, we paid great attention to the billboards that appeared along stretches of otherwise empty roads. We especially anticipated the Burma Shave signs that advertised the popular shaving cream with simple jokes spread a half-mile or so along the long, lonesome highway in five or six consecutive posts.

If you think
She likes
Your bristles
Walk bare-footed
Through some thistles
BURMA SHAVE

As we drove through the deserts of Arizona and New Mexico we looked for the images of various animals that appeared on plywood cut-outs just off the road next to the tumbleweed and the cactus plants. The silhouettes were something of a false lure, alerting travelers in the middle of the desert that there would be a gas station and some trinket shops in—let's see—eighty, seventy, sixty, or fifty miles, the countdown continuing, the anticipation building, even though the eventual destination would be little more than a shack at the side of the highway with a gas pump and a small store. If nothing else, the silhouettes gave us something to debate as we twisted and stretched and smacked each other. None of us argued that a rabbit or a Gila monster might actually be in the shops, as advertised in the stark roadside figures. Rather we gave each other odds as to whether my dad would take the time to let us go inside the store and look, even if he stopped for gas. We knew that he definitely wasn't buying anything.

Reaching Los Angeles, we drove along the amazing, modernistic freeway system—an almost futuristic concept in those days—and then searched for a hamburger joint along the city boulevards. We found the intersection of Hollywood and Vine, where we looked vainly out the windows, expecting to see a gaggle of movie stars.

While traveling back east we toured the French Quarter in New Orleans, or at least as much of it as could be absorbed in a walk around the block while my dad took my mom into the famed Café Du Monde for fifteen minutes, buying her a special treat of a beignet and a cup of coffee. Meeting us on the sidewalk outside of the restaurant when they were done, he assured us that this epicurean experience, while seemingly very tasty, was better saved for adulthood, especially since coffee made kids hyper and doughnuts made you fat. We were not fooled; we could see scads of calm, skinny kids sitting at the tables under the outdoor canopy. But we also knew that by sending the four of us for a walk around the block he had given us some much-needed exercise and had also cut two-thirds off his bill.

We drove past black-water swamps and spent long hours on old Highway 90 where it bordered the very edge of the Gulf Coast of Mississippi. We passed stands of trees whose limbs sagged almost nostalgically under the long grey fronds of Spanish moss, reminding me of Tara in *Gone With the Wind* and the romantic tales of the Old South. We stared out at the vast, placid waters of the Gulf of Mexico, which were dotted here and there with a whole bunch of oil rigs that towered within eyesight of the beach. It all seemed beautiful at the time, although I suppose this mix of oil, sand, and water would give the Environmental Protection Agency and most present-day Democratic senators a fit of apoplexy.

★   ★   ★

Aunt Carolyn was like my big sister, only thirteen years older than I. She had been a loving, teasing force in the long years in St. Joe when my dad had been constantly deployed. She taught me how to tie my shoes and took me for my first ice-cream cone. Famously in our family, I became such an instant ice-cream addict that I ate not only the cone but the paper napkin on which the ice cream had melted. While staying with her in California, I sold newspapers on street corners in Oceanside, earning three cents for every paper sold. For some inexplicable reason my biggest sales day was when the headline announced that President Eisenhower had suffered a stomach ailment. I could hardly hold a copy of the paper out in front of me before a customer would swoop it from my hand. Thirty customers cleaned out my entire supply within an hour. "Extra, extra! Eisenhower has stomach upset."

The Florida visits with Uncle Bud were among the high points of my childhood. Uncle Bud was worldly, witty, and wise. He and my dad were superb outdoorsmen and fiercely competitive chess players. Their unique friendship spilled over to both families, creating a deep and broad spirit of kinship. During those breaks my dad and Bud were also on a mission. It often fell to Dad to drive Uncle Bud into Florida's lake country, through remote areas near Ocala, taking soil samples and helping him overcome the devastating impact of the loss of his vision. Bud would later build two different businesses from the ground up, one of them pumping, bagging, and selling silica sand and the other selling fuller's earth.

Every day, on the docks and in the rowboats along Sarasota Bay or along the remote beaches of Longboat Key, my friends and I fished and camped. We gigged crabs and, when we were very lucky, speared a mullet or two. We caught every imaginable type of shallow-water fish, from catfish and pinfish to croakers and flounder, cowfish and dogfish, grouper and speckled trout. For bait we used shrimp and chicken gizzards and pieces of small pinfish. We went barefoot, the soles of our feet becoming leather-hard. And we constantly slapped away droves of mosquitoes, our arms and legs becoming scabbed as if from chicken pox from their persistent bites.

On family outings we drove through thick scrub trees along sandy trails to the wide salt-white beaches, where on any given afternoon on Longboat Key we might have the entire beach to ourselves. At the edge of the surf we dug charcoal pits into the sand, grilling chicken over open fires right on the beach. We harvested hundreds of coquinas to boil into a stew. We dipped our slices of watermelon into the saltwater of the Gulf of Mexico, standing waist-deep in the waves as we ate. We swam through the lapping surf to the sand bars, watching for sharks that might cut, fin-high above the water, along the foaming crest of the waves that washed onto the beach. And there we played, being careful not to step on the pesky stingrays that nestled into the sand bars.

Uncle Bud had three daughters, and in some ways I became the son he never had. When I was older, he gave me wise advice about the sorts of things that my Calvinist father would never shed his self-consciousness to discuss.

Over the next few years my scholastic efforts would tumble, as would my grades. School became a blur of new classrooms, strange teachers, interrupted or overlapping courses, and constantly changing peers. But for everything I lost academically, I gained even more in my understanding of human nature and of our country.

I attended Cloverdale Junior High School in Montgomery, Alabama, where many of the kids went to school barefoot. Football was the consuming passion in Alabama, producing many accomplished athletes, but at Cloverdale the entire team played barefoot. In these days of segregation, all of the students at Cloverdale were white, but many were bused in from hardscrabble neighborhoods at the rural edges of the city. On the school playground one afternoon we watched an overage eighth-grade student beat the tar out of a pretty tough physical education teacher after he had refused the teacher's orders to do some meaningless task. Expelled from school, the boy soon enlisted in the Navy. The South has always turned out excellent if somewhat irreverent soldiers and sailors. I have little doubt that the boy learned how to obey orders while in boot camp.

Living in a neighborhood that bordered the cattle and sheep farms at the outer rim of Montgomery, my brother and I spent hours hiking through the farmlands and the snake-infested ponds and streams. Copperheads and water moccasins were common. We and our friends carried long, shellacked walking sticks to deflect the snakes, although the best course of action was to walk carefully away from them. In the endless pastures we avoided the fulminating fire-ant hills and the ubiquitous cow pies.

Even at age eight my brother was a genius with animals. In the pasture near our home, Gary amazed all of us with his ability to call different cattle by name and to feed them from his hands. None of the rest of us could come within fifty feet of the animals if he was not with us. Often grazing in the tall grass just across the barbed-wire fence from our house on Guymar Road were Stacey, Lacy, and Tracy. Each knew their name when Gary called it. He was the cow-whisperer.

I sat in the Baptist Sunday school as our teacher solemnly informed us that God had made the races separate for a reason and that He did not intend for them to be mixed. Why should man dare to blur the divisions that God Himself had created? In Alabama it was impossible to ignore or rationalize the cruel realities of segregation and the Jim Crow laws. The blatant unfairness and degradation were apparent in every "whites only" drinking fountain and toilet and in the run-down black neighborhoods at the edges of Montgomery, which we drove past on our way to Maxwell Air Force Base.

Many of the seeds of the civil rights movement were sown in Alabama. Not long before our arrival, Rosa Parks had made national headlines—and history—by refusing to sit in the back of a bus, as then required by law. But another, less understood truth was also evident in the struggling edges of this otherwise historic place. The age-old three-tiered structure of the South that had so harmed my mother's family in Arkansas was alive and well in Alabama. The South had never been and was not then simply white against black; it had always contained a thin veneer of whites manipulating other whites against blacks. The country-club whites at the top of the power structure had for too many decades fired the emotions of poor whites and poor blacks, but in different ways. The result was a misdirection that constantly set them off against each other. When two starving dogs are fighting over a bone, neither has the time or the inclination to focus on who ate the meat off it before the bone was tossed their way.

This was a point that far too many political commentators, academics, and policy mavens were missing. To a discerning eye, even at my age, the harsh realities of segregation were fueled by a far more complex set of reasons than those that dominated the national discussion. It was hardly economic disparities that caused a barefoot white kid and a barefoot black kid to carefully watch each other as they drank from segregated water fountains.

I do not make this observation as someone who was welcomed with open arms by the teachers and students at Cloverdale Junior High School. Not being an Alabama native I often found myself derided as a Yankee in this frequently rough public school. My Arkansas-born mother found this humorous. My father explained that my treatment was due to my non-Alabama dialect, which he described as "cosmopolitan" due to our frequent moves. I did not particularly care, at least to the point of debating anyone about it. I simply found it ironic and confusing, one more irritation that attended the reality of being a military brat. Most of my ancestors on both sides had fought for the Confederacy up in Virginia, Kentucky, and Tennessee, although one great-grandfather, Tennessee-born but enlisting from Kentucky, had become a battle-hardened infantry sergeant in the Union Army. In the Civil War no state had seen more fighting, or higher casualties, than Virginia, and two of my ancestors had died fighting for the South. It was puzzling to comprehend how that history made someone a Yankee, even if he wanted to be—except by Alabama standards, where at that time the way one pronounced a few different words might tag him as a foreigner.

Just after my father began the one-year program at the Air Command and Staff College in Montgomery, the military world in which we lived changed overnight. On October 4, 1957, the day before my brother's eighth birthday, the Soviet Union trumped the United States in the space race. Since the end of World War II the overtly expansionist Soviets had repeatedly created turmoil and fear in an unstable postwar world. Their Comintern indoctrination programs were sending well-trained revolutionaries (Vietnam's Ho Chi Minh among them) from Moscow into contested regions across the globe. In war-ravaged Europe the Soviets had created a string of socialist republics out of the countries that had fallen under their control. They had blockaded Berlin in 1948 in an attempt to seal off East Germany and to oust the United States and other former allies from the German capital. More recently they had stolen the secrets of atomic energy from the United States, turning on the spigot for their development of thousands of nuclear weapons. Now they had put Sputnik 1, the first man-made satellite, into orbit.

The combination of a relentless German invasion, a trudging, accepting peasantry, and the vicious inhumanities of the Stalinist system had brought about the deaths of millions of Russian soldiers in World War II. Soviet military technology had been scarce and markedly inferior.

It was often said that the Soviet Army would rather lose twenty soldiers than see a supply truck go up in flames. But now, only twelve years later, the Soviets were being recognized as the world leader in the life-or-death race to combine nuclear weaponry with intercontinental ballistic missiles (ICBMs). That perception alone would affect international relations. More important, its realities threatened America's national existence.

The orbiting payload from Sputnik 1 was hardly bigger than a basketball and weighed less than two hundred pounds. But the military implications of being able to launch ICBMs into orbit, and potentially to arm such missiles with atomic warheads, were sobering and truly frightful. Then, on November 3, 1957, just to emphasize these implications to the rest of the world, the Soviets launched Sputnik 2, which included not only a bigger payload but a dog named Laika.

In this day and age it is hard to explain the sense of peril that attended the successful orbiting of Sputnik 1 and 2. If this accomplishment went unanswered, the United States and its allies would be just as vulnerable as the Japanese had been in August 1945, when confronted with their inability to either defend themselves or match our development of nuclear weaponry.

In standoffs between great powers, the history of warfare from time eternal has been dominated by the advancement of technology. The club beat the fist. The slingshot beat the club. The sword, spear, and shield beat the slingshot. The bow and arrow beat the spear. The longbow beat the crossbow. The musket beat the longbow. The rifle beat the musket. The machine gun beat the rifle. Breach-loaded field artillery beat random, muzzle-loaded cannon. Airpower and modern naval guns expanded mass slaughter's anonymity and reach. Radar beat even the most sophisticated telescope. The atomic bomb beat everything. And in October 1957 the greatest threat to our nation's existence was that, in terms of range and time and thus surprise, the ICBM might clear the entire slate between large nations, enabling incomprehensible levels of complete destruction.

Whatever it was that my father had been working on from the moment he arrived in Amarillo and during his temporary duty assignments at the Inglewood Defense complex in Southern California now quickly came to a head. Within days after the launch of Sputnik, our national leadership announced a renewed and vigorous commitment to America's military missile programs. Unknown to us, my father had already been selected to be a part of this effort. But the necessity for the development of such programs was no longer a matter of conjecture, and the timeline had now been urgently compressed.

The United States would double down on its missile programs. We would be fielding our own ICBMs, and soon. We absolutely had to. Our existence depended on it. And my father would dedicate the rest of his military career to it.

The needs of the service had once again been made clear. We were going to the wild central coast of California.

Chapter Six

MISSILEERS

We awakened early, driving north from Los Angeles past Santa Barbara, finally leaving Highway 101 at a small crossroads called Buellton. From there we took a narrow road to the left, heading west toward the distant sea. The road wound through hills and mountain passes. Soon the vista widened, revealing another small, flat town called Lompoc. A welcome sign at the city limits indicated that we had entered "The Valley of Flowers," population 5,000. As always my dad had done his homework, and during the long drive across the desert we had all heard his briefing. We knew that Lompoc's principal business over the past few decades had been the cultivation and exportation of flower seeds, largely made possible during the lean labor years of World War II by sending Italian and German prisoners of war from their nearby internment camps to work in the fields. We knew also that the local economy had benefited from Lompoc's hosting of a maximum-security Army "disciplinary barracks," a brig that soon would be taken over by the U.S. Bureau of Prisons as a federal penitentiary.

We had entered the valley of jails and flower seeds. Other than the flower fields, there was not a lot to see in Lompoc. We blew through the town in an eyeblink, not even thinking to stop. The road grew even narrower, winding this way and that. The scrub-filled, unpopulated mountains grew steeper. The car moved ever more slowly. And after ten miles or so we found what my father had been looking for.

A gate.

Not a garden gate or a Golden Gate or a Watergate. But neither was it the kind of brick-walled, iron-fenced, elaborately defended gate that we had grown accustomed to entering when we reached the outer perimeter of a military base. The gate itself was a little concrete island with a sentry post, sitting amid a field of raw, torn soil. Behind the gate, wide roads were being scraped from the dry orange earth. The foundations of buildings were being laid. Caterpillar tractors and bulldozer scrapers churned busily, far into the distance. A yet-to-be-populated community was coming alive before our eyes.

At three o'clock in the afternoon we were the only car waiting to enter the gate. The air policeman checked my father's identification and waved us through. As we drove along the roads inside, we could not make out the sort of headquarters buildings and other infrastructure that usually signified a major military installation. Indeed the very sign above the guardhouse at the gate had been small, temporary, and unconvincing: COOKE AIR FORCE BASE. Until a few months before, the installation, then owned by the Army and most recently operated by the California National Guard, had been named Camp Cooke. Within another few months—on October 4, 1958, not incidentally the first anniversary of the launch of Sputnik 1—the 85,000-acre facility in this wild, remote corner of Central California would formally be renamed Vandenberg Air Force Base.

Through my father's many vignettes I had already learned that the

Air Force and the Army did not like each other and rarely seemed to agree on much, especially on how to spend the Department of Defense budget. Indeed this was the very reason that the Army Air Corps had so persistently lobbied to separate itself from the Army in the years leading up to the 1947 National Security Act, which had created not only the Department of Defense but also the Department of the Air Force. But the motivations of these two services had been similar in securing this vast piece of unpopulated land that bordered a rough and untamable stretch of the Pacific Ocean, even though their actual uses could not have been more different. Both the Army, beginning in 1941 as the country was mobilizing for World War II, and the Air Force, which was now taking it over in 1958, had sought out this territory north of Santa Barbara and south of San Luis Obispo due to its value as a vast and otherwise useless wilderness.

During World War II, Camp Cooke had been a heavily used training center for infantry, artillery, and tank units heading to war in the Pacific. Beginning in 1942, units from the Army's 5th, 6th, 11th, 13th, and 20th Armored Divisions trained at Camp Cooke, as did the 2nd Filipino Infantry Regiment and the Army's 86th and 97th Infantry Divisions. In all, during the course of the war more than 400 military units, including medical, combat engineer, field artillery, ordnance, armor, infantry, and antiaircraft artillery, underwent training there. With the onset of the Korean War, Camp Cooke had again been activated in order to provide training for units headed for Korea. After the war the camp had been largely deactivated, although it continued to be used by the California National Guard.

Soon to be named Vandenberg Air Force Base in honor of General Hoyt S. Vandenberg, the second chief of staff of the Air Force and once director of the Central Intelligence Agency, Camp Cooke was ideally suited to become the principal base for the Air Force's missile program. The base covered an immense space at a time when no one knew how large America's missile program might eventually become. The property was already owned by the U.S. military, which eliminated any complications that might arise from interdepartmental transfer or the acquisition of nonfederal lands. It was both expansive and remote, valuable attributes, given the risks and safety zones necessary for the experimental launches of large missiles in an age of unproven and highly risk-filled technology. Its western border was on the sea, not only a safety consideration for missile launches but also a long-term guarantee against any future encroachment from civilian enterprises of a sort that could not be fully anticipated.

Additionally Vandenberg's far-western position on the elbow of the California landmass fit well with the Air Force's objective of putting satellites into polar orbit, whereby a missile would be launched in a north-south direction. Complementing this plan, the civilian launches from Cape Canaveral, Florida, would be sent eastward over the Atlantic, into east-west orbit. Thus by design, at each launching site few American cities and indeed few people would be at any risk if a missile launch went badly, requiring the control officers to abort the launch and destroy a missile in midair when it exceeded the acceptable beams of its trajectory.

This was a wise precaution. Especially for the U.S. military, the late 1950s and early 1960s were a time of missiles behaving badly. Our country was frantically trying to catch up with the Soviet Union. Risks needed to be taken. In those early days a lot of our Thor, Atlas, and Scout missiles were doing weird things. Sometimes they would blow up on the launching pads; sometimes they would veer suddenly toward the mainland just after launch, requiring them to be detonated, scattering pieces all over the Central Coast. Sometimes they exploded high in the sky because of a malfunction as their systems transitioned from stage one to stage two, or from stage two to stage three, treating those of us who were watching from the ground to a thunderous atmospheric display as if they had been giant firecrackers.

But this was the summer of 1958; none of that had happened yet. Camp Cooke had just awakened from the sleep of its World War II and

Korean War origins, to be converted into Cooke Air Force Base and then, eventually, to become the dynamic and vitally important facility of Vandenberg. Over the next year the base would grow from a population of nearly zero to 12,000. The atmosphere was chaotic, like that of a California Gold Rush town. And in the years following, it would grow even larger.

Odd cream-colored buildings dotted the landscape as we drove inside the base, holdover structures from World War II. Tall eucalyptus trees lined the narrow roadways, swaying from the sea breeze, planted during the war as windbreaks in successive lines that melted into a far horizon that eventually met the sea. There was, predictably, no military housing that would offer us a place to live, although we could see from the activity of the bulldozers and tractors the areas where the Capehart homes were being built. There were no schools, although my father assured us they would soon come, along with the housing. There was no operating infrastructure that would absorb the medical and recreational needs of military families. And there was no local population outside the gate itself that might have offered, say, a fast-food joint or a bowling alley or a movie theater—or, more important, a motel where we could spend the night.

All around us there was, basically, nothing.

Our car finally reached an old building where my father presented his orders and reported for duty. He was told that the nearest place that could accommodate a family of six was probably Pismo Beach, fifty miles north along narrow unimproved mountain roads that passed first through the small towns of Santa Maria and Arroyo Grande.

In Pismo Beach we found a motel room for $5 a night. The dingy, mildewed place sat on a hill overlooking the fog-filled pier and streets lined with penny arcades. Expert settlers by now, we quickly adapted to the dark motel room. Without a car for ourselves, we spent idle hours at Pismo Beach as my father drove more than a hundred miles every day along the rough two-lane roads to and from his new assignment. The room was technically called an apartment, since there was a tiny kitchen in one corner. My father negotiated the motel manager down to $25 a week for all six of us, since he could guarantee that we would be staying for a while.

Pismo Beach was more interesting than the Gila monster shop next to Route 66 in the Arizona desert. In fact it became an adventure. We played Skee-Ball at the penny arcades and spent long hours walking along the dull-grey beach, comparing it to the glorious salt-white sands of Sarasota that we had just left behind. We stared westward toward the open sea, watching half-interested fishermen pull an occasional fingerling from the ocean as they conversed with each other on the pier. We rarely saw my father, and we never discussed with him what he was doing in the scrub brush amid the rattlesnakes and wide patches of ice plant at the edges of this same ocean, far to our south.

As the school year neared, my father found a rental home in Santa Maria, which was being vacated by an Air Force officer who had just been reassigned from Vandenberg. Our house in Santa Maria cut my father's commuting time in half, but it still required him to drive twenty-five miles over the rough mountain roads before he reached the gate at Vandenberg, and then several additional miles to the missile pads that bordered the sea. A few months after that we were among the first group of families to move into the new Capehart housing project on the base itself. Thankfully and finally, we would stay in a new three-bedroom home at 612 Arbor Drive for a year and a half—the longest time we would occupy one home, other than Felix Street in St. Joe, in my entire childhood.

I began the eighth grade in Santa Maria, a quiet farming town of 25,000 people known mostly for its expansive strawberry fields. Sometimes as we drove past the fields I would watch my mother in the front seat, staring knowingly through the car window at the Mexican workers bringing in the fruit. I could see the memories floating through her eyes and feel them coursing through her veins. White County, Arkansas, was known mostly for its cotton and its lumber mills, but the small town of

Judsonia, just a few miles north of Kensett, had once labeled itself "The Strawberry Capital of America." My mother had picked and chopped a lot of cotton, but she also remembered well what it was like to work long hours in the strawberry fields, stooped over in the heat, carefully removing the fragile berries and filling up the baskets.

The education degeneration that had begun with our return from England hit a rapid down-slope in California. I attended three schools in the eighth grade alone, each of them a step downward toward academic oblivion. In Santa Maria they tested the whole class and then put four of us into an experimental routine, something of a precursor to today's gifted/talented programs, where we sat separately from the rest of the class and proceeded at our own pace. When my father was assigned to on-base military housing at Vandenberg, the kids at Capehart were initially bused into the overwhelmed school system in the tiny town of Lompoc. The classes were so crowded from the military surge into Vandenberg that the entire school was put on double shifts. In effect the school became two schools under one roof, the morning school and the afternoon school. Classes were so disorderly that often one could not even hear the teacher speak. There was no personal interaction; a student was nothing more than a name on the attendance sheet. Learning was impossible. This was not a school; it was a holding tank.

Just before Christmas, Vandenberg converted a sprawling, old World War II hospital into its own elementary and junior high schools. The one-story cream-colored hospital complex had consisted of a series of open wards connected by long, narrow hallways. Those wards were now our classrooms. School desks replaced the hospital beds. A portable green chalkboard stood in front of the desks, next to a larger desk for the teacher.

Mischief was rampant, both inside and out of these makeshift classrooms. Misconduct was the order of the day. Learning was not.

Entering the ninth grade, I established the school record on the California State Physical Fitness Test. As I was a year younger than my peers and rope-muscled, weighing in at about 120 pounds, it surprised more than one person to see my name in large letters at the top of the poster board that was mounted on a wall just inside the gym door.

Our physical education teacher, Mr. Purdy, was a hard-nosed disciplinarian who had most recently worked in the Lompoc Prison. In the shortened year before, the kids at Vandenberg Junior High had proved too irascible for several PE teachers, all of whom had quit. Mr. Purdy was the answer. He was a natural motivator. In the Marine Corps he would have made a great drill instructor. Inspirational posters filled the old World War II gym: "When the going gets tough, the tough get going" and one that I especially liked, "It's not the size of the dog in the fight, it's the size of the fight in the dog."

To my surprise and mild embarrassment, after the physical fitness tests were scored, Mr. Purdy lectured every class in the school on the subject of determination, and I was his teaching point. He told them that after eight pull-ups I should have dropped off the bar, but that I had refused to quit until I reached seventeen. I still don't agree with him on that. I did seventeen because seventeen needed to be done, Mr. Purdy. But I have never forgotten how valuable a bit of praise can be, especially from someone who grudgingly gives it.

At Parents' Night Mr. Purdy pulled my poker-faced father aside. "I did not know how your son got that score," he said, as my now glowing father recounted when he got home, "until I saw him take his shirt off."

The most memorable moments in the Vandenberg classrooms came from the missile sites, miles away along the coastline, where many of our fathers were spending impossibly long hours performing vital tasks that they could not tell us about. Without warning or fanfare, now and then as we sat in our hospital-ward classrooms the ground would begin to tremble and a dull roar would fill the airspace, becoming so loud that our teachers could not speak. We would pour out of the classrooms into the yard closest to the sea, looking westward and cheering as if we were spectators at a football game. Sometimes a Thor or an Atlas missile would loft majestically into the sky, pitching and yawing and rolling, finding its beam, then arcing into its second stage as it headed southward over the ocean. Sometimes the roar would suddenly stop, and we would know the mission had failed on the launching pad. Sometimes the missile would rise slowly and then go off-track, veering out of sight, and we knew that soon it would be destroyed.

In those moments I would quietly burst inside with pride. That was my dad out there on those pads. On October 16, 1958, the 1st Missile Division officially accepted the first Atlas ICBM launcher from the contractors who had built it. As I would later discover, my father had gained enormous credibility within the Strategic Air Command by having written the book outlining the procedures that the Air Force used to put the Atlas missiles into place. On September 9, 1959, the first Atlas-D missile was successfully launched from Vandenberg. A month later the Atlas ICBMs were equipped, on their launching pads, with nuclear warheads.

The officers and airmen out in the wilderness of Vandenberg had proven that the United States would neither be intimidated nor deterred. The challenge of the Soviet Union with the launch of Sputnik 1 and 2 less than two years before had been met, and surpassed. Later that year, during a visit to the United States, Soviet leader Nikita Khrushchev took the train past the tiny town of Surf on the outer edge of the base as he rode from Los Angeles to San Francisco. As the train passed near Vandenberg Air Force Base, he ceremoniously turned his back to us, staring out of the train car toward the sea. In the homes of Vandenberg we quietly celebrated this open and yet futile rebuke, for it could not have been a greater compliment. We had paid a price, all of us, but our fathers had made our country more secure.

★   ★   ★

In the midst of all this scientific and military achievement, Vandenberg remained remote, undeveloped, and surrounded by wilderness. There were no small commercial outlets such as McDonald's or Burger King where we might eat or, better yet, make a few bucks flipping burgers. There was no gate ghetto outside the base perimeter, and there were no strip malls. In fact there were no stores at all, other than the commissary, where people bought their food, and the Base Exchange, which sold basic clothing and essential sundries. A military-run Teen Club was the only place where kids could gather for social functions; the small, left-over World War II building held little more than a jukebox and a dance floor and usually was open only Friday and Saturday nights.

The base movie theater had one screen, where twice a night it most frequently showed second-rate B movies. Admission was 25 cents for an adult and 15 cents for a child. In the ninth grade, at the age of thirteen and then fourteen, I found work there as a cleanup boy, coming in after school to sweep and swab among the seats and scrub the toilet areas in preparation for the night's customers. The pay was minuscule, but there was little other opportunity for a job at Vandenberg. I mowed lawns here and there, and I tried baby-sitting, which for a boy was difficult work to find.

But the wild things in the dusty scrub and the sea life along the tidal pools and riptides of the Pacific shoreline were there to explore. The wilderness began at the edge of our housing project, continuing for miles until it reached the sea. I regularly took long hikes, often alone, some-times carrying a shotgun or a rifle, my brother sometimes with me, carry-ing a bow. On the far side of a few stands of eucalyptus trees the trenches and the foxholes of the Army training areas still remained. Deer, lynx, bobcats, and rabbits often sprang before us. The rough seacoast was dot-ted with large tidal pools, busily diving cormorants, and thick colonies of sea lions.

The base shuttle bus made regular runs to a small beach area near the town of Surf, but few people took that ride and the beach was usu-ally empty. Signs warned us that the often violent surf, riptides, and seven-mile-an-hour undertow precluded swimming. The target lanes and the impact butts from World War II firing ranges still lined some of the beaches, where soldiers had once fired their rifles toward the empty, turbulent sea.

Our family took weekend drives well to the north along the narrow, sand-filled roads that bordered the sea, the only greenery among the parched sand of the coastline from scraggly shrubs and vast fields of ice plant. My brother and I often went camping with our friends in the sand dunes. We explored the tidal pools and did our best to fish in the rough, almost explosive sea.

At home, my cow-whisperer brother now became the fish gatherer, building a saltwater aquarium for the creatures he took out of the tidal pools. At one point he captured an eel, which over the space of a few days managed to devour every other creature in the tank.

For a few months I operated what certainly was the worst little paper route in the world. Delivering newspapers door to door was one of the few ways that kids just entering their teenage years could make money in this remote place. Competition was fierce, and the methods of obtaining a paper route were shrouded in mystery. There was no place to actually apply for the job. Like the inheritor of a royal title or a family-held monopoly, a kid with a paper route at Vandenberg could not be challenged by a competitor or forced to subdivide his realm. Once he obtained a paper route, unless he grew tired of folding, bundling, and riding his bike through the neighborhoods or his family was transferred to another military base, the job was his.

The moneymaking newspapers at Vandenberg were the *Los Angeles Times* in the morning and the *Santa Barbara News Press* in the afternoon, followed by the *Santa Maria Times* for those interested in more local news. I made myself constantly available as a substitute carrier for the boys who owned the routes whenever they were sick or when their families were on vacation. This brought in some cash from time to time. It also allowed me to get to know the local distributors, who dropped off each day's load of newspapers on the driveway of the carriers. A distributor finally gave me the franchise for sales in my neighborhood of the weekly *Lompoc Record*, a thin local rag whose business model was so skimpy that it did not allow for the complicated paperwork of subscriptions. Instead it required that the paper be sold door to door.

The financial results were slim, but I did sell a lot of *Lompoc Record*s. My brief experience selling newspapers on street corners in Oceanside while staying with Aunt Carolyn had taught me a valuable lesson about face-to-face marketing. This was a military community that had precious little expendable income. With the *Lompoc Record* the challenge was convincing people to buy something that they did not particularly want or need, all in the space of about ten seconds and often in the middle of a hectic family dinner. This meant keeping potential buyers from giving an immediate no to the kid at the front door and balancing their lack of interest in the paper with the fact that it was only a quarter, given to a kid who at least had the industry to be walking through the neighborhoods in the darkness to try, Oliver Twist–like, to make a few pennies.

To this logic I added one more emotion-laden factor. Military family members opening up the door might not be particularly moved when staring into the face of a thirteen-year-old with an earnest but easily dismissed attitude. What they needed to see on their doorstep on a dark Tuesday night was a puppy that they instinctively wanted to pet. That part would be played by my irrepressibly lovable nine-year-old brother.

I carefully prepared Gary for the task, loading him up with canvas bags carrying copies of that week's edition, fitting the bags front to back over his shoulders, burdening him as if he were a pack mule. I taught him how to hold the newspaper, in both hands just below his chin, as soon as the door opened. We rehearsed how he should look: wide-open eyes and hopeful half-smile. I made him practice again and again a slow, cautious phrase to utter as soon as someone answered the door, followed by the smile: "Do you want to buy a *Lompoc Record*?"

I walked with Gary along the streets, holding a larger bag and refilling his as it steadily emptied. Like a parent with a trick-or-treating kid on Halloween night I waited on the sidewalk as he approached each house.

We could not sell the papers fast enough. With each sale I would give Gary a nickel, keeping a dime for myself as the agent and manager. But a few dollars one night a week was a pittance compared to the money being made by the lucky few who had the big routes of the well-known dailies.

Finally one of the distributors offered me a base-wide route that had opened up due to the sudden resignation of the boy who owned it. A kid abandoning something as valuable as a paper route in Vandenberg should have given me pause, but the lure of having my own route made it impossible to even consider saying no. The distributor caught my excited look. He emphasized again that the route was base-wide and that I would have full rights to expand the subscriptions, with a bonus for every new one I could get.

Thus I was suckered into delivering the *San Francisco Chronicle* and the *Los Angeles Mirror News* to homes spread out in various corners of the vast acreage of Vandenberg Air Force Base. I began with a few limitations, one of them being that I did not own a bicycle, and thus on a daily basis had to borrow my brother's white secondhand twenty-incher that my dad had recently given him for Christmas. The second limitation was far more frustrating. Although my territory included the entire housing area, I had only thirty customers. So every afternoon I would load up my newspaper bags and pedal all over the sprawling base in order to throw thirty copies of these two newspapers into the driveways of people who, for reasons unknown even to me, were interested in reading them.

Sunday mornings were the worst. I would wake up before dawn, folding and loading the small pile of newspapers that had been left on my driveway, and then bicycle mile upon mile to deliver them before breakfast. I did not mind the waking up or the pedaling, but all of this effort in order to deliver a mere handful of newspapers seemed foolish compared to my peers, who in the same amount of time were making big money delivering hundreds of copies of the *L.A. Times* and *Santa Barbara News Press*. One cool, foggy morning I pulled myself inside the old green kapok parka that my dad still kept from his days in the frozen regions of Alaska. Coasting down a hill on a long stretch of houses where I had no subscribers, I fell asleep on the bike, crashing immediately into the pavement. Embarrassed, I was saved from real pain by the absence of traffic at six in the morning and by the pillow-like parka that had lured me to sleep in the first place.

The shock came at the end of the first month, when I went to the homes of my customers in order to collect payment. Fully half of them refused to pay me, informing me that they had tried to cancel their subscription to no avail. I had thrown newspapers onto their driveways for a month, certain that each of them would net me almost $2, and had received nothing. I was now down to sixteen customers, spread out over an area several times larger than the landmass of Arlington National Cemetery.

My distributor had obviously heard these complaints before. He promised me that I was first on the waiting list for the Santa Barbara newspaper if the boy who held the route ever quit, which I knew he would not do since he lived across the street and had told me so. The distributor also promised me that since I had the rights to deliver the *Chronicle* and the *Mirror News* throughout the base, I could continue to recruit new customers and thus grow the route. And with that, a light went on in my brain.

In order to grow the route, I told him, I needed extra papers to feed potential customers. He agreed, giving me a stack of complimentary copies every day. Rather than tossing them into random driveways in the housing areas in hopes of eventually finding one or two new customers, I took the extra papers to the military mess halls, where often bored airmen were gathering for their evening meals. This was a win-win solution for both me and the distributor. Instead of making 3 cents a day for every new subscriber, assuming anyone ever decided to subscribe, I now could make a dime for every paper that I sold in the mess hall. And the distributor did not care. If he lost me as the delivery boy for the sixteen scattered subscribers in the housing area, he would have to deliver them himself, because nobody who learned about the realities of this route ever wanted to keep it.

Selling newspapers in the mess halls was easy work and great fun. After a few days a couple of the military cooks adopted me, sneaking me an occasional piece of cake or pie. And convincing a handful of airmen to buy a newspaper taught me valuable new negotiating skills. Approaching the tables, I would quickly figure out which airmen had taken notice of my shoulder bag and would head for them immediately. In newspapers as in politics, there is no substitute for eye contact.

"Hey, mister, how about a *Chronicle* or a *Mirror News*?"

I would inevitably get a dismissive smile. "Not interested."

"It's only a dime."

The resistance would weaken. "I can't read."

"If you buy one I'll read it to you. Come on, mister, it's a dime."

There would be a shared laugh among military friends at the table: *The kid has spunk.* "Oh, all right. If you promise to leave me alone to-morrow."

Pocketing the dime and handing him that day's *Mirror News*, I suggested, "Check out the comics section. Mister, once you read this paper you're going to be looking for me tomorrow!"

★   ★   ★

As we finished nearly two years at Vandenberg, the base itself was growing up. The trees and the yards in the housing areas were becoming more mature. Commercial zones were responding to the increased Air Force presence in the towns of Lompoc and Santa Maria and even in a few spots near the base. The base was becoming known, though not always in a positive way. One weekend afternoon our rather monotonous

regimens were broken when a contingent from the Ban the Bomb movement located somewhere far away, probably San Francisco, made a curious march outside the main gate. We watched from inside the chain-link
fence as they tried to enter the base with their protest signs. We cheered
with relief as they were washed back across the road by air policemen
with a fire hose. Surprisingly they then made a rather orderly departure,
perhaps having captured their political moment with a few good camera
shots.

Along the way, my father had gained a superb reputation for innovative problem solving in a professional arena where, at least in these early
months, raw intellect was valued over formal education. In early 1960 he
was promoted to lieutenant colonel. Along with a handful of others, he
had become a true pioneer in the missile program and was among the first
to be awarded the coveted badge of a Missileman to wear on the upper left
pocket of his uniform jacket, below his ribbons. Above the ribbons, like
a long-lost memory from another time, he was still entitled to wear the
pilot's wings that I had been so worried they would take away from him.
Now he was assigned to Strategic Air Command headquarters at Offutt
Air Force Base, near Omaha, Nebraska, where he would continue to
work on Top Secret issues related to our missile programs.

My ever-nomadic father was nothing if not predictable. Not having
taken anything resembling a vacation in two years, the first thing the Old
Man did before reporting for duty in Nebraska was to load us in the car
and drive from California through Texas and all the way to Florida.

It was a brutal trip. The three shut-ups rule was gone, but with the
improvement of our national highways the goal of 600 miles a day was
now extended, my dad pushing for 700. The backseat of the car had not
grown any bigger, but all four of us kids had.

Reuniting with the Colwell family, we spent a month fishing and
water-skiing in the lake region near Ocala. Life was good in the normal,
outside world. Uncle Bud's silica sand plant was up and running with
three full-time employees, not far from Florida's famed Silver Springs.

I was fourteen. I caught a lot of bass. I learned to pull two water-skiers behind the powerful outboard motors of a fiberglass boat. I hitchhiked here and there along central Florida's tree-lined highways. I fell in love a dozen times a day. Then we turned around and headed halfway back across the country to the farmlands of Nebraska.

Chapter Seven

GONE FOR A SOLDIER

A poem written at age seventeen, the night before graduating from high school:

I want to go back, I want to go back,
Go back to a day left behind,
Forgotten in life's rush to the grave.
Go back to a crisp, cutting autumn day,
With burning leaves and winter's promise in the air.
I want to go back to a day when nothing happened,
A day spent lolling in the grass,
When "the nothings" were my greatest worry,
And "the somethings" were for the Other World,
The world of Cannibals known as adults.

I want to go back—
I'm a fool.
I'll be very old when I return,
When once again a nothing will mean something,
When a day will be spent lying, and thinking, and smelling.
But then I will envy my cannibal sons,
And think only of my man eating days,
When I could brag of sending someone back,
Back to lie, and think, and smell.

I do not want to become a cannibal,
But I will learn to like the meat.
I will learn to live for the kill, and the advance,
And I won't want the "good life."
I won't want to go back.

A bright, bare lightbulb dangled on a wire from a rafter just above my head. The air was brittle and dry as it entered my lungs, stale from years of cloistered confinement, musty with the odor of old wood and stored artifacts. I sat directly underneath the bulb, cross-legged on the wooden floor. A copy of *Life* magazine published during World War II was open on my lap. There in front of me, as if I were alive during those days, was a story recounting, with appropriate maps and heroic black-and-white pictures (all shaped by careful wartime censorship), the American military's battlefield advances on the broad fronts that were being pursued in Europe and in Asia toward the end of the war.

Just as fascinating, on page after page were comic-strip drawings of unusually happy scenes back here as the war went on, and the catchy slogans designed to sell the most popular commercial products of the time.

RCA Victor "Golden Throat" Radio Is Here!

BEST FORM Girdles and Brassieres, No Finer Fit

Park and Tilford, America's Luxury Whiskey

Squibb Angle Toothbrush Cleans Better!

Be Lovely to Love with FRESH Cream Deodorant

Carnation Milk—From Contented Cows!

I'd Walk a Mile for a Camel

Lucky Strike Green Goes to War

Ah, the Lucky Strikes, bringing with them memories of the meticulous smoking habits of my granny. I remembered well those short, unfiltered hits of nicotine, in a pack that was now white instead of prewar green, with a red circle on its front. I didn't know much about girdles or rub-on cream deodorants, but when it came to cigarettes I knew that these advertisements clearly worked. Since my earliest childhood days my granny would smoke no other brand than a Lucky. On the other hand, my dad seemed regularly willing to walk a mile for his also-unfiltered Camels, while my mom would adamantly defend the clean, fresh taste of a new brand called Newport Menthols.

I was just as pliable. Even as kindergartners my friends and I had carried packs of candy cigarettes that duplicated the logos of the brands our parents smoked. Now, whenever I could sneak a pack, I favored Herbert Tareytons, impressed as I was at the age of fourteen by their scientific approach in having created not one but two filters, end on end, one of fiberglass and the other made of "activated charcoal."

There was nothing unique about the magazine on my lap or the stories told inside the pages. In fact I had picked it randomly from among hundreds of magazines, so many that I could never hope to read them all. In every direction from where I sat were neatly stacked piles of America's most famous journals, some dating back to the late 1920s. I could have been sitting in the stack room of a public library. Within fifteen feet of me I could find carefully archived copies of *Time*, *Life*, *Look*, *Coronet*,

Collier's, the *Saturday Evening Post*, *National Geographic*, *Vanity Fair*, *Esquire*, *Newsweek*, *Harper's*, *Pageant*, and others.

But this was not a library, nor was it a school. I was in the attic of the rural farmhouse we were renting five miles outside Plattsmouth, Nebraska, a place we had come to call The Ranch. The people who owned this house and had preceded us as its residents may have been geographically isolated, but without question those old-time farm folks were smart, cultured, and incredibly well-read.

True to the journey of the postwar Air Force, there was not yet sufficient military housing for mid- and lower-ranking families to move immediately onto Offutt Air Force Base. Family quarters were sparse, from an old multifamily Wherry Housing section near a place called Radar Hill to the magnificent historic brick houses along General's Row just across from what many years earlier had been a parade field. Long ago Offutt Air Force Base had been an Army post named Fort Crook. The mansions of General's Row on one side of the field faced a row of wide, porch-lined barracks on the other, where the unmarried enlisted men still lived. The parade field was now an athletic field, where the next summer I would play Babe Ruth League baseball.

But just as at Vandenberg, the Capehart projects were quickly going up. We would soon move into military housing now being constructed outside the base, on the left side of a new duplex that had been built on reclaimed farm fields a few miles outside Offutt's base perimeter. True to my ever-restless father, in Nebraska we would end up living in three different homes during a period of less than three years. While we awaited base housing my father had rented this mammoth old farmhouse for $75 a month, with an agreement that we would pay $100 for every month we remained during the autumn and the winter, when the expensive oil furnaces kicked in full-time.

The Ranch sat on ten acres with an old windmill and several outbuildings, including a barn and a grain shed still used by neighboring farmers, who also tilled the land that surrounded us. Screened summer sleeping porches spanned the second floor above the front entrance to the non-air-conditioned house. Two smaller porches extended from the bedrooms in the back, looking out upon an old chicken coop and a wide vista of rolling corn and milo fields. The museum-like remnants of a corn-mash whiskey still sat in a dim-lit side room in the basement, long out of use. The otherwise empty concrete basement, from which I would clear a series of mousetraps every morning, was large enough for me to build a properly buttressed shooting range where at night I would practice marksmanship with my .22 rifle.

Our ancient wall-mounted telephone belonged inside a Norman Rockwell painting. Its chest-high wooden frame was mounted in the hallway just outside the kitchen, featuring a removable handle to place against one's ear and a voice-box on the frame. The phone lacked even the circular dial that characterized what then were considered modern telephones, which themselves would soon give way to push-button numbers. We did not need the National Security Agency to monitor our phone calls: we were on a party line. All of the farmhouses along this rural route shared the same main phone line. In order to make a call, one was required to give the number to an operator. If a call were coming into our house the operator would signal us with one long ring and two short ones, the identification for our number on the party line. Each subscriber to the party line had his own characteristic ring. Thus a party line could easily become a gossip-maker. If any curious occupant of another farmhouse heard our ring and wanted to listen in on our calls, there was nothing to stop him. Not that we had much that a neighbor might want to listen to in this new rural habitat, other than the moonstruck, teenage chitchat I might direct toward the latest girl I had met in school or at the Offutt Air Force Base swimming pool.

Hey, I really liked that green bathing suit you wore today! Did you hear the new Maurice Williams song, "Stay"? They played it on KOIL this afternoon. I love it when his voice gets way up there like a falsetto—"Oh, won't you stayyy-y-y-y, just a little big longer." And man, I love Dion and the Belmonts. Do you know that song called "The Wanderer"? That's my song, you know. "The Wanderer." Yeah, "I roam around and around and around and around." Oh, did you hear that click? Somebody on my party line just hung up. So, anyway, I hear your mom yelling at you.

My father was not only working at a demanding, Top Secret job at SAC Headquarters; encouraged by his recent promotion and determined to obtain a college degree, he was also attending school three nights a week at the University of Omaha. Fats Domino released a popular song during those months, which we would jokingly sing as we sat without him at the dinner table: "Three nights a week, you're gone / Three nights a week, I'm alone."

When autumn came, I nailed a bushel basket onto a tree and gathered hundreds of green-husked walnuts from where they had fallen into the yard. Measuring off twenty paces and piling the walnuts into another bushel basket, I would then throw them hard into the basket on the tree, again and again. I had read about how to throw a curveball; now I was teaching myself how to pitch. The walnut tossing would pay off, even if a walnut husk was smaller and did not have the raised seams of a baseball. The next year I would co-captain Offutt's Babe Ruth All-Star team, ranking in the top three in the league in batting average and pitching a no-hitter and a one-hitter along the way.

Red squirrels were plentiful and good to eat, sprinting and acrobatically diving among the branches of the nearby trees. With my ever-present shotgun I could shoot at them from the back porch, and sometimes from the front porch. I hunted fat quail and swiftly flying pheasant along the rows and in the drafts of the corn and milo fields, usually walking with a big wad of Red Man chewing tobacco between my cheek and gum. On some days, rifle in hand, I would hike alone five miles across the never-ending farmlands to the Missouri River, and then back again to The Ranch.

The weather grew colder. The heating bills and the rent increased. My father grew restless. My mother was bored and sometimes scared, all alone during the day. My brother and I took turns shooting field mice that were migrating into the tool drawers of the cabinets in the outer sheds, one of us pulling a drawer open and then stepping back as the other fired a bird-shot barrage from a .22 rifle. In the side yards of The Ranch I raked and burned huge piles of autumn leaves. As the leaf piles burned, I stood in the front yard with my lovable but pathetically gun-shy dog Sandy and watched the dusky frigid sky fill with thousands of distantly honking geese, heading south for the winter. Sometimes, in a futile gesture that only accentuated our isolation, I would shoot my .22 into the sky as the thick flocks of geese flew overhead. Firing my rifle into the air was little more than an effective way of scaring my dog. I knew I had about as much chance of dropping one of the geese flying at that impossible altitude as I would have had in convincing Brigitte Bardot to journey from Paris to Nebraska and be my date for the King Corn Carnival. Now, there was a dream.

Somehow, someday I would go to Paris, and to Tokyo, and to Bangkok and Berlin. I was born to be on the road. Every move we made only reinforced my belief that no matter what I had seen, I would someday fulfill a destiny that at that moment I could not clearly define. The white line fever filled my senses. Watching the wild geese and listening to their honking rhapsodies I would remember a song made famous by Frankie Laine:

> *My heart knows what the wild goose knows*
> *And I must go where the wild goose goes*

Perhaps it was the books and magazines that I never stopped reading, however chaotic my formal education had become, or maybe it was the nomadic life into which I had been born. In the meantime I embraced the mysteries of the outdoors, fishing and hunting and camping. I was at peace hiking by myself for miles along the tree lines and next to the streams and the swift, turgid waters of the Missouri River. I was just as comfortable immersing myself in great writing that told the tales of America's cultural and military history. To me, this was not isolation. In my young mind it was preparation.

On lazy weekend afternoons and in the evenings I often found myself alone in the large, walk-around attic of The Ranch, fingering the stacks of magazines as if I had just found buried treasure. We lived five miles outside of town. The TV had three channels, all of which were boring. The radio had two stations, one of which had popular music that I listened to every night before going to sleep. Entrancing, powerful tales awaited me in the archives of the attic. I loved all of it: the exotic, sometimes war-torn places these great writers had seen, the stories they had been able to capture, and the awesome beauty of the words they chose. Inside those pages was firm evidence that these had been years of greatness for America's magazines and for the brilliant and well-regarded talent of the people who had written the stories.

A nagging certainty tugged at me as I read these stories. I could go there. I could do those things. And I could write like that.

At Plattsmouth High School, as at the high school in Bellevue that I would enter later that year, my classroom efforts were perfunctory. If you were an admissions official at a first-string university you would not waste your time looking twice at this kid. My grades followed no pattern, and neither did I. More to the point, I did not particularly care. In my view grades were largely irrelevant to anything I would do in the rest of my life.

By the time I reached my senior year I was retaking second-year algebra and had been relegated to second-track English, despite scoring in the 99th percentile on the nationally administered Iowa State Tests of Educational Development. This was not a question of intellect; it was a measure of my attitude. I really did not know anything about college, but I did know that I hated the confinement and the rote regurgitations that were required in this endless succession of classrooms, from Illinois to England to Missouri, Texas, Alabama, California, and now Nebraska.

This feeling never went away, despite the education I eventually received at the University of Southern California, the Naval Academy, and at the Georgetown University Law Center. I simply was not that interested in being taught and my self-respect never depended on a grade I received in a class that I did not particularly want to take in the first place.

My mind had its own metabolism. I devoured books, statistics, and good journalism, but I learned at my own pace. The constant changes in schools, teachers, subject matter, and classmates had created within me an aversion to sitting at a desk, surrounded by people whom I did not know and who in the next year would inevitably change anyway. I had become, as journalist Elizabeth Drew described me many years later in an article for the *New York Review of Books*, an autodidact.

During my junior year my teacher in American history began one class by commenting that during the Civil War in 1863, Abraham Lincoln had freed all the slaves in America by issuing the Emancipation Proclamation, which was the assigned topic of discussion from our textbooks for that day. Despite my usual reticence I could see where her lecture was heading. She was the teacher and I was a fifteen-year-old naysayer, but I did not agree. As she finished her opening comments to the class I raised my hand. "He didn't free all the slaves," I commented.

This was not the best argument to be making. Her eyes rolled and her face hardened. My own demeanor immediately sagged. Whoops.

From my many moves I knew how to read a room, and in this case I knew full well the look on my teacher's face. Within five seconds I resigned myself to the reality that the rest of this hour, and probably the rest of the year, was not going to go well for me. But despite the teaching point she was trying to make, she was wrong on the basic facts. I was not a frequent talker in class, but I could not stop myself from disagreeing. She was teaching out of a "how-to" textbook. I had read the Emancipation Proclamation, all of it, the night before.

"I do not need any disruptive behavior today," she finally said, for she knew that although I seldom spoke, when I did it was usually to disagree.

"He didn't free all the slaves," I continued. "He didn't free any of the slaves in the Union states. That's what the Proclamation says. He wasn't talking about Missouri, Delaware, Maryland, or Kentucky. They didn't join the Confederacy, but they were still slave states. He didn't free any of the slaves in those states. And not only that, he didn't free any slaves in the areas of the South that the Union Army had already taken over by 1863, either. That was a lot of territory. So he only freed the slaves in the areas of the South that were conquered after his Proclamation. How many was that?"

She said nothing. Ignoring the age-old maxim that if you dig yourself into a deep hole the best thing to do is to ask for a ladder instead of continuing to dig, I doubled down one more time. "He didn't free all the slaves. Why do people keep saying that?"

She continued to stare at me, as if attempting to measure my motives. The thought did cross my mind that Nebraska had fought on the side of the Union. But this wasn't about Nebraska or about the Union or even about slavery, which obviously had ended when the Civil War was over. To me it was about the puzzle of the Emancipation Proclamation and how the issues that had spawned the Civil War were being interpreted a hundred years after the fact. Now that would be a good discussion, I thought, kind of like the piece of a puzzle that could give us a true glimpse into what was really going on in the minds of people a hundred years before. Why hadn't Lincoln freed the slaves in the North in 1863? And what did that really say about the reasons the Civil War was being fought in the first place? I didn't know the answer, but for some reason my teacher and everybody else seemed to be afraid of even discussing the question.

If I could have walked out of the classroom and gone home or to work I would have done so in a heartbeat. Several students were now looking at me as if I had just said there was no God. I had been through a few versions of this before. I knew how it was going to turn out, even before the end of the school day, much less by tomorrow's class. *Did you hear what Jim Webb said in class? That Abraham Lincoln didn't really free the slaves? Sheesh, how can anybody be so stupid?*

I finally shrugged. This was why I hated classrooms.

"I was talking about that Proclamation. Did anybody else read it?"

Many years later, while serving in the Senate, a retired Air Force colonel who had served in the early years of the missile program with my father wrote me a letter. He wanted to know how I could have survived in the American political system when I possessed the disastrous trait of, as he put it, "constantly blurting out the truth." On this morning I had blurted far too much. There was no upside in criticizing the most revered American president in history.

But on most days in high school I blurted out far too little. A year earlier one of my teachers at Plattsmouth High School had stopped class during a particularly distracting Indian summer afternoon. Creeping carefully to my desk as the rest of the class watched delightedly, she waved her hand in front of my face to get my attention. I had been gazing longingly out of the window toward the nearby woods and imagining the swirling eddies and the freedom of the Missouri River far beyond. "Jim Webb," she finally said, "you remind me more of Tom Sawyer than any boy I've ever taught. It would not surprise me to see you jump out of that window and not stop running until you reach the river."

I had actually been thinking of doing just that. A friend and I had been planning for months about how we might take a canoe trip all the way downriver to where the Missouri joined the Mississippi, and then float onward to New Orleans. In retrospect two teenage boys in a canoe filled with camping gear would probably have gotten mugged and maybe even killed by the time we reached St. Louis. But there was no harm in dreaming. We were going to have fun in New Orleans. All this business about "life on the Mississippi River" was Mark Twain's fault, or maybe my dad's for having made me read all of his books from the age of nine, or, most probably, my own for having enjoyed them.

Learning little in school did not stop my thirst for knowledge. I had burned through every interesting book I could find in the meager base library at Vandenberg. I carried books to bed with me at night, including my mother's page-worn copies of Tony Wons's *Scrapbook*, a collection of down-home, inspirational poems and essays that I still keep to this day, and the dry, fragile volumes that my father and I had found on the shelves and tables of the used-book stores and estate sales in Henlow and Hitchin. Now in the attic of The Ranch I had found an inspirational dream world of recent history and exceptional writing talent.

From the time I was ten my dad had challenged me to read a book a week, and if that did not remedy my restlessness to try to read two books a week. Read, read, read, he urged me, and I had, including poetry, fiction, history, and anything I could get my hands on that was about sports or the military. Even at that age my father and I would sometimes have poetry challenges at the dinner table, one of us starting a poem from Rudyard Kipling or another of the great British and Irish poets, or perhaps one of my father's favorite inspirational poems, and the other having to continue the lines.

> *If you can keep your head when all about you*
> *Are losing theirs and blaming it on you*
> *If you can trust yourself when all men doubt you*
> *Yet make allowance for their doubting, too . . .*

While in Nebraska my father also reconnected with his love of Minnesota's lake region, a place where he, along with Uncle Bud and other friends, had first camped and fished in his young adulthood before the war. Even in my infancy my father had taken us to remote fishing camps on Lakes George, Bemidji, and Itasca, whence flowed the headwaters of the Mississippi River, often with Aunt Carolyn and Granny. It was only one day's drive from Omaha to Bemidji. While in Omaha, we usually managed to fit in two fishing trips to the lake country of Minnesota every summer. This family tradition continued throughout my adulthood, well into the next generation, until my father passed away in 1997 at the age of seventy-nine.

We always knew when my father was ready to go to Minnesota. At the dinner table he would begin with one special poem:

Do you fear the force of the wind, the slash of the rain?
Go face it and fight it
Be savage again.
Go cold and hungry like the wolf
Go wade like the crane
The palm of your hand will thicken
The cheek of your face will tan
You'll grow ragged and weary and swarthy
But you'll walk like a man.

* * *

The Baby Boomers were a young generation raised in the wake of the most devastating war the world had ever endured. Not surprisingly World War II was never far away from our consciousness. The war dominated every form of media, from books to film to television, and from serious drama to documentaries and even comedies. For those with an interest in military history, weekend TV was filled with reenactments and detailed documentaries from that epochal event. Powerful narratives recounted such themes as victory at sea, airpower, the tales of heroes such as Audie Murphy and of such historic places as D-Day at Normandy, Iwo Jima, and the Battle of the Bulge.

I absorbed these programs, minute by minute. I knew, as I had always known, that I was born to be a soldier. Generations of family members who had served as citizen-soldiers from before the American Revolution reminded me that I was bred to it, like a bird dog. In China the Confucian scholars often intoned that it was a waste to use good metal to make a nail or to send good men to be soldiers. But one of the highest honors in the Anglo-Celtic tradition that had carried over to the founding of the American frontier was to serve honorably in our military.

Years before, in an old drawing room in England, my father and I had discovered and purchased a leather-bound, gold-embossed collection of poetry called *The Book of the Seven Ages*. The verses in the book were built around a passage from Act II, Scene 7 of Shakespeare's *As You Like It*, which began with the timeless, often-quoted phrase, "All the world's a stage, / and all the men and women merely players." I still keep this two-hundred-year-old book on my shelf. In this famous passage Shakespeare placed a soldier's important formative years between the young life of the lover, "sighing like furnace, with a woeful ballad," and the later, seasoned years of the justice, "full of wise saws and modern instances." I did not know if I would ever reach the level of the justice, but I did know that I would be the soldier, "jealous in honor, sudden and quick in quarrel, seeking the bubble reputation even in the cannon's mouth."

But what road would I take to do so? Unlike my father and eventually my brother, who later became a Marine Corps helicopter pilot, I never felt the romantic lure that both of them attached to the mechanics of flying an aircraft. I teased my father that being a pilot was little more than driving a fancy bus or a truck with wings. He and my brother both dismissed me as if I were incapable of understanding the uniqueness of their special calling, which was true. And although I still had fond memories of our ocean voyages to and from England, I did not want to spend long months at sea in the cramped quarters and on the swaying grey behemoths of our combatant fleets.

I liked the idea of keeping the ground beneath my feet, even if it meant standing inside a muddy, mosquito-infested foxhole, awaiting wounds or death at the hands of the sweating, bug-eyed charge and the pointed weapon of an attacking enemy soldier. I loved to camp and to hike. I had grown up with a rifle or a shotgun in my hands. The logic of ground combat came naturally to me. And I was learning how to think. I decided that whatever else I did in my life, I would someday serve in either the Army infantry or the Marines.

And there was another memorable lesson. Such is the power of the written word that the works of a single thoughtful writer—and indeed sometimes just one powerful book—might focus the direction of a young person's life. James Michener's early novels enthralled me, opening my eyes to the nexus between the American military and modern Asia, and then through his sweeping novel *Hawaii* to the intersection of so many different Asian cultures with the larger history of America itself. For a high school kid who was hitchhiking from school to work every afternoon and then bagging and carrying groceries to people's cars throughout the bone-chilling, windswept Nebraska winters, there could have been no more powerful magic, no sweeter siren song of seduction than to read Michener's early novels—and so to dream.

A Navy veteran of World War II, Michener wrote a series of short stories that became his first book, *Tales of the South Pacific*, which was awarded the Pulitzer Prize for fiction and was the basis for the enduring Rodgers and Hammerstein musical *South Pacific*. His novel *Sayonara*, a beautifully rendered *Upstairs, Downstairs* tale of two cross-cultural love stories set in postwar Japan, was rumored to be based partly on his love affair with Yoriko Sabusawa, who became his third wife. In 1957 *Sayonara* was adapted into a popular film starring Marlon Brando, earning four Academy Awards, including one for Red Buttons as best supporting actor and another for Miyoshi Umeki as best supporting actress. His Korean War novel *The Bridges at Toko-Ri* is a powerful drama of the challenges of combat for carrier-based naval aviators, and also became a well-regarded and enduring film, this one starring William Holden and Grace Kelly.

But above all I found myself mesmerized by Michener's vast, sweeping novel *Hawaii*, a masterful, multigenerational tale that weaves together the stories of the different cultures that had come to populate that tropical paradise. Irritating some, Michener's tapestry begins with a hundred-page essay that resembles a postgraduate student's dissertation in geology, describing the ancient volcanic surges that produced the islands themselves as they bubbled up one eruption at a time from the seabed, and then the typhoons that blew the bugs, birds, and vegetation that initially populated them. But for those who continue reading, Michener describes in powerful, intimate detail people after people leaving their vastly different origins, mostly in Asia, and making their way to the Hawaiian Islands. This mix of cultures came alive with a vibrant reality that offered up an achingly sensuous and energetic alternative world to the bitter struggles of a harsh Nebraska winter. On page after page the stories piled on top of each other, introducing me to arcane social customs, different traditions, and the varying skills that were carried across the seas to this one unique, isolated group of islands, thereby creating a new and unusual society.

Throughout my high school years in Nebraska I had found steady work in grocery stores, first working fifteen-hour Saturdays for 50 cents an hour at Ruback's Grocery in Plattsmouth and then as a bag boy in Offutt's base commissary after school and on the weekends. One freezing afternoon while working in the commissary I noticed a strange, oval-shaped red fruit on a brightly lit shelf as I walked past the produce section. Slowing down, I read the label on the shelf and saw that it was a mango.

An impossible thrill coursed through me. *A mango!* I had never seen one before. I could not believe my eyes. There in front of me, like a page ripped out of a Michener novel, was an exotic fruit that had traveled thousands of miles to be placed on a shelf in the commissary on a winter's day at Offutt Air Force Base, Nebraska.

There was only one mango on the shelf. Perhaps there had been others that had already been bought. I stared at this strangely shaped fruit, enraptured by the thought that I was peering through a prism that on the other side reflected all of the yet-to-be-reached places and people that I was reading about and dreaming of. What would it feel like to simply pull a mango from the low branch of a tree or to buy one for a pittance at a local street market? How had this mango made its journey? And what did it taste like?

The mango was selling for more than a dollar, an exorbitant sum at a time when an entire week's worth of groceries for a military family typically cost around $20. Bagging groceries for tips alone, on a good day I could make perhaps $5. But how could I say no? I dumped my tip money from that day onto the checkout counter, a handful of hardearned nickels, dimes, and quarters, and took my little tropical treasure home.

Standing at the kitchen sink that night, I had trouble just figuring out how to eat it. No one in my family had ever seen a mango. I tried to bite into it like an apple, with no success. I tried to peel it like an orange, but that did not work. Finally I simply attacked it with my knife, slicing it into thin pieces and staring with frustration at the reality that I had just spent nearly an entire day's pay on an apple-size fruit that consisted mostly of a large, inedible seed. But in the end that did not matter. Biting into the stringy mango meat and tasting the sweet exotic juice, I felt as though I had just become a blood brother to the people who unknowingly awaited my arrival in the far realms of the Western Pacific.

I was hooked. I had fallen in love with Hawaii and indeed with all of Pacific Asia, a place I'd never even seen, and also with its pulsing, energetic cultures, which I had experienced only through books and magazines. I had now eaten a mango. I was going to go where they grew wild and plentiful on trees that lined the sand-packed roadways. Nothing was going to stop me. I vowed that whatever course I took in my life, I would find a way to become a part of it.

So the puzzle had begun to sort itself out. I wanted to be an infantry-man and I wanted to go to Asia.

★ ★ ★

At age fourteen, beginning in the base gym at Offutt and continuing for another eight years, I started fighting under the lights. In today's po-litically correct world and given the scientific truth that strong blows to the head might leave one brain-damaged, nerve-trembling, and word-slurring in old age, it is not a popular thing to admit, but I loved to fight. Win or lose, there was a majesty in being in the ring, something akin to serving in the infantry in combat. Those who follow either or both of these pursuits understand the challenges and the risks. But despite the hazards and the inevitable price that must be paid, the fighter and the infantryman know that in every respect they are at the tip of the spear, ath-letically and militarily, and that they must answer in their honor to no one.

On the other hand, spending day after day getting punched in the face by a determined opponent wearing only eight-ounce gloves, the practical equivalent of a smooth fist, was not the most productive way to be expanding my intellect. One of my closest friends, a fine athlete and thrice-wounded Marine from Vietnam, summed up our physical legacy years ago. "I think maybe I should have played the saxophone and then dodged the draft," he cracked. "Every morning when I wake up, the trip between my bed and the bathroom is like a walk down Memory Lane."

Boxing, and the rough-hewn world in which the sport resided, taught me valuable lessons about human struggle and the thin line be-tween success and failure. In the ring you learned quickly that life was not always fair and that it did not always offer you a face-saving time-out when things were going badly. Once the bell rang you were out there by yourself, exposed for all the world to see, until it rang again. No excuses, no sitting out for a couple of plays just because somebody hit you so hard that you couldn't see straight and your toes felt numb. A well-placed hook that popped your mouthpiece onto the canvas did not mean that the referee would stop the fight so you could wash it off and put it back in—and I picked up the chipped teeth to prove it. One lucky punch that dropped you when you were winning, or a couple of disagreeing judges at ringside, could make the difference between a champion and an also-ran. And the Golden Rule among fighters was simple: you shut your mouth and lived with the result, win or lose. Everybody could give a reason why they lost, but nobody liked a complainer.

Not that anybody wanted to go through the demanding regimen and the painful rigors of a fight only to lose. My coach Harley Cooper, a truly great fighter and valued moral mentor who won the national Golden Gloves title as a heavyweight during my senior year in high school, put it as succinctly as anyone I have ever met: "Who ran the first four-minute mile? Roger Bannister. Who came in second? Guess what? Nobody cares."

So you trained hard, fought hard, developed self-discipline, and learned to take a punch. You kept at it because you loved the sport; if you did not, the brutal price of entry was simply too high to pay. I was good, but I was not Harley Cooper and I was not Muhammad Ali. What mattered was that I was willing to step into the ring and to fight my heart out. Even in retrospect, the lessons I learned were worth the price that I paid. Boxing also brought me into intimate contact, so to speak, with many different cultures, whose people I would be required to inspire, motivate, and take care of when I was leading a rifle platoon and company in combat. And in practical terms, boxing was the only sport that did not require me to quit my job while I was in high school, since I could go to the gym after work and still complete my training regimen.

Despite Omaha's seeming isolation at the center of the tranquil farm communities of the Midwest, the city was very much a boxer's town. Winters were cold and frequently boring. There were no hockey teams to root for, and only rarely did Creighton University field a worthy basketball crew. But boxing had found an anchor in this midsize city. The African American communities centered on an area loosely referred to as North 24th Street put forth a continuous stream of notable athletes, including Hall of Fame football star Gale Sayers and his brother, "Rocket Roger," who during those years flirted with world records in the 100-yard dash. North 24th Street also turned out a steady stable of fighters, managed by a one-armed white man who oversaw the Hulit Boxing Club. The Mexican and Eastern European neighborhoods in South Omaha, descended from settlers lured to the city in the early 1900s to work on the railroads and in the stockyards, were known for the tough kids on their streets, in the pool halls, and in the ring. North of Omaha, the Winnebago Indian Reservation hosted a thriving boxing program dominated by young men who would say little to anyone around them while sitting on the wooden benches in the warm-up areas but who were explosive and fiercely determined once the bell rang.

I fought regularly during my last three years of high school, from scraps in local gyms to the much-advertised and well-attended smokers that brought in fighters from the entire Omaha region, and to the more formal programs such as Junior Gloves and Golden Gloves, which expanded the talent pool into nearby Iowa and South Dakota. The Omaha Civic Center was a great venue for boxing. Thousands might turn out for Fight Night during the cold Nebraska winter, even for a series of amateur bouts. Omaha also sponsored strong professional cards, which at that time featured such promising fighters as Adolph Pruitt, a hard-punching welterweight managed by the legendary boxer "Hammering Henry" Armstrong, and Alejandro Lavorante, an Argentine light-heavyweight who later would be killed in the ring by an unknown named John Riggins after having been knocked out in consecutive fights by ring greats Archie Moore and Muhammad Ali.

It was an awesome thing to be fifteen years old and to be treated like a minor rock star, even for twenty minutes, as I punched and bobbed and weaved in front of hundreds and sometimes thousands of boisterous, cigarette-smoking, otherwise winter-bored spectators. The announcer would call for the next fight. My trainers, alternatively Whitey Lohmeier or Harley Cooper, both of them deservedly legendary figures, would rub a final coat of Vaseline onto my eyebrows, cheeks, and lips, smacking my gloves to make sure they were tight against the rolls of gauze that had been wrapped around my wrists and palms, and then push me toward the aisle. I would follow the narrow walkway from the dressing room past interminable rows of packed, expectant fans, climb the wooden stairs, slip under the middle rope, and step into the canvas ring. There I would raise a fist and dance inside the resin box in my corner, making sure that my leather-soled shoes were coated so that I would not slip on the canvas as I fought.

People who did not even know me would cheer as my name was announced. But not just for me, and I knew it even at that age. Whitey, a local boy from Iowa who had been an all-Navy fighter, was beloved in Omaha. He was also a crowd-pleasing rascal who often worked corners wearing Alaskan mukluks and keeping a mix of water and glycerol inside a catsup squeezer, as if he were pouring blood inside a fighter's mouth rather than rinsing it out. Sometimes I would wear his white terry-cloth robe with US NAVY embroidered in large blue letters on the back, and the crowd loved that. Harley, a sharecropper's son from Georgia, was a quiet, homily-speaking role model, rightly revered as perhaps the finest fighter ever to have stepped into the ring in Omaha. In his first fight on the way to the National Golden Gloves title Harley had hit John Gatus, the previous year's Midwest Golden Gloves champion, so hard that Gatus dropped like a stone. This very fine fighter lay unconscious on the canvas floor for more than ten minutes as the doctors tried to wake him up, his left foot twitching uncontrollably as if he were in the middle of a seizure. Fight promoters with big money were begging Harley to turn pro, and I have no doubt he could have been a world champion. But both Harley and Whitey were dedicated career military men. And the crowd loved that as well.

I could have been anybody on those cold winter nights, as long as I was willing to step inside the ring and face somebody my own size. It was a magical little microcosm, with the bright lights overhead illuminating us as the arena lights darkened. Little handheld cameras flashed here and there from the distant seats, glowing like fireflies. Layers of tobacco smoke hung like mist below the ring lights as if we were fighting in wispy strands of fog. The bell would ring. We would step toward each other, chins down and hands high, dancing and snorting as we threw our punches, bobbing and weaving, sidestepping, sometimes lying back against the ropes as we waited for our opponent to attack. This was the whole world squeezed into a brightly lit, smelly square of canvas, just me and the other guy and the referee, the slick wetness of Vaseline and sweat causing our arms and faces to slide in a soapy embrace when we clinched.

I won far more fights than I lost, but win or lose, we were small-time gladiators, with nothing really to gain or to prove except for the esteem and self-respect that came from the fight itself. They cheered us because they saw themselves through us, and what they saw was that we had the guts to take the blows and to accept the sometimes harsh consequences. Omaha was a town that loved the fights.

My dad hated the very thought of boxing, despite the fact that his older brother, Tommy Lee Webb, was known for his fighting skills. In the stockyard communities of St. Joseph he had once been regaled as a "packinghouse pro." My dad should not have complained. He had bought me my first pair of boxing gloves at age six and had taught me how to use them. But he was so opposed to my fighting under the lights that he left it to my mother to sign the necessary medical waivers. He did not come to any of my fights for almost six years. But in truth and in retrospect, his concerns were not misplaced.

When I was fifteen I fought as the only "dependent" member of the Offutt Air Force Base boxing team, the next youngest fighter more than five years older than me. One night as I returned home after a particularly grueling day in school, at work, and then inside the ring, my dad was waiting for me just inside the front door. I was beat, literally. I had a black eye, down in the bone at the edge of the socket. My left ear had puffed up at the top from a hard punch and later had to be drained, giving it a slight but permanent droop. Several teeth were chipped.

My dad reached up and grabbed my chin where it joined my neck. Holding it in one hand as if it were a detached skull, he carefully examined my face. "What the hell are you doing? Someday some guy with an IQ of one is going to hit you so hard that he'll scramble your brain into mush. And then what have you proved?"

We did not wear protective headgear. Sometimes after a hard fight it would take days before my ears stopped ringing, even to the point where I could again hear my teachers at school. Sitting in English class during my senior year, my ears ringing loudly from a fight a few days before, I purposefully yawned, trying to clear the ringing, and suddenly realized that I could breathe through my right ear. The eardrum had been blown out by a punch, and later had to be surgically repaired. At age eighteen a hard left hook when my mouth was partially open tore the ligaments in one side of my jaw and broke it, causing the right side of the jaw to permanently sag. I won the fight. The sagging was the first thing my mother noticed when I walked in the door, home on Christmas leave from the Naval Academy. I hadn't seen her in six months. Her first words, at six in the morning, were "What happened to your jaw?"

In our youth we seldom worry about the wages that we might someday be required to pay for acts that at the time seem oddly normal. Muhammad Ali comes to mind, as do other great fighters, such as Joe Frazier and Jerry Quarry, whose later years were spent in mind-numbed helplessness. In that category of concern we might also include the entire

National Football League, not to mention almost every person who has ever endured long months of infantry combat.

★   ★   ★

In the midst of all this dreaming my father was busy, having left the launching pads of Vandenberg for the world of strategic plans and operations. Then, in the autumn of 1962, came the national moment of truth known as the Cuban Missile Crisis.

American missiles were in place at Vandenberg and elsewhere, including in nuclear submarines at sea. That was a good thing, for relations with the Soviet Union during the early 1960s were growing progressively worse. Since the end of World War II the political tension between our two competing systems of government had steadily gone global and become more direct. The debates had transitioned from the quasi-academic, prewar philosophical disagreements over economic policy and theories of government. There had been a pause in these debates due to the alliance of necessity with the Soviets during the war. But the postwar era had brought an unremitting series of volatile confrontations, often conducted through international surrogates. Much of what was now being called the Third World was in political and economic flux, some countries under the direct sway of one side or the other, but others subject to intense, bloody, and politically inspired insurgencies. And while these lower-level insurgencies shook the stability of the Third World, the First World standoffs grew ever more dangerous. Nuclear weapons of all sorts were being built and fielded at a frenetic pace.

Most disturbing, there was no predictable arc in these ever more serious disagreements, no real historical model that could show us how it might turn out. The horrific carnage of the world wars was testimony to how costly a miscalculation might be. With the advent of nuclear weaponry there was even less margin for diplomatic or military error. For us, the threat of a nuclear attack from Russian-launched ICBMs was not a fantasy. Even more worrisome, such an attack could be conducted and finished, from launch to impact, in less time than it took my dad to climb into his car and drive to work. The policy of the United States had become "mutually assured destruction," better known as MAD, which meant that if the Soviets were going to destroy us, our best-case deterrent was the lose-lose promise that we were going to destroy them just as badly. Threats and dangerous diplomatic posturing were the order of the day.

While the rest of the world debated the nuclear arms race in theoretical terms, we were a part of it, living inside the impact zone of its disastrous potential. In our daily world amid the reclaimed cornfields outside of Offutt and at the edges of the stockyards of Omaha, this boiled down to a pretty simple reality, to be accepted, lived with, and worn, psychologically at least, as one more merit badge on the hidden sash of what it meant to be a military brat. It was widely known that if hostilities between the Soviet Union and the United States were actually to erupt, the Strategic Air Command Headquarters at Offutt was second only to the Pentagon just across the Potomac River from Washington, DC, as a target for nuclear-armed Soviet ICBMs. In fact, given the number of missiles that would be headed our way, we probably were tied with the Pentagon for first place.

In other words, we knew full well that if a nuclear war began, and if the Soviets were even half as good as they claimed to be, then we may as well forget it. Those of us who lived in the vicinity of Offutt would quickly be fried and forgotten.

On the other hand, my dad, ever the science-oriented optimist, frequently counseled us that we did not have that much to worry about. If the air-raid siren were to go off or if the radio were to warn that we were about to be attacked, we should just remember to find a ditch or another piece of low earth and to pull something heavy, perhaps a rug or an overcoat, over the top of us. We were then to lie still. If the initial blast did not kill us, after an hour or so the nuclear fallout would have settled, vastly reducing the potential for radiation burns. After that, he assured us, we would no longer be at risk.

There would be no second strike, or so my dad counseled. They didn't really have *that* many missiles. Just get up out of the ditch, shake off the dust, and get on with the business of cleaning things up. That is, if the initial blast does not kill you, and if there is any real business to get on with.

Thanks, Dad. This is all very reassuring.

In reality we did not spend much time thinking about the prospect of the End of the World. Not many people roll out of bed in the morning wondering how they will respond if a lightning bolt strikes them as they cross the street. Very few airline passengers seriously consider what they will do if the airplane they are boarding actually does crash into the sea. But every now and then there do come clarifying moments.

With the young and relatively inexperienced John F. Kennedy having replaced former five-star general Dwight D. Eisenhower as president, the early years of the 1960s became a time of testing, all along the international creases and borders of what we then were defining as the Free World. The most volatile flash point, just as it had been in the months during my early childhood, when my father had flown in the Berlin Airlift, was the inner German border between East and West Germany, and particularly in Berlin.

The Soviets had a special problem in East Germany, and that problem magnified itself inside the divided city of Berlin. The selling of the communist system worldwide depended on its moral credibility as the evolving smaller nations in the international community shook off the vestiges of their colonial past and looked into the unknown future. That credibility rested largely on Third World perceptions of the untested philosophical snake oil that the Soviets were marketing as the inevitable tenets of societal change.

The revolutionary zealots who wished to recruit, motivate, and sustain an insurgency had to do more than attack the validity of existing governments, be they in Cuba, Vietnam, Angola, or Greece. History informs us that in order to inspire and sustain revolt, one must offer the incentive that after the inevitable bloodshed, the efforts of those who had risen to the cause would be rewarded with more than mere positions of power, which are a part of every political system, however corrupt. The flame of revolution is always lit by the belief that fresh generations of determined leaders might actually bring about a better system of governing and a fairer way of life. Bearded, fiery activists could preach a new doctrine and rant endlessly about the evils of the age of imperialism, but at some point they had to deliver results. And yet, in every place it had prevailed, the record of communist ideology thus far had produced little more than massive bloodshed accompanied by the deliberate destruction of organized religion, the family unit, and the freedom of the press.

On every one of these points, those who had concocted and were directing the spread of international communism had their hands full when it came to explaining the obvious dichotomy of postwar Germany. Indeed, if one wished to compare the merits of totalitarian socialism with those of democracy and free markets, Germany could have served as the perfect laboratory specimen. Not unlike what the world has seen after decades of separation between North and South Korea, the division of Germany at the end of World War II glaringly juxtaposed these two vastly different systems of government on top of one reasonably homogeneous people.

In this visible laboratory experiment the West was clearly winning, as it always would, even in the face of its own widely examined flaws. To paraphrase Winston Churchill, democracy remained the worst system of government in history, except for every other system of government in history. East Germans were voting with their feet, often at the risk of their lives, in support of democracy and the freedoms that came from the minimal government interference inside free market systems. Despite measures to try to prevent their leaving, in the sixteen years between the end of World War II and the summer of 1961 more than 3.5 million

East Germans had fled across the inner border to West Germany. This represented approximately 20 percent of the entire population of East Germany, and a much higher percentage of those who were of working age, particularly among highly educated and skilled workers. And, to state the obvious, no one from the West was trying to hide inside the bed of a covered truck or in the luggage compartment of a train in order to flee into the East.

For those who remained behind, all of East Germany had become a veritable prison. During the 1950s the East German government, largely controlled through the edicts of the Soviet Union, had erected a barrier of barbed wire and concrete walls between East and West Germany. But such physical barriers had not been built inside the city of Berlin, for a complicated set of economic and political reasons. Although the entire city of Berlin was well inside East Germany, this historic capital was not fully controlled by the Soviets but was under the shared administration of the United States, Great Britain, and France, as well as the Soviets. Additionally, valuable railroad traffic from the west moved regularly through Berlin to other points in East Germany. Erecting barriers inside Berlin itself would stop the railroad traffic and damage the already struggling East German economy.

Not surprisingly, in the absence of such impediments, by 1958 more than 90 percent of those who were defecting from East Germany were leaving through Berlin. The city was not only suffering a brain drain; it was dramatic proof that the communist system was an utter failure.

The Soviets and the East German leadership decided to fix this. At midnight on August 12, 1961, while Berlin slept, East German police and army units massed along the borders of the Soviet-controlled sector of the city, tearing up the streets and erecting barbed-wire barriers and fences. By the morning of August 13—my sister Pat's seventeenth birthday—West Berlin had been sealed off from East Berlin and from East Germany. Soon thereafter the barriers would be replaced by a continuous twelve-foot-high concrete wall. Multiple rows of barbed-wire and chain-link fences would soon appear on the East German side of the Wall. Minefields would be laid. Sentry towers would be erected. Guard dogs would prowl the perimeter. Hundreds of people would die for the crime of trying to climb a wall, on the other side of which lived their own countrymen, and in some cases their own family members.

This was the infamous Berlin Wall, erected not as a defensive perimeter against invasion or as an immigration-control measure to protect a country's borders from illegal entry, but as the boundary of a massive national prison, guard towers and all. The sole purpose of these hundreds of miles of cement and barbed wire was to keep people inside a jail that some insisted on calling a country, and thus to preserve the unelected power of so-called leaders who ruled through the perpetuation of individual misery, domestic spying, and the incompetent management of a communist system that had utterly failed.

Obvious as it may seem in the rearview mirror of history, the failures that resulted in the building of the Berlin Wall, and the draconian measures the communist system employed in order to repress their own people, were irrefutable evidence that the sacrifices being made by our fathers and our families in this often-overlooked "nonwar, nonpeace" era were worthwhile. I was a little boy when my dad was sent away from us to fly in the Berlin Airlift. As I approached manhood I could more fully understand the strength and the yearnings not only of the people of Berlin but of all those who were then living under the harsh umbrella of the Soviet Empire. And I knew that if it had not been for the brave pilots and airmen who had fed and sustained the city twelve years before, there would have been no need to build a Berlin Wall, because all of Berlin would have already fallen underneath the weight of a brutal and repressive communist regime.

Twenty-five years later, as an assistant secretary of defense responsible for evaluating American war plans in NATO Europe, I would often travel to Germany to meet with my West German counterparts, and I would frequently visit Berlin. As I passed through Checkpoint Charlie from the placid, thriving neighborhoods of West Berlin into the stark Soviet-controlled streets and ugly postwar buildings of East Berlin, the intimidation and fear among the people forced to live on the communist side were palpable. No one could ignore the nervous looks and the self-conscious, whispering words of East Berliners even as they simply shopped in local stores.

The Berlin Wall fell in 1989, becoming the symbolic precursor to the demise of the Soviet Union itself. Electrified by the suddenness of this historic tectonic shift, the world watched on television as thousands of Germans raced to embrace one another, tearing down the Wall and celebrating the sudden reunification of the country under democratic rule. In 1996, while working on a film project for Paramount Pictures, I revisited the city, spending a good bit of time in what had once been East Berlin and East Germany. On more than one occasion I took long strolls along sections of the now-dismantled Wall, pocketing a chunk from the Wall itself. One of my most gratifying moments was when I brought this little square of once-stultifying cement back home and awarded it, like a long-overdue combat medal, to my father.

Of course in 1961 and 1962 we did not know that any of this would happen as we watched the buildup of vast nuclear arsenals and the ever more dangerous rhetorical escalations between the United States and the Soviet Union. Instead, what we were seeing during those years was an intentional and extremely dangerous escalation of confrontations, largely designed to test the mettle of our recently elected president. Young, the son of immense privilege, the glib, well-managed John F. Kennedy came to office with a reputation as a womanizing dilettante and in foreign policy as a somewhat ethereal, Harvard-embellished academe. The Soviets, after being reined in by eight years of Eisenhower's no-nonsense realpolitik, were ready to pounce. Above all, they viewed Kennedy as a weak, inexperienced leader who would crumble under pressure and be prone to the sort of compromise that might provide him short-term political success from resolving tactical spats while gaining the Soviets a series of long-term strategic advantages that they could use to solidify their growing empire.

In April 1961, just after Kennedy took office and only four months before the erection of the Berlin Wall, his new administration authorized a disastrous CIA-sponsored invasion of Cuba led by a group of overconfident Cuban exiles who sought to topple the Castro government. Former president Eisenhower had warned Kennedy that if he were to order the Bay of Pigs invasion, which had been discussed during Eisenhower's own time in office, he could not afford to fail, for it would "embolden the Soviets to do something that they otherwise would not do." But the Bay of Pigs invasion was a complete and humiliating failure, whose strongest impact was to convince the Soviets of Kennedy's lack of experience and weakness.

Khrushchev, along with the rest of the Kremlin, had watched carefully Kennedy's stumbling performance during the Bay of Pigs debacle. The new president's halfhearted response to the erection of the Berlin Wall four months later further emboldened them. Berlin was the ultimate strategic prize, but the United States had made a glaring error in sponsoring the disastrous invasion of Cuba. For a tangled but not illogical set of reasons, the Soviets became convinced that if they raised the stakes in Cuba, even the worst-case outcome would be a negotiated series of quid-pro-quo compromises in Europe that might over time allow all of Berlin to fall within their orbit. Above all, the Bay of Pigs invasion had given the Soviets a military and diplomatic free shot, an opening that would allow them to significantly increase their influence and even their military presence in Latin America, since in the eyes of much of the world there was some justification in their making a gesture of support for their Cuban ally.

In early 1962 the Soviets began building missile facilities in Cuba, less than a hundred miles off American shores. Despite their repeated assurances that these facilities would contain only defensive antiaircraft weapons, by October 1962 it became clear that the Soviets intended to emplace offensive nuclear weapons that could potentially strike a large number of targets inside the United States itself. Our country had thus entered the most serious nuclear face-off in history. If unanswered, the presence of Soviet nuclear missiles in Cuba would have been tantamount to accepting Soviet domination in Latin America. More grievously, a vast segment of the United States would then be living at risk of a sudden and unstoppable nuclear attack.

During a crucial two-week period recounted in numerous books, films, and strategic recantations, the Kennedy administration successfully expelled the Soviet military from any threatening presence in Cuba. We also made clear that our country would continue to enforce the age-old Monroe Doctrine, warning that we would not accept an offensive Soviet military presence anywhere in our hemisphere. A military blockade was implemented around Cuba. A full-scale invasion of the island was seriously considered. And in the end, our national leaders signaled conclusively that the United States was prepared to respond to Soviet pressures and threats by all means necessary, including the possibility of the onset of a full nuclear war.

At 7:00 PM on October 22, 1962, I stood transfixed before our small black-and-white television set in the living room of our Capehart housing quarters just outside Offutt Air Force Base as President Kennedy delivered a nationwide address announcing the discovery of the missiles. His speech was chilling. The president flatly stated, "It shall be the policy of this nation to regard any nuclear missile launched from Cuba against any nation in the Western Hemisphere as an attack by the Soviet Union on the United States, requiring a full retaliatory response upon the Soviet Union." Solemn and clearly agitated, Kennedy then described the administration's plan: "To halt this offensive buildup, a strict quarantine on all offensive military equipment under shipment to Cuba is being initiated. All ships of any kind bound for Cuba, from whatever nation or port, will, if found to contain cargoes of offensive weapons, be turned back. This quarantine will be extended, if needed, to other types of cargo and carriers. We are not at this time, however, denying the necessities of life as the Soviets attempted to do in their Berlin blockade of 1948."

My first reaction as the president finished his speech was little more than an odd reflection of my youthful naiveté: Was there going to be a war while I was stuck in high school, too young to fight? My second was more personal: it was eight o'clock at night, my dad was not at home, and none of us knew where he was.

In fact during the nationally nerve-racking two weeks that followed, my father largely disappeared. We could not predict with any specificity where he was going, or what he was doing, or when we might see him again, other than that he was constantly in the air on military flights between Offutt and Vandenberg. What did become clear to all of us was that if war came, its outcome would depend heavily on whether the missiles on the launching pads at Vandenberg could do their ugly but essential job. What we later learned was that a cadre of officers, including my father, was tasked with making certain that this would be so. Sleeping only on the military aircraft during the shuttle flights, my father eventually collapsed at a conference table at Offutt and was hospitalized for exhaustion.

The crisis passed. Although a quiet quid pro quo resulted in the United States removing an obsolescent missile system from Turkey, the overwhelming message from the Cuban Missile Crisis was that our country refused to be intimidated in a showdown with grave implications for the emerging international order that had followed World War II. The world had watched as the Soviets were turned away from their bald challenge in Cuba. And in leaving Cuba, Khrushchev had also tacitly yielded on the future of Berlin. The young, untested president had risked it all. Our nation had prevailed, both militarily and in terms of international credibility. And in the most measurable way possible, given the secrecy of that era, we knew that my dad had done his part during two of the most crucial weeks of the entire cold war.

• • •

It had now been five years since those days in Alabama when the first Sputnik had been launched and the Air Force had decided to send my dad to the remote Camp Cooke, which subsequently became Vandenberg Air Force Base. During that time my father had been noticed and respected among the leadership of the Strategic Air Command. Along the way, over a period of twenty-six years, he had also mixed night school with his military assignments and had finally fulfilled his dream of gaining a college degree.

My father's graduation ceremony at the University of Omaha's gymnasium was one of the most memorable moments of my young life. We sat in the front row of the bleachers as the Old Man walked proudly to the podium in the midst of wrinkle-free fellow graduates with not one grey hair on their twenty-something heads. Degree in hand, he then strode across the basketball court, explosively happy after his decades of effort, and waved the diploma in my face.

"You can get anything you want in this country, and don't you ever forget it!"

A couple of years later I would frequently shame myself with the memory of that moment as I contemplated how much I despised the brutal rigors of plebe year at the Naval Academy. My father idolized the Naval Academy, which he referred to as The Trade School. He would have swapped plebe year in a heartbeat for the rigors and uncertainties of his own academic journey. Now, for those who were keeping professional score (and in the Air Force a lot of people did), he was a certified college graduate. After two decades in uniform, that magical little piece of paper had finally placed him as something of an equal among the Academy graduates and the trained engineers who were his Air Force peers and with whom he had been competing in the ever-shrinking percentage zones of those who might be promoted to the next-higher rank.

All the while, things were changing quickly in our household. The Webb kids were growing up. Decisions had to be made about the future. My parents, now married almost twenty years, were becoming nostalgic.

Their social life rarely included visits to restaurants or nightclubs, instead focusing on weekend dinners at the Officers Club and parties at the homes of friends. In the living room they kept stacks of LP records featuring the Big Band Era that had dominated music during their earliest years together. My father loved to pull out the trumpet he had played in a dance band before joining the military, filling the house with better than average renditions of such classics as "Stardust," which he claimed was the most beautiful song ever written. My mother loved to dance; graceful and athletic, she could quickly master the steps of any dance routine. Coming into the house on late Saturday nights I would often find the two of them embracing in the living room, dancing to the Big Band songs that had marked the Hit Parade during their earliest years together.

They were remembering, and in a way they were also preparing for what could be described only as a new set of memories that the ineluctable cycle of life would soon require them to embrace. For just as quickly as the four of us had been born, one after the other we would be leaving to find our own way into full adulthood. The journey of parenting that had so consumed them, and that in fact had completely dominated my mother's waking hours from the time she was eighteen, was going to end.

Coming home from work one night I walked into the small Capehart bedroom that I shared with my brother, unexpectedly finding my mother standing at the clothes closet. She had been hanging my shirts after washing and ironing them, but now she was holding one of the shirts to her face, weeping. Alarmed, I asked her if anything was wrong.

"I just realized that in two years I'll never do this again," she said. Then she caught herself, a false toughness pushing back the tears. "So you've got to learn to do it for yourself. You wash and iron your own clothes from now on."

And so I did. Sensing her fateful mood and remembering how little life had really given her, I also decided to do another thing. My schedule at the base commissary caused me to work weekdays after school, then every other Friday night until eight o'clock and all day every other

Saturday. I decided that I would work weekdays and on Saturdays just for me but that my tips on Friday nights were going to be spent on my mom. On Friday nights toward the end of work I would take a quick break from my job, walk across the street to the Base Exchange, and buy my mother a gift.

Within a few months after the end of the Cuban Missile Crisis my father was deep-selected for promotion to full colonel, which, since he had served only two years as a lieutenant colonel, was a rare accomplishment. In May 1963, the month I graduated from high school, he was ordered back to Vandenberg Air Force Base and given command of the prestigious 4300th Support Squadron, the only composite squadron in the Air Force, responsible for launching Thor, Atlas, and Scout Junior missiles.

I have never met a more capable hands-on engineer than my father. He could fix any electrical problem, overhaul any piece of machinery. And he could work his way through the sophisticated, code-worded scientific formulas in order to actually shoot an intercontinental ballistic missile. He would demonstrate this talent again and again upon his return to Vandenberg, with eleven consecutive perfect launches of the Atlas missile into the faraway atoll of Kwajalein, having taken command of a squadron whose success rate before his arrival was less than 20 percent. Ever the avid outdoorsman, my dad and his first sergeant also worked a deal with local game wardens to bring a truckload of wild boar to the missile sites from nearby Lake Cachuma in order to control the rattlesnake population. The wild boars flourished, feasting on the rattlesnakes. For better or worse they are famous at Vandenberg today.

★   ★   ★

It was not long before I was on the move as well. Almost despite myself, I would soon report to the University of Southern California, one of the country's most well-respected (and expensive) colleges, on a full academic scholarship with my tuition, books, and a stipend toward lodging paid for by the U.S. Navy.

I learned of this on a wintry Saturday morning as I stood at the same kitchen window where months before I had tried to peel and eat a mango. I was washing my breakfast dishes, getting ready to leave for work. Just below the window the driveway dropped down a small hill onto the street. The mailman stopped in front of our house, busy on his weekend rounds, stuffing a few envelopes into our mailbox. I knew what that meant. The chatter in our school was that this was the weekend for the letters to arrive.

Even after all the decades that have passed, I can still see the mail truck pulling away from the front of our house and driving around the corner to its next destination, and still feel the soapy white cereal bowl that I now carefully placed inside the sink. I was wearing a white sweatshirt, wheat-colored Levi's, and white tennis shoes. Soon I would pull on a coat, climbing into my old 1953 Plymouth, and drive to the base commissary. But now there was important mail to fetch.

Leaving the kitchen I opened the side door, stepped into the carport, and walked carefully down the driveway, avoiding a few little patches of ice that might send me suddenly sprawling. It was bitter cold outside, the kind of Nebraska winter morning when the wind blows steadily all the way from the Arctic regions of Manitoba past North Dakota and South Dakota into Nebraska without a mountain or even a high hill to slow it down or one little heat wave along the way to warm it up.

I reached the mailbox, taking a deep breath, and opening it. There among the advertising brochures and a few other pieces of mail was the letter that I had been awaiting and at the same time dreading for more than a month. I immediately grew hopeful, since it was a pretty big envelope. The return address was from the U.S. Navy's Education and

Training Center. I knew this was the right letter, because the envelope was addressed to me.

James Henry Webb Jr.
12435 South 35th Street
Omaha 47, Nebraska

A thrill coursed through me as soon as I fingered the envelope. Even before I opened it I sensed that I had been chosen over nearly a dozen others from our school, including the valedictorian and salutatorian, all of whom had scored high enough on the Navy's standardized test to be offered interviews with two senior Navy officers who would make a final judgment. Unlike regular college admissions, the Navy weighed not only academic grades but also a full range of other qualifications that in their view indicated future leadership potential. My first interviewer, a former enlisted sailor who, like my father, had worked his way to higher rank despite a lack of prestigious academic training, was a boxing fan and had seen me fight. Just as important, he placed my having held a job all through high school as a strength rather than the disqualifier it might have been to others since it limited my school-based extracurricular activities. The other interviewer, an Annapolis-educated senior captain, tested my composure with a couple of unanswerable riddles, and at the end of the interview assured me that I should not worry about my less than brilliant high school grades. The captain was looking for leaders who might turn into scholars, not scholars who might or might not turn into leaders. Einstein was brilliant, the captain pointedly said, but he couldn't even work a yo-yo.

Rejection letters were known to be thin, consisting of one page. The envelope in my mailbox was fat, filled with what I sensed would be long forms and detailed instructions. Although I viscerally understood what this meant, a small part of me still feared that it was not so. I held the envelope in my hand as the wind whipped at me. Finally I could wait no longer. I tore the envelope open and read the letter. There it was, in black and white. I had been selected to receive a full Naval ROTC scholarship at any one of fifty-two colleges and universities across the country, depending only on whether I could get accepted by one of them. In return, I had to agree that I would participate in on-campus NROTC programs and then serve as an officer in the Navy or Marine Corps for a minimum of four years upon graduation.

I still could not believe my luck or fully absorb the finality of their decision. *Are you kidding*, I thought. *ARE YOU KIDDING?* The Department of the Navy was going to pay me to live out my dream. Famed middleweight boxer Rocky Graziano had recently published a memoir called *Somebody Up There Likes Me*. I decided that Somebody Up There liked me too, a lot. At that moment I vowed that I would never betray the trust of those who had put their faith in me.

A neighbor peering out of the window might have thought that young Jim Webb had lost his mind, for I could not control myself. I danced and cheered all the way up the driveway, from the mailbox to the side door of my house, holding the envelope skyward and shaking my fist.

There may be smarter people, I thought to myself as I danced up the driveway. There may be better athletes. There may be people who have been better prepared for college. Along the way there would be people who liked me and there would be people who hated me. But in the end, I decided, none of that counted. I had one thing to offer that nobody else could top: *nobody was going to outwork me*.

And there was another thing, a little guarantee, insignificant unless you have never before known the feeling. For the first time in my life I could actually predict where I would be living and what I would be doing in a year, two years, maybe even eight years. I was going to go to college. And I was going to be a Marine.

They had sent me a stack of forms to fill out. Going through them when I came home from work later that evening, I saw that I was required to list my top six college choices and to apply for admission to each, and after that to check the yes/no box on the remainder of the schools that had NROTC programs. My family had no academic history that I might fall back upon. I had never even heard of half of these schools. The cold winter wind rattled constantly outside my window as I studied the forms. And simple as it might seem for such a life-altering decision, the cold wind finally convinced me. I put down, in order, the six warmest schools on the Navy's list.

My first choice thus was the University of Southern California. Other than its prowess as a football powerhouse I did not know anything about the school. But I had no doubt that it would be warm. And to my pleasant surprise, USC quickly accepted me.

Three days after I graduated from high school our family left Nebraska for my dad's new assignment at Vandenberg Air Force Base, and I never looked back. I had just turned seventeen. On the road once again, the Webb family's fully loaded car headed west, this time leaving my sister Pat behind in Omaha, where she was working as a secretary. Ever emotional and deeply proud that I was going to college, Pat had splurged an entire week's pay on a top-flight Remington typewriter as my high school graduation present. Just as my father's career was finally solidifying, our family was beginning to move into the inevitable dispersion of adulthood. Indeed this would be the last trip I would ever make as part of a family move.

In the rearview window as we headed west, the flat skyline of Omaha disappeared forever from my life. Nebraska was becoming a memory, along with St. Joe and Scott Air Force Base and Henlow and Amarillo and Montgomery, just as suddenly and completely as the end of a movie for which there would be no sequel. Gone in the space of a day were the long, gun-toting hikes to the river, the afternoons and weekends working at the commissary, a teenager's nervous pool games played alongside the hustlers at Paxton's famous downtown hall in the midst of fifty-three slate tables, double-dating to the world's best doughnut shop on 13th Street, sneaking with improper ID into the Muse Theater to watch playfully naked women on soundless screens, camping among the stinger-nettles in the Fontanelle Forest, necking with a girlfriend on the riverbank underneath Bellevue Bridge, shivering in the stands next to my father as we watched the Triple-A Omaha Dodgers play baseball in the early spring, drinking Omaha-only Birch Beer in the summer, driving hell-bent along corrugated dirt roads that often blew my tires out on the curves, going to proms held amid the dung-filled aromas of the Omaha stockyards, and, to my parents' chagrin, hanging out every now and then at the Crooked Ear, a harmless folk-music imitation of what the beatniks in San Francisco were at that time inventing and more hedonistically enjoying.

In late August I reported to the University of Southern California, taking the oath of a midshipman and becoming a member of their NROTC unit. The nine months I spent at Southern Cal became an idyllic interlude in the midst of an odyssey of otherwise constant, grit-filled turbulence. The years had been hard since our return from my dad's magical tour of duty in England seven years before. In contrast, the university was a veritable playground. No one had ever told me that such tranquility and happiness were even possible, despite that fact that I was fulfilling a requirement of the Navy as a precursor to the responsibilities of being a military officer.

As I later liked to tease my Naval Academy classmates that yes, I did have a year of actual college, and yes, I did know what I was missing as we spent all those lonely plebe year weekends staring at the stark walls inside the Marble Monastery of Bancroft Hall.

I loved every day I spent at Southern Cal; it was a heaven that I could only have dreamed of. At the same time, as a scholarship member of the NROTC unit, I took to the prospect of a military life with a voraciousness that was complete. I wanted to be a Marine. I lived, breathed, ate, and drank everything about the Marine Corps. I was ranked first in leadership during both semesters, causing the Navy and Marine Corps officers who ran the NROTC program to strongly recommend that I apply to the Naval Academy.

Personally I was ambivalent. I had everything I wanted at Southern Cal. I did not know very much about the Naval Academy and had never even seen the place. On the other hand, the football games at the Los Angeles Coliseum were legendary. Fraternity life was actually better than the movie *Animal House* would later portray it. At seventeen and finally turning eighteen, I perfected the technique of drinking myself sick every Friday night, sometimes barfing expertly from my frat room window into the trash cans just below. Weekends often began with loud, raucous keg parties on Fraternity Row. I partied with friends on the nearby beaches west and south of the campus. On Sunday I often took Harry Truman walks, picking a direction and heading for hours into different neighborhoods, including the simmering streets of Watts, which would explode shortly after I left USC, sometimes ending up hitchhiking all the way to Venice and back.

But I also knew that beyond the beery, almost incomprehensible enjoyment of fraternity life at USC the world was changing. The civil rights movement was hitting an early crescendo with Martin Luther King's memorable "I Have a Dream" speech at the Lincoln Memorial in Washington. The Beatles were competing with, and surpassing, the popularity of the Beach Boys. In the troubled country of South Vietnam, President Ngo Dinh Diem was assassinated in a coup, causing some of the older members of our ROTC unit to predict that we might end up going to war in that remote place that none of us had ever heard of. And then, only a few weeks later, President Kennedy was assassinated in Dallas.

In an impulsive moment after the assassination, while I was watching the Army-Navy game on TV, my competitive urges overwhelmed my common sense. I decided to apply to the Naval Academy. As the TV screen repeatedly showed the Brigade of Midshipmen cheering on their team from the stands at the Philadelphia stadium, my mind flashed forward into the unknown of the career I had chosen. The crisply uniformed young men in their woolen overcoats and white midshipman caps were, inarguably, the Varsity. Indeed the television announcers repeated again and again that this was "the cream of American youth," being groomed to assume "the highest positions of command, citizenship, and government."

As I watched the game the thought nagged at me, whether true or not: Were they going to be better prepared than I was? Was I being lulled into complacency by the existence that I had come to so fully enjoy? And there was another uncertainty: no matter how well I did in the ROTC program, there would always be a question in my own mind of whether I could have competed, and thus grown, in the twenty-four-hours-a-day, seven-days-a-week regimen in which the Academy midshipmen lived.

So I applied, and was accepted as a member of the Class of 1968. My friends were very excited. The officers in the NROTC unit were confident that I would do well. My father and mother were beyond overjoyed, for this was The Trade School, after all, and in the military environment in which they lived, their son had reached the apex.

In June 1964 I said good-bye to college things and flew east to Annapolis. As the aircraft lifted off from the Los Angeles Airport, heading toward Dulles International, it seemed as though I was the only one with mixed feelings about what I was leaving behind and the four years I would now be spending at a place I had never seen.

Chapter Eight

WHERE SEVERN
JOINS THE TIDE

Four years together by the Bay where Severn joins the tide
Then by the Service called away, we've scattered far and wide.
"Navy Blue and Gold," alma mater of the U.S. Naval Academy

The front doors of the Naval Academy chapel are high and heavy. I walk up the wide, tree-shaded steps toward them, looking left and right to see if anyone is going to stop me, and then I carefully pull them open. I do so not only with some physical effort but also with trepidation, for at this moment I am nothing more than an interloper. It is a bit surprising that the doors are not locked. As I pull them open, the cavernous chapel reveals itself, markedly unchanged despite the decades that have passed since I first sat in its pews.

And I step inside.

Even after more than 150 years of what seems to have been continuous construction, including landfills dredged up from the Severn River and the Chesapeake Bay, the chapel remains the emotional and geographic centerpiece of the Naval Academy grounds. Tradition once had

177

it that only upon sighting the chapel dome upon one's return from a summer at sea following plebe year would a midshipman truly become an upperclassman. Long ago, midshipmen were seldom allowed to go beyond
the infamous "seven-mile limit" even on weekend liberty, the seven miles
being measured by the distance from the chapel's dome. Sunday services
at the chapel were mandatory until the 1970s, when a U.S. Supreme
Court case overturned the regulation on First Amendment grounds.

Those weekly services remain memorable, even for those of us
who probably would not have attended regularly if given the option of
catching a couple more hours of much-needed sleep on Sunday mornings, particularly during plebe year. Political correctness and religious
diversity certainly argue against requiring the entire brigade to march
to chapel on Sunday morning in their Full Dress Blues as a band plays
"Onward Christian Soldiers," although for me the song was always more
martial than messianic, bringing back memories of my schoolboy days in
England as we sang a dozen different military songs in Mr. Hanley's class
at RAF Henlow.

But no matter; in a much larger sense the memories of attending
chapel as a midshipman strike deep and hard. Some of them are indeed
religious. Some of them are military. And some are intensely personal, for
the chapel is a welcoming and yet intimidating place, a staid and unwav-
ering benchmark from which to measure the trajectory of one's later life.

And here I am, a much older man, laden with such memories, pulling open the heavy front doors of the chapel on a weekday summer
afternoon, then stepping quietly inside. Its size and very magnificence
overwhelm me, as do the memories themselves. The pews are empty,
although capable of seating more than two thousand worshippers at a
time. The images on the stained-glass windows gleam above me, just as
they did when I was a determined but largely unknowing young man,
staring up at them while sitting in the pews, dressed in my Full Dress
Blues. But now, instead of challenging me about my future intentions,

they are asking me an unavoidable, retrospective question: Have I indeed lived up to the promises that I secretly made during the weekly moment of silent prayer all those years ago?

As I stand alone among the empty pews, in my mind the chapel comes alive with visions from those earlier days. The pews were full. The prayers were intense. The days were harsh, but the dreams were fresh. We were all earnest and yet for the most part unscarred, and thus forgivably naive. I had not yet learned the disappointments that seem to follow one's inability to find clear answers to the complex demands of some of life's harsher realities.

Someone once said that every successful life is in reality a series of minor failures. In the chapel as I stand surrounded by these recollections I do not think of the résumé-enhancing achievements summarized elsewhere on mere pieces of paper, or even of such things as whether I held a position of responsibility or won an election. Instead my mind goes back to the early years, when I sat inside the pews and wondered whether I could live up to the words that were being spoken from the pulpit, and the examples that had been set by those who had gone before me. When I became Secretary of the Navy, young for the job at forty-one and in retrospect admittedly brash, I mentioned to a writer for *Newsweek* that when I died, God was not going to ask me if I had been Secretary of the Navy. The thought remains, standing here in the cool quiet of the pews. Nor would the summation of a truly good life necessarily include having been a member of the U.S. Senate.

The call to serve the higher good can hardly be described in a résumé, and those who speak fervently about their faith or how much they have done for their country while in public office usually make me nervous. But service to country has always been my life's clearest calling. And if that calling did not begin here at the Naval Academy, certainly this is the place where it was most intensely honed and challenged.

One of the most memorable mottoes of the Naval Academy has

always been *"Non Sibi, Sed Patriae"*—not self, but country. Appropriately, that motto is inscribed over the chapel doors. And thus for me and many others the chapel has always transcended religious ceremony. Instead, it encapsulates a stern, age-old reminder that true service is by definition a sacred obligation—in peace or at war—which requires one to sublimate himself to a larger good. Even at this stolen summer moment, standing among the pews and surrounded by a rush of memories, I worry that however I answered the call all those years ago and even more recently, I have not done enough.

Like whispering ghosts, the voices of thousands of midshipmen singing the Navy Hymn on a long-ago Sunday morning echo across the now-empty walls:

Eternal Father, strong to save
Whose arm hath bound the restless wave
Who bid'st the mighty Ocean deep
Its own appointed limits keep;
O hear us when we cry to thee
For those in peril on the sea.

It is not so much the song, beautiful and timeless as it may be, but instead the vanished voices that haunt me. The chapel will always be here, as it has been for more than a hundred years. The Navy Hymn will always be sung, as it now has been sung since before the Civil War. But just as my surreptitious visit has been quick and unrecorded, those of us who spent our young years at this institution were at bottom merely transients.

We ourselves passed through this place in four years, which for us may have seemed endless at the time but which in historical context was nothing more than a mere moment. In differing ways the Naval Academy left its mark on every one of us. In much less significant ways, each of us left a little bit of ourselves behind. And in a far greater sense, as we poured out from Annapolis into the Fleet, class by class and year by year, we carried with us the harsh and timeless lessons that are the bedrock of this institution, to be infused, one person and one day at a time, into the very soul of what it means to serve one's country.

★   ★   ★

In the late afternoon of June 30, 1964, 1,334 young men stood together in the packed confines of Dahlgren Hall, the Naval Academy's armory, and took the oath of office as midshipmen in the Class of 1968. The swearing-in ceremony was in a way symbolic of the larger journey on which they had all begun. From the outside looking in, this was a three-hanky meltdown moment, as sentimental as an *Old Yeller* Disney movie, showcasing an aggregation of the Cream of America's Youth, a descriptive phrase that would be repeated often over the next four years. From the inside looking out, the mood had already become a mix of uncertain panic and even regret from a room filled with teenagers who had just committed themselves to a full year of unremitting harassment and abuse, four years of monk-like separation from the rest of American society, and a minimum of nine years of military service.

Cynicism was a valuable commodity at the Naval Academy. Within only a few hours it had spread like wildfire among even the most naive and the most inspired of those who had made the journey to Annapolis to become midshipmen. Four years later it would have become the most common form of humor and repartee. No tragedy or disappointment was so great that it could not be half laughingly dismissed. Even as the graduation caps went into the air in 1968, the mumbled punch line among the new ensigns and lieutenants ran something like *Congratulations, you just finished four years of abstinence, discipline, and isolation. Now for your reward: go to Vietnam.*

Early that morning in the summer of 1964 the class had reported for duty in half-hour time increments at the Library Assembly area, moving in an orderly fashion from one station to another in the wide, dim-lit, air-conditioned room. Conversing with staff in near-whispers, the members of the new class processed their paperwork, paid their $200 entrance fee, and signed their lives away. At the rear of the room, the paperwork complete, each new plebe had carried his suitcases through an exit door and walked onto a sunbaked terrace that marked the inner domain of the grounds surrounding Bancroft Hall.

The cacophony that awaited them on the terrace made the whispering courtesies of the Library Assembly area seem like a cruel, intentional joke. In the space of five seconds the hell of plebe year descended upon each new "piece of meat" with an unanticipated suddenness. Screaming, nonsensical orders and shocked, submissive replies filled the terrace. Young men ran in loose military formations, gasping for air, bogged down with the luggage they had brought from whatever hometown they had left behind, their best suits already soaked with sweat.

My turn came. I stepped onto the scream-filled terrace and was immediately lost in the confusion. My mind fell into free fall, as if I had just jumped off the edge of a sharp cliff and only now was permitted to look down to see if there was water or a net below. I had never been to the Naval Academy before. The sum of my knowledge about plebe year was contained in a guidebook sent to me along with my acceptance packet, but it was mostly filled with dry narrative. At my final station in the Library Assembly area I had been given a cream-colored IBM computer punch card that noted my platoon and squad number, 2223, as well as my assigned room number, 3206, my Naval Academy "alpha number," 688533, and my laundry number, 9718. Armed with only this quizzical entry ticket, I stood next to my suitcase and stared out at the pandemonium, trying to figure out what to do and where to go.

A second-classman in a starched, short-sleeve Tropical White uniform walked briskly up to me. He hit me hard in the center of my chest, taking the card from my hand and examining it. He was wearing a red name tag above his left shirt pocket, identifying him as a member of the Plebe Detail, the Naval Academy equivalent of Marine Corps drill instructors.

"You're in First Battalion," he said, handing the card back to me. He pointed to a spot where a dozen other plebes were standing awkwardly, awaiting further orders. "Stand with that group. Now, get over there. Move it, move it! Expedite, EXPEDITE!"

I looked at him for a moment, picking up my suitcase as I measured his eyes, and made my very first mistake as a midshipman. Hitting one's subordinate was not a part of the military in which I had lived and come to love over the past eighteen years. I nodded toward my chest, where he had just hit me. "Are you really allowed to do that?"

"Do what?"

"Hit me?"

"*What did you just say?*" He called to a few of his nearby classmates. "Hey, Sam, hey, Lobo, we got a sea lawyer here!" He hit me again as his classmates converged on me, screaming in my face. "There's only one answer I want out of you! MORE, SIR! HARDER, SIR! FASTER, SIR! I LOVE IT, SIR!"

I had definitely gotten his point. "Aye, aye, sir." I mimicked him, without his energy. "More, sir, harder, sir, faster, sir, I love it, sir."

"Are you a wise-ass? Get your fat little feet over there. MOVE IT."

So I learned, with two swift blows to the chest and one cold rebuke, that the military was the military, but the Academy was the Academy, and that in order to survive both it was necessary to separate one from the other.

"Aye, aye, sir. Thank you, sir."

"Don't thank me. I'm not your friend."

Thus the day began and so it passed, with exhausting and yet remarkable precision. Inside the closed corridors of Bancroft Hall the new plebe class sprinted back and forth in twenty-man groups, chopping to every destination under the relentless screams of their new squad leaders. By late afternoon each midshipman had checked into his assigned room, then raced from one checkpoint to another, drawing military shoes and clothes, changing quickly into the sailor-like "white works" uniforms and circular Dixie Cup hats, opening up "box issue" supplies of sheets, towels, sweat suits, pajamas, socks, underwear, toiletries, and other necessities, getting a buzz haircut at the barbershop, and undergoing the first of what would become hundreds of "Plebe Ho" sessions in the open corridors, our backs in a brace up against the walls as the upperclassmen paced along the center of the hallway, lecturing us on the do's and don'ts of the year that had just begun.

As this pandemonium went on behind the sequestered walls of Bancroft Hall, hundreds of family members, high school sweethearts, and friends spent the hours strolling along the brick walks and the grounds outside. Inside the Hall, a new way of life was forever swallowing up their loved ones. Oblivious to the chaos, the friends and family members stared with awe and amazement at the tranquil beauty of the lush, historic grounds that bordered the Severn River where it opened up into the sailboat-dotted Chesapeake Bay. To the west the sun began to drop below the skyline of Maryland's capital city. As the sky dimmed and the air cooled they converged on Dahlgren Hall, climbing its stairways to the upper terrace. From that vantage point they stood behind the railings and looked down below them at the newly formed Class of 1968 as it marched wearily in from Bancroft Hall to take the oath.

Most of them did not know it yet, but those young men were no longer the same people their families had dropped off at the Library Assembly area only eight hours before. The new plebes looked pretty much the same, jammed tightly against each other in the warm confines of Dahlgren Hall, although many were dangerously dizzy from dehydration and exertion. For the ceremony they had changed back into their now salt-stained and rumpled civilian suits. But once they had taken the oath they would march immediately back into Bancroft Hall, where the suits would come off again, this time for good. As the long day came to a close the suits would be jammed hurriedly into a box. The box would be shipped back home, along with every other item of civilian clothing, including underwear, shoes, and socks. The new plebes would not be allowed to wear any article of civilian clothing until they arrived home for Christmas leave six months later. And they would not be permitted to keep civilian clothes in their rooms for another three years.

With a nostalgia normally reserved for childhood I was already missing the lost, languid afternoons on Fraternity Row at Southern Cal. And for the first time I realized that I had fallen inside an unanswerable conundrum. On the one hand, this was indeed The Trade School, a place of constant challenge and personal growth that my father could only have dreamed of attending. On the other, I knew that I was never going to actually like the Naval Academy. But the bottom line was that however much I hated it, I knew why I had come and I knew I would never quit.

The time for contemplating alternatives was over. My mind was shuddering from the reality of the contract I had signed. It would be nine years—four at the Academy and another five in the Marine Corps, fully half as long as I had already lived—before I would be able to regain control over the direction of my life for even the simplest decisions. The unknowns of those next nine years unfurled before me, overwhelming my emotions even though it was useless to think about them. I would probably stay in the military, as had my father. But who knew? By the time I regained enough control over my life even to decide, I would be twenty-seven, which in my eighteen-year-old mind would make me as old and as mentally manacled as a zoo-kept elephant.

Inspirational speeches were being made by the Academy's senior officers as the commandant of midshipmen prepared to administer the oath. Above us on the second-floor terrace, many mothers and girlfriends were crying, some of them waving brightly colored handkerchiefs, trying to find and gain the attention of their favorite plebe.

I had no such challenges; my family was three thousand miles away at Vandenberg Air Force Base in California. But it was no use for any of the weeping, hanky-waving moms and girlfriends to try to make eye contact, even if they could. A wall had just been erected between us and every aspect of our previous lives. Over the years that wall might be crossed from time to time, but it would never again come fully down. The moms would grow older; most of the girlfriends would disappear. As one officer cynically put it on our way back to the innards of Bancroft Hall, "You could hear the umbilical cords snapping from one end of Dahlgren Hall to the other."

I was definitely not in college anymore.

Four years later, on June 5, 1968, only 821 of the 1,334 young men who took the oath as midshipmen that day would have survived the brutal rigors of plebe year and a newly invigorated academic curriculum in order to graduate from this historic institution and receive commissions in the Navy or Marine Corps. (Another twenty-one completed probationary training and graduated at the end of that summer.) The countervailing pressures of military indoctrination on the one hand and stringent academic requirements on the other would cause the Class of 1968 to suffer an attrition rate of 37.9 percent, the highest among all of the Naval Academy classes in the entire thirty-year period spanning the final months of World War II to the end of the Vietnam War. To put this number into modern perspective, the Class of 1968's attrition rate was more than three times higher than that of the Class of 2012, which lost just 12.2 percent of its enrollees during its four years at the Academy.

Over time the Class of 1968 would become famous for many reasons. Its high attrition rate was certainly one of them, causing some later historians to label the class "68-X" for the disciplinary and academic experiments that had been initiated at the expense (and demise) of some of its members. Another remarkable factor in the class's journey was that its time at the Academy, from June 1964 to June 1968, coincided exactly with a number of historic institutional and societal junctures. Some of these sea changes reflected new policies at the Academy; others mirrored the dramatic turmoil in American society brought on by the culmination of the civil rights movement and the vitriolic debate over the Vietnam War.

I reported to the Naval Academy in 1964 with a short haircut that happened to be the most common look on Fraternity Row at Southern Cal. I graduated from the Naval Academy in 1968 with the same short haircut, but by then it marked me among many of my age-group peers as a supposedly out-of-touch, militaristic Neanderthal.

Institutionally the Class of 1968 was caught inside what its more imaginative scientists might have termed a military-academic ther-mocouple. On the one hand the popularity of the post–World War II military and the rigorous screening for entrance into the Class of 1968 had brought to the Academy a highly talented representation of young American society. The 1,334 young men who took the oath that day in-cluded more than 100 high school valedictorians or salutatorians, more than 500 members of the National Honor Society, more than 1,000 var-sity athletes, and the second-highest cumulative average on the College Board (SAT) exams in the thirty-year post–World War II era. (The Class of 1969, entering the next year, averaged just seven points higher.)

Academically, as some commentators like to put it, the Academy was aspiring to become "MIT on the Severn." As the Class of 1968 ar-rived, this new emphasis on high-demand academics brought with it a restructuring of the Academic Board and a somewhat controversial deci-sion to appoint a civilian to the post of academic dean. With the growth of the nuclear Navy and the requirement for greater technological skills in an ever-modernizing military, every Naval Academy midshipman was required to major in engineering, while being allowed to choose a minor among twenty-three different options (mine, counterintuitively for the rest of my studies, being literature). In addition to the rigid full-time mili-tary life and the requirement to participate in a sport or extracurricular activity throughout the year, midshipmen carried a minimum course load of eighteen hours a semester.

Even though the Academy was moving away from a time-honored lockstep academic curriculum, the intense regimen of this new approach was untested and intensely demanding. Among other modifications, it required the entire class to study both physics and chemistry during plebe year. Coupled with the harsh demands of the plebe system, studying two lab sciences at the same time became a killer for some potentially fine military leaders whose academic skills lay outside the realm of science and mathematics. If a midshipman's cumulative grade point dipped below 2.0 he was required to face an academic performance board, which examined not only his grades but also his standings in leadership and conduct. And if he failed any course at the Academy, he was expelled.

On the other side of the institutional spectrum, the Academy's infamous and demanding plebe indoctrination system reached a historic peak during the 1964–65 academic year. Indeed, as the result of internal reviews brought on by a series of highly publicized congressional investigations, plebe year began to change, limiting some of the more severe physical punishments and focusing on structured leadership accountability through what became known as the Squad System. In a Catch-22 moment for the Class of 1968, this meant that plebe year began all over again during the last third of the academic year, typically a time when plebe indoctrination grew more lax, as the Academy's leadership experimented with this new policy.

Despite these rigors, or perhaps because of them, the collective achievements of those who endured and graduated as members of the Class of 1968 rank it as one of the most successful classes in Naval Academy history. As in any other top-level university, the class had its share of salutary individual achievements, including a Rhodes scholar and an Olympic athlete. But most important, it provided our country with hundreds of accomplished, dedicated, and intensely screened young leaders. Indeed, the mission of the Naval Academy has always been not to offer up great athletes, poets, scientists, venture capitalists, or jurists but to develop leaders imbued with a firm sense of duty, honor, and loyalty who over their careers can function at the highest levels of command, citizenship, and government.

In this endeavor the Class of 1968 was inordinately successful. In terms of military achievement, its members eventually accounted for twenty-three Navy admirals and six Marine Corps general officers, as well as the first Naval Academy alumnus in history to serve in the military and then become Secretary of the Navy. Among those twenty-three admirals were two four-stars, Jay Johnson and Mike Mullen, who became chiefs of naval operations, the highest military position in the Navy, a rare double success matched only twice in the Academy's history, by members of the classes of 1885 and 1916. Mullen went on to become chairman of the Joint Chiefs of Staff, the highest-ranking military officer in the country. Another of the class's four-star admirals, Rhodes Scholar Dennis Blair, served as commander in chief of the Pacific, an eminent and vitally important operational billet, and after his military retirement became director of national intelligence.

While only eighty-one members of the class were accepted for commissions in the Marine Corps, it is probably a record that six of them went on to become general officers in this small and elite corps that at any one time fielded only sixty-seven generals. Among those six, Major General Charlie Bolden, a renowned astronaut, later served as the administrator of NASA. Following his active-duty service Lieutenant General Chip Gregson became an assistant secretary of defense. And most tellingly, infantry leader Mike Hagee ascended to the revered position of commandant of the Marine Corps.

Such titles reached at the peak of one's career are illustrative, but they do not in and of themselves reflect the collective motivations that drove all of these young men during four years of rigorous indoctrination and preparation as our country went through so many upheavals. While undergoing the rigors of Academy life, few were thinking of what positions they might earn thirty years down the road. The true challenge that faced every one of them was whether they would be prepared to lead America's sailors and Marines as ensigns on the ships, submarines, or aviation squadrons of the Navy or as second lieutenants in a Marine Corps that was facing the constant, grinding challenges of ground combat in Vietnam.

In larger terms, while the members of the Class of 1968 studied and drilled and trained inside what we teasingly called the Marble Monastery of Bancroft Hall, these four years encompassed a time of almost unprecedented turmoil in American society. Less than a week after the class was sworn in at Dahlgren Hall, President Lyndon B. Johnson signed the historic Civil Rights Act of 1964. Scarcely six weeks later, the much debated Gulf of Tonkin incident signaled a massive increase in America's commitment and troop presence in Vietnam. On March 8, 1965, more than 3,500 Marines landed at Da Nang, Vietnam, a harbinger of a long and costly ground war that for the next six years would be led predominantly by American troops. On March 7 here at home—adjusting for international time zones, literally within hours of the Marine landings in Vietnam—the bloody confrontation between civil rights marchers and local authorities in Selma, Alabama, marked an irreversible, sometimes violent uptick in the civil rights movement. In August 1965 President Johnson signed the landmark Voting Rights Act. A few months after that, our combat troops went on the offensive in Vietnam, marked by engagements with the North Vietnamese Army during Operation Starlight near Da Nang and the well-remembered battle of Ia Drang farther south. These dual challenges, one to our social fabric and the other to our international posture, continued throughout the coming years. Our cities frequently reverberated with violent racial protests. College campuses and even the nation's capital became the focus of organized demonstrations against the Vietnam War. And inside Vietnam the war itself escalated steadily and uncontrollably, taking thousands of American lives and giving no hint as to when or how it might end.

In June 1967 the Arab-Israeli War spilled over into the Mediterranean, among other results causing the Soviet Navy to begin full-time operations there and heightening the tensions of the cold war. In December 1967 the North Koreans captured the USS *Pueblo* and took its crew hostage, leading many to believe we were going to war in North Korea as well as in Vietnam. The early months of 1968 saw a crescendo on all of these fronts. In late January into February, just four months before the Class of 1968 would graduate, the Tet Offensive brought the Vietnam War to its peak, with thousands of American casualties in the space of a few weeks. With an immediacy unknown in previous wars, the blood of American soldiers was splattered daily on the TV screens inside the living rooms of America. Respected luminaries such as television anchor Walter Cronkite—"the most trusted voice in America"—decided and reported that the Vietnam War was a lost cause.

On March 31 a beleaguered, disenchanted President Johnson surprised the country by announcing that he would not run for reelection. Five days later, on April 4, only two months before graduation day, Martin Luther King was assassinated in Memphis, Tennessee. Riots broke out across the country. Cities burned. The National Guard was on the streets, including in Washington, DC, only a few blocks from the Capitol building itself. And two months after that, in the early hours of June 5, the very morning that the Class of 1968 assembled on the field of the Navy–Marine Corps football stadium to graduate, Robert Kennedy was assassinated in Los Angeles.

Inside the Academy walls during those four years, when it came to views about service to country and the reasons for service not much changed. The grand tradition of our nation's military has always been that military service trumps politics and that politics can never be allowed to diminish the honor and obligations of service. Contrary to so many false assumptions at the time (and especially in later years), despite its physical isolation, the Brigade of Midshipmen was not philosophically insulated from these debates and their reverberations. Nor were its members blindly deluded by the admirals and generals who so frequently came to lecture the brigade on the progress of the war. Loyal as they were, the midshipmen were also smart. Four thousand of the brightest, most cynical young minds in America are hardly susceptible to being politically brainwashed. Indeed, when it came to the cost of war, there were few places where the impact was more directly felt than at the service academies. By the time the Class of 1968 graduated, there was hardly a member who had not already lost at least one good friend in Vietnam.

The reality of the challenges we faced as we prepared to serve as commissioned officers was both complex and hard to explain when we went home during Christmas break and over summer leave. Intellectual debate was for more leisurely souls, or at least for another time, perhaps after we had done our part in the war itself. We had practical lessons to learn and time-honored traditions to understand and uphold. Most important, we would soon have leadership positions to fill, the consequences of which involved the lives of those young Americans who were entrusted to our judgment.

Whatever one might have felt about the war in Vietnam, the inescapable truth was that it was not going to go away. The taxpayers of America were paying for our education (as the ever-cynical saying went, shoved down our throats a nickel at a time). But what they were really buying was leadership. If we did not provide it, no matter how smart our intellectual and political arguments might have seemed, we would have failed.

★　　★　　★

Thumb-tacked on more than a few cork bulletin boards just inside the doorways of midshipmen's rooms in Bancroft Hall during the 1960s (including my own from time to time) was a quote from Admiral Hyman Rickover, the irascible and brilliant father of the nuclear Navy. Rickover, who recruited heavily from the academic and leadership cream of the Academy, was famous for personally interviewing and deliberately berating every young applicant who was seeking acceptance into the prestigious nuclear power program. And he made no secret of his disdain for what he viewed as the Academy's counterproductive day-to-day disciplinary environment.

"The Brigade of Midshipmen is made up of 4,000 young men kept in a state of suspended adolescence by petty rules and regulations."

Rickover's words rang irrepressibly true, even among those of us who believed strongly in the Academy's mission and successfully made our way through the disciplinary minefields in order to score high on our leadership evaluations and eventually become "stripers" in the brigade's command structure. For as college campuses across the country grew ever more carefree, the Naval Academy remained mired in a rigid disciplinary system that had changed little since the days before World War II. Even setting aside the harsh regimens of the plebe indoctrination system, in retrospect the restrictions placed on midshipmen seem almost incomprehensible when juxtaposed against the steady evolution of the rebellious, free-spirited, sex, drugs, and rock-and-roll college tempo of the mid- to late 1960s.

Much of the disciplinary environment inside Bancroft Hall seemed designed to replicate the daily schedule of what a midshipman might expect if he were stationed on a warship far away at sea. Keeping or drinking alcohol of any sort in Bancroft Hall was a Class A conduct offense. In an era of bawdy fraternity parties on civilian campuses and the prevalence in our age group of a wide variety of drugs, particularly marijuana, it was against Maryland state law to sell even a beer to a Naval Academy midshipman, regardless of his age. At a time when individual liberties and freedom of association were the subject of great debate and numerous lawsuits, attendance at chapel on Sunday morning was mandatory. It was not unusual—indeed it was normal—to go an entire week during the academic year and not even see a member of the opposite sex, other than perhaps to pass a tourist who was watching a parade or viewing the historic memorabilia inside Bancroft Hall's main entrance.

No matter a midshipman's academic schedule or personal habits, when the reveille bells rang at 0615 all 4,000 members of the brigade were required to be out of their beds and on their feet within forty-five seconds, subject to a physical "muster," when a midshipman from every room was standing in the hallway and reporting that everyone in his room was "all turned out." From reveille to morning meal, if a midshipman was caught even sitting on his bed it was a conduct offense. And a false report by a roommate standing in the corridor after the bells stopped ringing and reporting the room "all turned out" during muster was a violation of the Honor Concept, subjecting the person making the report to expulsion.

A half-hour later, at 0645, every midshipman in the brigade was required to be showered, shaved, and dressed in full uniform and to form up squad by squad, platoon by platoon, in company formations. After morning-meal muster was taken, the entire brigade marched down the stairways inside Bancroft Hall for breakfast in the mess hall. Meal formations were mandatory for all three meals. Careful personnel inspections took place every day at noon-meal formation. Saturday noon-meal inspections were especially tedious and exhaustive, and the brigade was not released for weekend liberty until they were completed.

The brigade dined en masse for all three meals inside the huge three-wing structure of the mess hall. The dining hall was a key feature not only of the Academy's day-to-day existence but also of the plebe indoctrination system, much of which took place at the company tables. The mess hall accommodated all 4,000 members of the brigade in an intricately organized structure. Every midshipman was assigned to a specific seat at one of the twelve-man tables. Two or three first-class (seniors) sat at one end of each table, next to the outer boundaries of the mess hall, which were then called First Class Alley. Two or three second-class (juniors) sat at the other end, along an inner corridor called Second Class Alley. A few third-class "Youngsters" (sophomores) sat along one side of the table, and usually four plebes sat on the other.

Morning meal always began with a prayer, offered by a chaplain standing at a microphone located at the Anchor, a small station at the intersection of the three wings of the mess hall. Once the prayer was finished, every meal began with an explosion of fierce, sometimes funny, always unpredictable chaos as the plebes were run by the members of the upper classes.

During meals the plebes sat in a rigid "brace" on the last four inches of their mess-hall chairs, their backs stiff and chins pressed tight against their throats. Their faces were required to remain impassive, their eyes staring fixedly straight ahead, "in the boat." They ate only when permitted by the upper class. It was their duty to "pass chow"—the heavy metal plates of food brought from the kitchens by Filipino stewards—from one end of the table to the other. The plebes served the upper class their food and poured their drinks. Plebes were also required to recite the "rates" of the day and to answer any "professional questions" asked by the upperclassmen by the next meal.

A professional question could involve any subject. I once was required to learn all the countries and capitals of Africa between evening meal and breakfast the next day, even though I was facing three midterm exams at the same time. Through the vestiges of colonialism there were several dozen countries on the continent of Africa in 1964. I had never even heard of at least half of them. Study hours for plebes ended at 2300—11:00 P.M. in civilian terminology—with a mandatory lights out. I spent several hours after that sitting in the dim lights of the toilet down the hall with my Naval Academy atlas on my lap, facing the reality that the next day would begin with the reveille bells at 0615 and that plebes were not allowed even to sit on their beds, much less nap, between reveille and taps. I did not do well on my midterms, particularly in oceanography and chemistry, both of which I was in danger of failing. But on the company tables the next morning I gained the grudging respect of a first-classman who was running me with the possible intention— common at the time—of causing me to flunk out of the Academy. His first words to me that morning, even before "Pour my coffee," were "Upper Volta, Webb."

The poet in me had quickly filed that one away as I studied my atlas in the dark of night. "Ouagadougou, sir." And after all the intense hours of midnight memorization, that was it. As I poured his coffee he moved on to other topics.

Being even one second late to any military formation was a punishable conduct offense. Falsely reporting another midshipman as being on time, even if he was only thirty seconds late, was an honor offense, punishable by expulsion. Every midshipman showed up for every meal in the mess hall. Those who were not hungry were required to wait with the others until the class bells rang from the Anchor podium at the center of the mess hall before they exited and returned to their rooms: three bells for first class, two bells a bit later for second class, and one bell for third class. Dawdling was not allowed. When the brigade commander stepped up to the Anchor and announced "Fourth class, march out," the entire brigade was required to immediately vacate the mess hall.

Midshipmen were not allowed to date during plebe year, except for one or two formal dances, after which they were allowed perhaps two hours of liberty before reporting back to Bancroft Hall. Plebes were not allowed to keep any electronic equipment in their room, including radios and record players, nor were they allowed to wear rings or any other ornamental jewelry. In most companies plebes were not allowed to drink coffee during meals.

During their second year and beyond, midshipmen were allowed to date but not to leave the "seven-mile limit" without special permission. Their dates usually stayed, for $5 a night, in local homes that had been certified as "drag houses." Any public display of affection—known as PDA— was a serious conduct offense. This included the simple act of holding

real world of military leadership, the burden, and the lessons of the experience, turned inward. A midshipman was required to struggle with his own conscience, and then decide whether to ignore the violation, to confront and counsel the violator, or to report the incident to the Brigade Honor Committee.

As one who was selected by his classmates to sit as a member of the Brigade Honor Committee for all four years at the Academy, this seriousness of purpose on ethical issues among the brigade was perhaps the most enduring feature of my Academy education. I sat on numerous cases during those four years. Some of them were heartbreaking examples of young men caught up in their own personal quandaries that resulted in regrettable ethical lapses. Some of them involved plebes under enormous stress who were, arguably, entrapped by cunning upperclassmen but who nonetheless lied or dissembled when under pressure. And some of them involved outright thievery or other behavior that was indicative of serious character flaws.

But in every instance in which a midshipman lied, cheated, or stole and his case was referred to the Brigade Honor Committee, we knew our duty, both to the integrity of the institution and also as stewards of the future of the officer corps of the Navy and Marine Corps. A midshipman might be put on academic or leadership probation, but there were no second chances when it came to honor violations. There was no room for lying or dissembling in the Fleet, and the pressures of combat operations were in many instances much greater than those at the Academy. Did we want to serve with someone who would give a false report in the operational environment merely to deflect the anger of his senior officer or to preclude an unfavorable fitness report?

Some cases were indeed formulaic, like the Marriage Rule, where in a form of entrapment a violation of regulations was turned into an honor offense. Midshipmen were required to sign a statement after every leave period, certifying that they were not now nor had they ever been married. Obviously, lying on such a statement was an honor offense, although the sweeping way in which the Marriage Rule was enforced was something of an ethical dragnet.

On the other end of the spectrum, some cases were downright painful. A struggling plebe classmate who despite some academic weaknesses would have turned into a fine officer and leader was failing chemistry. Knowing that the failure of one course was grounds for expulsion, he decided to compile a detailed cheat sheet on a three-by-five index card, which he took with him to the final exam. As a testimony to his ignorance of chemistry, there was nothing on his cheat sheet that could have been of any use on the exam. But when he turned in his exam, the professor noticed the three-by-five card in his upper shirt pocket, took it from him, and turned him in.

If this were a legal case, a defense might have been raised that he had never actually cheated since the card never came out of his pocket and he had not in any way used the useless document. But he had indeed prepared it for an unethical reason. A key question from his fellow plebes during his honor hearing was whether he would have used the cheat sheet if there had been useful information on it.

"Of course I would have," he responded, incredulous that we would even ask. "I'm not going to lie to you."

And thus, hoisted partially on the petard of his ethical standards, did our classmate leave the brigade.

Other cases would have raised the eyebrows of students at almost any other institution in America. One example, which was read to the entire brigade as they sat in the mess hall during evening meal, involved an upperclassman who had lied to a pretty girl.

Leaving chapel services one Sunday morning, the midshipman noticed the girl standing on the sidewalk in front of the chapel steps. She was lost, trying to find an unfamiliar face among the sea of young men in their dress blue uniforms who were streaming back toward Bancroft Hall. Seizing the opportunity, he asked her if he could help. She told him that she was there on a blind date, waiting to meet a certain midshipman—let's call him Midshipman X.

"Oh," said the perpetrator, who actually knew Midshipman X. "I know X. I guess he wasn't able to tell you, but he was put on report, and he had to restrict in his room this weekend. But since you're here, why don't you let me show you around the Academy?"

A half-hour later Midshipman X saw the girl and introduced himself, saying he had been looking fruitlessly for her.

The girl looked at her newfound friend, then back to Midshipman X. "I thought you were restricting in your room."

The old maxim "All's fair in love and war" did not apply to Annapolis. Midshipman X did not appreciate being unethically snaked. And within a few weeks her new friend was no longer a midshipman at the Naval Academy, expelled for having lied to Midshipman X's blind date.

Almost on a par with the Honor Concept, time management was the whipping post of everything every midshipman did at the Academy, all day, every day. Whether deliberately or merely ineluctably, there simply was never enough time to completely fulfill any assigned task, contrary to the more relaxed manner of most of the civilian world. One of the favorite expressions among midshipmen was that every day involved trying to fit "ten pounds of [stuff] into a five-pound bag."

Being late for any required event, even by one second, was taken seriously. Being late for a meal formation or when returning from leave or liberty could cost a midshipman dearly: ten demerits for the first minute and a demerit a minute thereafter. The importance of time was reinforced not only every day but several times a day, beginning with the ear-splitting demands of the reveille bells at 0615. Before every meal formation, in every corridor of Bancroft Hall, with an exactness and unanimity that was astonishing, plebe "chow callers" ritualistically recited their "rates" as the clock ticked over from one minute to the next, counting down the minutes before the brigade was required to be in company formation for that meal.

> Sir, you now have ten minutes before morning meal formation.
> Sir, the menu for morning meal is . . .
> Sir, the Officers of the Watch are . . .
> Sir, the movies in town are . . .
> Sir, the days are . . .

The chow callers would return at the five-minute call, then again at four, three, and two minutes. Finally, with one minute left, the chow callers would utter the age-old warning before sprinting off to their own place at company formation:

> Sir, you now have one minute before morning meal formation. *Sir, time, tide, and formation wait for no man, I am now shoving off, SIR!*

This subservience to the schedule was so powerful that at times the entire brigade became Pavlovian robots. During our second class year a careless midshipman standing watch in the Main Office in the middle of the night accidentally tripped the switch that started the incessant reveille bells at 2:30 in the morning. Despite the time on our own clocks, the entire brigade turned out for reveille. We did not trust the clocks; only the bells. Wiping the sleep from our eyes, my roommate and I went through our usual morning rituals, he sweeping out the dust from the room into the corridor while I quickly shaved and stumbled into the shower. Only when a voice came over the loudspeaker in the hallway, announcing that the reveille bell had been tripped by mistake, did we fall with numb relief back into our beds.

Midshipmen resisted and complained about every one of these petty rules and regulations, but actually that was a part of the tradition as well. Who were we but a bunch of whimpering, whining puppies who by

tradition and design were being locked up inside Mother B for our obligatory "four years by the bay" in order to earn the right to stand alongside
our predecessors in the conning towers and wardrooms of the Fleet? In
short, what appeared to be insanity actually was studied preparation, designed by officers who knew the tribulations of long periods at sea. They
knew. And it was our sworn duty to learn.

The guiding hands of the vastly experienced salty Sea Dogs who had
sailed the China Sea and fought the great battles of World War II and
Korea still steered the Academy's rudder through their adamant, collective wisdom. The importance of discipline motivated them. Integrity
inspired them. And the unforgiving demands of the clock compelled
their insistence on ensuring that every Academy graduate understood
the crucial importance of time management. In the earliest days of sail
and then coal-powered steam, if an officer or sailor "missed movement"
as his ship deployed, a night of frolic or a momentary inattention to his
schedule could bring months of delays before he could be reunited with
his ship across the vast Atlantic or Pacific, which in and of itself would
probably mean the end of his military career.

*   *   *

Space does not allow a thorough rendering of that long-ago era's lonely,
sometimes vicious version of hell called plebe year, a subject about which
I wrote in detail in my novel *A Sense of Honor*. There was method in this
madness, but at times there also was unconstrained madness, wrongly
justified by accepted methods designed, at least in theory, to test one's
ability to function under extreme stress.

It was not uncommon for a plebe being run by an upperclassman
to rise before reveille and pull on two or even three pairs of sweat suits,
soaking them down in the shower and running a lap or two around Far-
ragut Field, about a mile per lap, before reporting to an upperclass room
for the thirty-minute sessions called "Come Arounds." No matter his
starting point the previous June, by fall every member of our class was

capable of doing sixty-eight push-ups on command, plus one to Beat Army and, for those of us who were aspiring Marines, one more "for the Corps." During the three Come Around sessions every day, it became as common as breathing to race against the clock to our rooms, change into any uniform recognized by Academy regulations, and report back to the upperclass room within two minutes.

"White Works Echo, Webb. Go." Then, two minutes later, "Full Dress Blues. Two minutes. Go."

We also raced the clock, sometimes individually and sometimes in groups, to see how long it would take us to negotiate the corridors and stairways of Bancroft Hall and then out toward the buildings bordering the Severn River, in order to memorize a historic brass placard or to slap the gonads of the brass sculpture of Bill the Goat, the Naval Academy's mascot. In the dead of night our class was also charged with the symbolic responsibility of Brasso-ing Bill's balls, keeping them as shiny and gleaming as the belt buckles of the Working Uniform Blue Alphas that we wore to class each day.

Sometimes the rigors of plebe year veered into reprehensible cruelty. And sometimes the wisdom of the Old Salts who were so brilliant in their shipboard acumen seemed hilariously out of place when it came to the well-intentioned but outdated standards of social behavior that they sought to perpetuate.

Nine years after I came back from Vietnam, shortly after my novel *Fields of Fire* had been published, I returned to the Academy as a visiting professor, teaching courses on poetry and the novel. Among my colleagues was a soft-spoken, thoughtful classmate, still on active duty in the Navy, who during our first two years at the Academy had been a member of the infamous Fourth Company. During our plebe year the upperclassmen of the Fourth Company, along with the Eleventh Company in my battalion, had physically run out more than half of their plebes, triggering one of the congressional investigations that eventually brought about a revamping of the plebe system.

My classmate and I had both seen combat in Vietnam. Before assuming my position as visiting professor I had spent two years as a legislative counsel on the Veterans Affairs Committee in the House of Representatives. One of the key issues we had focused on was the recognition and study of post-traumatic stress syndrome, the understanding of which was in its infancy. Curious, over lunch one day I asked my classmate if he had nightmares about his combat service in Vietnam.

"Not really," he said, with the pervading sense of calm that had characterized him since we first met at the age of eighteen. "But I do still have nightmares about plebe year."

For many in our class, such continuing nightmares were understandable and deserved. One of the more celebrated comments in 1973, when our prisoners of war returned from long years of incarceration in Vietnam, reputedly came from a Naval Academy graduate. Upon his return visit to the Academy, the alumnus was told that plebe year had been relaxed and that there was now a computer in every basement wing of Bancroft Hall. As the story went, he shook his head in disbelief. "If there's one thing that screwed up the Vietnam War it was computers," he said. "And if there was one thing that got me through my POW experience it was plebe year."

Plebe year was serious business, the consequences of which potentially extended to an individual's entire professional career. This was not the sort of celebrated "hazing" that took place in civilian colleges when one pledged a social fraternity. The upperclassmen responsible for a plebe's indoctrination had absolutely no obligation to like the plebe or to want him to remain at the Academy. In many cases during this era, the reverse was true.

In the autumn of my plebe year I managed to irritate five of the two dozen or so first-classmen in my company at the same time. During predinner Come Around, one of them put me into various stress positions for a half-hour while he lectured me about my unsatisfactory conduct and then about the irrelevance of pain. I began our little session by rigging three M-1 rifles, a total of thirty-three pounds, holding all three of them straight-armed in front of my face as he taunted me. Within seconds, the muscles in my arms constricted and the rifles fell slowly toward my thighs. Taunting me, he took one rifle off, then another. When I could no longer hold one rifle in front of me, he replaced it with seven books. As my muscles gave out he took off one book, then another, then another, and when I could no longer hold one book in front of my face, he replaced it with a pencil. All the while he droned on in a flat, unemotional voice, as if this were a class in philosophy, which in a way I suppose it was. "What is pain, Webb? What's the matter? Does it hurt? Stop making those faces. Nobody gives a shit whether your arms hurt, do you understand me? Keep your problems to yourself, Smack."

After twenty minutes, Dr. No-Pain called in his four classmates, two of whom lived across the hallway. I now stood in front of them holding only a toothpick, which I was unable to keep in front of my face even though I was using both hands. They collectively derided me, urging me to resign from the Academy and go home, and warning me that if I did not quit, they would run me until I flunked out anyway. "We don't want you here, Webb. Go home."

During dinner the five sat together at my company table, placing me next to them and running me throughout the meal, among other challenges making it impossible for me to eat. As I poured their drinks I spilled iced tea on one of them, bringing an eruption of abuse from all five.

After dinner I reported to the room across the hall, where the four who had joined evening Come Around toward its end took turns beating me with a cricket bat.

"Touch your toes."

"Aye, aye, sir." I would lean over and touch my toes. They would hit me, swinging the bat as if taking batting practice for a slow-pitch softball game. I would then come to attention and resume my brace. "Beat Army, sir."

"Did that hurt, Webb?"

"No, sir."

"Touch your toes."

"Aye, aye, sir." The bat would connect again. "Beat Army, sir."

"Did it hurt?"

"No, sir."

"Okay. Touch your toes."

"Aye, aye, sir." The blow would come. I would straighten up again. "Beat Army, sir."

"Did it hurt?"

"No, sir."

After they had each hit a couple of slow-pitch home runs, it had apparently stopped being fun and their exuberance diminished. One of them finally told me that if I would simply admit that it hurt, they would stop beating me. But for all I knew, even this guarantee could have been doublethink. If I told them it hurt, would I really be allowed to leave, or would it bring on yet another lecture and another round? Or worse yet, did they really want to send me back across the hallway? I had already dealt with Dr. No-Pain before dinner began. I did not want to survive the cricket bat only to go back to the toothpick.

The pain had actually left my body. Or maybe it was merely my brain's reaction, as I would later find out with Marines who were wounded so severely that that their nervous systems became overloaded and shut down so that they could not feel any pain. I had detached myself from the moment. It was as if I were watching myself from another room.

"Did it hurt, Webb?"

"No, sir."

"Just tell us that it hurt, idiot. Did it hurt?"

I could hear the worry in his voice. Somehow the very abuse that they were now weary of perpetrating had inspired me. By refusing to lose, I felt that I was somehow winning. "No, sir."

"Touch your toes." Another blow.

"Beat Army, sir."

Behind me I heard them discussing that the bat had split length-wise on my ass. "All right, get out of here, Webb."

"Aye, aye, sir." I ran back to my room. My backside and the upper part of my thighs were thoroughly beaten, and now my senses were returning. The noise and rhythms of evening study hour surrounded me in the hallway. Upperclassmen were calling amiably to each other, heedless of me as I passed. I paid them no attention. At that moment I was lost inside my own head. I was addled and angry, on the edge of something that I could not understand. Part of me wanted to flip the switch, pack my bags, and walk out of this place forever. Part of me wanted to turn around, and go back inside their rooms, taking the bat away from them and beating the ass of every one of them.

But as I ran I realized that in either case I would only satisfy their instincts and somehow justify their abuse. Instead I decided simply to mark their names forever in my memory, which I have done. I would get through plebe year, one way or the other. And then I would succeed, despite their predictions.

I fantasized for a moment. Maybe someday I would outrank all of them, and then I could write their fitness reports. "This officer is an asshole," I would write. "I know this from personal experience. Do not promote him." Yes, that would be their best rebuke.

I reached my room, stepping inside and closing the door. Sitting at their desks my two roommates looked up from their studies and caught my shattered look. Enraged, humiliated, and still in pain, I was unable to face their querulous stares. I did not want to hear their questions. I could not have answered them anyway. I stepped inside the closet, sticking my face inside my laundry bag so that they would not see the sputtering gasps that had begun now that I was inside our room, and spat my frustrations onto the dirty clothes inside. For a moment I cried tears of anger and revenge, wishing I could have fought back or that I could be anywhere else, doing anything else. What did all of this have to do with learning how to be a leader? And if my dad had seen it, what would he think of the vaunted Trade School now?

I calmed down. The clothes inside my laundry bag stank. I pulled my head out, catching my breath. I was flunking out and I needed to study. No matter what I felt, tomorrow morning the reveille bells would go off at the same time they always did, and the dog-and-pony show would resume. As in combat, I could not choose my moments of relaxation or respite. And maybe that indeed was the lesson. I regained my composure, stepping from the closet and sitting down at my desk.

One of my roommates, now my brother-in-law, searched my face for answers. "What happened?"

"I don't want to talk about it. I'll tell you later," I said. Then I pulled out a book and tried to study.

And yet, in the flash of a moment, plebe year could slide from the unforgivably harsh to the hilariously sublime.

In the midst of the chaos of the plebe system and the very real fear in the early months that due to the new academic standards a substantial portion of our class was in danger of flunking out (I was at this point the high man in my three-man room, with a 1.61 grade point average), the entire plebe class was required to attend mandatory dance classes. Our retired alumni would have it no other way. We were going to learn not only how to be engineers and technically proficient officers but also how to be smooth and svelte gentlemen, capable of navigating a formal receiving line and thereafter guiding the lady of our choice through the complicated steps of the waltz, the fox trot, the rumba, the cha-cha, and the tango.

Of course it was rather difficult to learn all of these maneuvers when we were forbidden to date, and when there were no females to practice with anyway.

Regardless of such drawbacks, when our names popped up on the signing boards in front of our Battalion Office, for a month or so we were required to report to Memorial Hall after evening meal, in shifts of more than a hundred plebes at a time. Our after-class athletic requirements did not go away. Monday marching drills and Wednesday parades were still in order. In the company living spaces the upperclassmen still waited to indoctrinate us. Our academic expectations did not decrease. The newest round of professional questions waited to be researched and memorized before morning Come Around or at breakfast in the mess hall. But now it was time to waltz and tango, to learn to rumba and do the cha-cha-cha. Surrounded by some of the most sacred symbols of naval history, we danced—by ourselves.

Well, not completely by ourselves.

Upon arriving in Memorial Hall we formed a wide line on the polished floor at the rear of the high-ceilinged, vast and empty room, all of us looking smart in our Service Dress Blue uniforms. Our instructor, a rather elegant, fortyish woman who stood before us, would offer a few welcoming remarks. The original ship's flag from the historic Battle of Lake Erie during the War of 1812 loomed on a high wall directly in front of us, reminding us forever, DON'T GIVE UP THE SHIP. Inside a low-lit glass case underneath the flag was a typed honor roll listing the names of Academy graduates who had been killed in our nation's wars.

On the floor beneath the glass case our instructor would set the needle on her small portable record player, playing a favorite instrumental song. Then she would walk across the room until she was just before us, her arms outstretched, her left arm around an imaginary waist, and her right hand in the air, grasping an imaginary hand. Moving backward as if she were dancing with every one of us, she would call out the directions in a piercing voice that echoed loudly inside the hall and down the long marble steps to the rotunda below.

"READY, BEGIN!"

We would hold out our own hands, matching her movements as if each of us were dancing with her. None of us really wanted to be there. But there was indeed a poetic resonance in the impossibility of those moments as the music echoed off the hallowed walls of Memorial Hall and we held our arms in front of us as if we were delicately embracing an imaginary female partner. This hopeless, collective pose may have been the most symbolic, defining ritual of our entire plebe experience. We carefully followed her step-by-step instructions. Empty-armed, as synchronized as a mildly competent Broadway chorus line, we would waltz across the gleaming floors in a room that commemorated the wars of those who went before us.

"One, two, side-together, add a box! Very good, gentlemen, very, very good! Stay with me, now! Progressive right—and left—and turn—yourselves—around, Boom-Boom!"

All of these newly acquired skills were soon tested. We were required—through postings on the muster boards in front of each Battalion Office—to attend four out of a series of six formal Sunday afternoon receptions known among the midshipmen as Tea Fights. Four hundred young women from nearby colleges would be invited to spend an afternoon mingling with a crowd of six hundred plebes, most of whom had not so much as said hello to a female for months. As members of the Naval Academy band played soft, slow melodies, plebes were randomly paired off with the visiting females, escorting them through a military reception line that included a senior officer and his wife, and then onto the dance floor.

The first Tea Fight took place in Dahlgren Hall, the armory in which we had been sworn in as midshipmen the previous June. Far from being an afternoon filled with niceties and romance, it became a veritable cattle call. The young women arrived at one end of Dahlgren Hall, all made up and dressed to kill. The swarming mass of plebes gathered at the other, wearing their Dress Blue uniforms, cramped inside that section of the hall by a white picket fence. Once the "reception" began, midshipmen members of the Brigade Hop Committee swung open the white picket fence, funneling the hundreds of plebes toward one edge of the hall that was marked off by another picket fence, this one green.

An expectant tension rose among hundreds of spirited young men who did not normally even see a female face other than during the couple of hours they were allowed to walk along the streets of Annapolis on Saturday afternoons, much less actually touch a woman or talk to her. When the white fence opened up, the mass of plebes rushed forward toward the other side of the hall, where the green fence channeled them four or five abreast to preserve some semblance of order.

Despite earlier warnings that there would be consequences for any misbehavior, within seconds hundreds of low "moos" spontaneously emanated from the plebes, and then they began singing the chorus from the popular TV show *Rawhide*: "Roll 'em, roll 'em, roll 'em . . . Moo, moo . . ."

It was indeed a cattle call. Wearing their Dress Blue uniforms, moving toward what in their imaginations might end up being the girl of their dreams, they nonetheless inched forward as if they were cattle being unloaded from a freight car into a slaughterhouse. Finally reaching the end of the green fence and popping out on the other side, the plebes just as suddenly ceased their belligerent noise as they were introduced, one person at a time, to a usually smiling, equally nervous, and sometimes equally disappointed young woman who would be their dance partner for the afternoon.

Somehow, despite this random, blatantly comic process, addresses were exchanged, letters were written, relationships were formed, and in more than a few instances the groundwork for marriage was actually laid.

As the Vietnam War gathered in intensity, the leadership of the brigade began posting pictures and biographies of alumni who had been killed or were missing in action on a large board in the middle of the Rotunda, just inside the main entrance to Bancroft Hall. The pictures and short biographies were taken from the Lucky Bag, the class yearbook from the year that each alumnus had graduated. The board on which the notices were placed was large, perhaps eight feet high and four or five feet wide. At its top was a boldly lettered inscription: TO THOSE WHO WENT BEFORE US.

As the Class of 1968 neared graduation, the "To Those Who Went Before Us" board had become two boards, and then three. A high percentage of the alumni listed there were either Marines or naval aviators. Many of their names and faces were familiar to all of us. More than a few included friends, and some of these friends were especially close.

During my plebe summer the controlled mayhem of plebe indoctrination on my twelve-man table in the mess hall was perpetrated by an intense, deliberately malicious second-classman named Chuck Warner. Warner was a dedicated future Marine. When he learned that another plebe and I on the table were aspiring Marines, he put us on either side of him and gave us, shall we say, especially close supervision.

"Eat a pat of butter, now! Eat a pat of butter eat a pat of butter eat a pat of butter." With each command my classmate and I would grab a pat of butter from a nearby plate and swallow it whole. "Rig the milk." We would hold a carton of milk straight in front of us until told to drop it. "Rig your knees." We raised our feet off the ground, pressing our knees against the underside of the table as we sat on the very edge of our chairs and rigged the milk in front of us.

"Come aboard."

"Aye, aye, sir." We would set the milk down and place our feet back on the floor. "Beat Army, sir."

"Clamp on."

"Aye, aye, sir." This required us to pull our entire body weight into the air as we balanced on the table, supported only by our elbows.

"Come aboard."

"Aye, aye, sir. Beat Army, sir."

"Chop."

"Aye, aye, sir." We ran in place, still sitting at the forward edge of the chair.

And so on and so on, just another normal day at Navy. Admiral Rickover was right, but he did not give full credit to what happens when smart, cynical young minds bump up against the challenge of administering stress to new plebes without violating regulations to the point that they themselves may be thrown out of the Academy.

Warner would repeatedly challenge us. "What do you have to offer the Marine Corps, Webb?"

"Thirty years, sir."

"Thirty years? You puke! How about your *life*?"

"Aye, aye, sir. My life, sir."

During plebe summer the Wednesday night fights were the greatest entertainment at the Academy, pitting top boxers from the four plebe battalions against each other in a continuous round-robin tournament. The entire plebe class attended, each battalion sitting together in a separate bleacher section, led by cheerleaders as they chanted and sang together. Hundreds of upperclassmen assigned to the Academy during summer training sessions came to the fights, as did local officers and many residents of Annapolis. On any given Wednesday night the four stands of bleachers that bordered the floor-level canvas ring would be packed with perhaps two thousand spectators.

In the final round of fights I faced an especially tough opponent, a thickly muscled former wrestler. On the mess hall tables that morning, Warner was all over me: "Are you going to win tonight, Webb?"

"Yes, sir."

"Do you bet your ass?"

I actually had no choice, but as a plebe, this simple challenge struck me as a unique opportunity. In the Naval Academy tradition, betting your ass had more potential consequences for Warner than it did for me. True, if I lost the fight Warner could "take my ass" by requiring me to touch my toes and then hitting me full force with the heavy, paddle

My parents, James H. Webb Sr. and Vera Lorraine Hodges Webb, 1943

From the left, top row: Aunt Carolyn, Granny (Georgia Doyle Hodges), Mom (Vera), holding Gary Lee; bottom row: Jim Jr., Tama Sue, and Pat, at Scott Air Force Base, circa 1952

Tama Sue, Gary Lee, Pat, and Jim Jr., Paeglow Housing, Scott AFB, circa 1953

Georgia Doyle Hodges (Granny)
with Jim Jr., probably 1947

James Webb Sr. with James Webb Jr.,
St. Joseph, Missouri, 1948

A fifteen-year-old Jim Jr. holding up
a few fish in Minnesota, 1961

The Webb brothers— Art, James, Tommy Lee, and Charlie—with their father Robert Webb, 1943

One of the only pictures ever taken of my grandfather Birch Hays Hodges, Kensett, Arkansas, circa 1936, a photo that along with the picture of my dad (facing page) has hung above my work desk for more than thirty years

Captain James Webb Sr. during the Berlin Airlift

Jim Webb during
plebe year, "passing
chow" while braced
up in the mess hall

"Youngster Cruise,"
summer of 1965
aboard the USS
Hornet

Brigade Boxing, U.S. Naval Academy (Jim Webb on the right)

The Brigade Staff, autumn 1967 (Jim Webb fourth from left)

JAMES HENRY WEBB, JR.

"Spike", an Air Force Brat, has lived just about everywhere, but claims Andrews AFB as his present home. He became a Theta Chi at USC, but it only took a year for Mother B to claim his talents. An all-around athlete, he specialized in boxing and always made it to the finals in the Brigade Boxing competition.

In his spare time Jim always managed to give a few haircuts, and this resulted in little sleep on Friday nights. Friday night liberty soon broke up his business, however, as he found more time to drag his pretty fiance. Perhaps his most valuable talents, though, were his desire and determination. These factors were always evident in his actions, and qualified him as a four striper.

There is no doubt in Jim's mind as to his choice of service. A "grunt" from way back, he was always recruiting for the Corps. Those who knew Jim will testify that his sincerity and selfless dedication will take him to the top. . . or farther.

Left: "Lucky Bag" photograph, first class year

Above: Receiving the superintendent's special commendation for leadership just before graduation, dress parade, U.S. Naval Academy, June 1968

Receiving the award as
honor graduate at
The Marine Officers
Basic School,
February 5, 1969

Jim and Granny,
Riverside, California,
February 1969, just before
deploying to Vietnam

Platoon command post, Henderson Hill, April 1969

Third platoon, Delta Company, First Battalion, Fifth Marine Regiment at the An Hoa combat base, early May 1969

Memorial service for Delta Company Marines recently killed in action,
Liberty Bridge compound, May 1969

Standing at the entrance to an enemy bunker, Go Noi Island, June 1969

Jim Webb facing camera, company commander of Delta, during a combat patrol in the Arizona Valley, October 1969

Command post at the center of a Delta Company perimeter during a monsoon-season combat operation in the Arizona Valley, November 1969. Jim Webb, company commander, standing at right wearing bush hat. The cloth on the poncho hootch is an "Air Panel" marking the Marine position for identification by low-flying tactical aircraft.

Great-aunt Lena and
my mother Vera, 1976

Gary Lee, James Sr.,
James Jr., Cocoa Beach,
Florida, 1979

Dad and Mom, circa 1979

Secretary of the Navy Jim Webb in front of the USS *Saratoga*

Senator Jim Webb and wife Hong Le in front of the U.S. Capitol Building, 2011

board–like Naval Academy atlas. But given the daily regimens of the plebe system, while this might have been painful it was not particularly humiliating. On the other hand, if I won he had just offered me the very rare opportunity to physically strike an upperclassman.

I wanted to be sure. "Aye, aye, sir. My ass against yours, sir?"

He hesitated for a moment, making some sort of private calculation, and then agreed. "All right, Webb. My ass against yours."

That night as I stepped inside the ring and the crowd roared during the introductions my corner man made a tiny miscalculation. When the warning whistle blew just before the bell signaled the start of my fight, he shoved my rubber mouthguard crookedly so that it did not lodge firmly against my teeth. In the first few seconds of the fight my opponent stepped quickly toward me, wanting to trap me in my corner and pummel me before I could reach the center of the ring. I danced away from him, jabbing him in the face as I sidestepped his initial attack, trying to bite the mouthpiece into place. But it wouldn't move.

I drifted back into the ropes, keeping my chin down and opening my mouth as I tried to set the mouthpiece into place with my tongue. Just then he stepped in and hit me with a fierce left hook, tearing the ligaments on the right side of my jaw and cracking the jaw bone up near my ear lobe. Unable to fully close my jaw, I boxed him like a matador, sidestepping his attacks, counterattacking, and then moving back to the center of the ring, again and again.

Between rounds my corner man kept urging me to finish him off. "Take him out! Take him out! He can't keep up with you!"

"You don't understand." I did not know my jaw was broken, but I did know the risk if he were able to land another solid punch on the jaw. "I can't close my mouth!"

I boxed him for three rounds, bobbing and weaving and keeping control of the center of the ring. And I won the fight.

Late that night, after visits to the dentist and sick bay, I finally returned to my room in the quiet darkness of the plebe living area. My roommate in this plebe summer room was asleep. I was exhausted. My entire head hurt. I was carrying my boxing gear in one hand and an ice pack for the right side of my face in the other. It was a good fight, but it was now history. In a week no one would care or particularly remember. But when the reveille bells rang at dawn, plebe year would begin again.

I dropped my gear and the ice pack onto the desk. Warner suddenly stepped out from the darkness and stood directly in front of me. I startled. As was required even in the middle of the night, I stepped backward until I "hit a bulkhead," pressing my entire body from ankles to the back of my head up against the nearest wall.

"Midshipman Webb, fourth class, sir."

Warner spoke quietly in the darkness. "That was a good fight."

"Thank you, sir."

He stared at me almost uncertainly. "Do you think you could take me, Webb?"

I stared back at him. On that I had no doubt. "Yes, sir."

He shrugged. "Well, I owe you my ass."

"Yes, sir."

To my surprise, Warner extended his hand, offering a handshake. In Naval Academy tradition, he was offering to "spoon" me, which meant that from that day forward we would be personal friends, thus ending my status as a plebe between the two of us. I knew that this was almost unheard of so early in plebe year.

"My spoon or my ass."

I looked down at his hand, sorely tempted. I wanted to be his friend. But this was too precious a moment to yield. "I want your ass, sir."

I broke my brace. In the darkness I fumbled around on the side shelf of my desk and found my Naval Academy atlas. My roommate was awake now, watching with a secret but glorious smile. I made Warner bend over and touch his toes, and I hit him as hard as I could.

"In the tradition, sir . . ."

"I know, I know." Warner gave me a fierce look. He came to the position of attention. "Beat Army." Then he left the room, slinking into the dark hallway as my roommate and I quietly celebrated one stolen moment of payback.

In return, for the next four months Chuck Warner ran me every chance he got, even though we were in different companies during the academic year. Finally, as the brigade prepared to go home for Christmas leave, he spooned me.

Almost exactly three years later, in the fall of 1967, as the brigade returned from summer cruise, I assumed the duties of a "four-striper" position on the brigade staff. As the brigade administrative officer, one of my duties was to clear out all of the incoming mail and official traffic that was sent to the Brigade of Midshipmen at the Main Office of Bancroft Hall. This included casualty reports from Vietnam, which I would then pass on to the brigade first lieutenant so that he could update the pictures on the To Those Who Went Before Us boards in the Rotunda.

One afternoon as I sorted through the mail, walking from the Main Office to the living spaces of the brigade staff, I opened up three casualty reports and saw that Chuck Warner had been killed. We were growing inured to such reports at Navy, but this notice shocked me. I had heard from Warner after he had been wounded and then hospitalized. I did not know that he had returned to combat. He had not lasted for long after being sent back into harm's way. Apparently he bled to death after being shot in the chest.

Reaching the brigade staff's living spaces, I entered my room and closed the door. I stood motionless for a while, staring out the window at the cobbled yellow bricks of Tecumseh Court and the placid Severn River on the far horizon. It was a beautiful Indian summer afternoon. Next door the radio in the brigade commander's room was blaring loudly. Glen Campbell was singing "By the Time I Get to Phoenix," a song written by the legendary Jimmy Webb, who years later I would learn was a distant cousin. The instrumental chords of the plaintive song somehow intertwined with my emotions, and with the view I was seeing from my window, and with the years I had now spent preparing to do what Chuck Warner had been doing. It all sank inside me, along with the coldly worded message I was holding in my hand.

My stomach rolled. I became physically ill. And to this day, despite all of the savagery that I myself have witnessed and endured as my life moved forward, whenever I hear the instrumentals that begin that song, my stomach rolls nauseously once again.

As was the usual practice I brought the casualty reports to the brigade first lieutenant, who was responsible for such things. Within a few days the pictures and the names were on the Board in the Rotunda. And every day until we graduated as I made my way to and from the classrooms on the other end of Stribling Walk I would stare at Chuck Warner's photograph, as well as the smiling, almost angelic young faces of a lot of others whom I had known but who now were forever gone.

Chapter Nine

THE FLEET—AND THE CORPS

The years from 1964 to 1968 were a time of ever-intensifying war in Vietnam and frequent international tensions elsewhere. This was also a period when the U.S. Navy dominated the seas just as certainly as the Royal Navy had in the two centuries that preceded World War II. The Royal Navy itself was growing smaller year by year as Great Britain continued to absorb the fiscal decimation brought about by the two world wars. America's most reliable global ally was inexorably withdrawing from such traditional orbits as its postings in Hong Kong and Singapore, the Indian Ocean, the Persian Gulf, and the Mediterranean. The German Navy, which had been so powerful in those wars (obviously, before Germany was on our side in strategic matters), was largely gone, although over time West Germany's army became a critical element of NATO's defense of Western Europe. Constrained by its postwar constitution and by raw regional memories of World War II, the Japanese Navy (again, in historical memory not to be bemoaned) was reduced in size and mission to the role of a local self-defense force. The ever-independent French retained a seagoing force of moderate size though modern and sophisticated.

On the other side of the strategic equation, the Soviet Union's navy was steadily expanding. By the early 1980s the Soviets would field a formidable global force, larger in total numbers than even the U.S. Navy but far less capable. The Chinese were beginning to stir, but unlike today were not aspiring to have a true "blue water" navy, although they would soon produce a fleet of nuclear submarines. In more recent years China would steadily expand its maritime size and influence, accompanied by increasingly aggressive claims of sovereignty over territories that extend throughout the islands and waterways of East Asia, from Taiwan to the southern reaches of the South China Sea.

But in the years when the Class of 1968 studied at the Academy, despite the operational tempo of the Vietnam War and the need to compensate geographically for Great Britain's shrinking fleet, there was no naval force that could even remotely challenge the U.S. Navy in size, lethality, or geographic reach. In 1968 our Navy fielded 930 combatant ships, a logistically self-sustaining and militarily powerful force that spanned the globe. Within ten years, in the aftermath of the Vietnam War, that number would dip to 479 combatants before climbing back up to 568 during the Reagan administration, peaking in 1988, when I was serving as Secretary of the Navy.

Today, with 288 combatant ships, our Navy remains the best in the world, but its commitments have not diminished even as the Fleet itself has grown steadily smaller. Frankly, Americans tend to take our Navy for granted as our attention has focused on the extensive tactical deployments of ground troops in Iraq, Afghanistan, and beyond. By design our Navy has always been our most valuable strategic asset, instantly maneuverable depending on the crisis of the moment and lurking on the other side of the horizon in a wide variety of potential hot spots. But its reach and, most important, its staying power under long-term, heavy deployments have been frequently strained, while China's naval power is on an upswing. In an ironic twist that illuminates the top-heavy command structure of the Department of Defense, there are now actually more admirals in the United States Navy than there are ships.

Setting aside policy debates, in purely practical terms this shrinkage of the Fleet affects the ability of Naval Academy midshipmen, as well as new Academy graduates, to serve at sea, for while the ships have disappeared, the size of the Brigade of Midshipmen has not diminished at all. Since the Class of 1968 graduated, the number of ships in the Navy has diminished by two-thirds, while the number of midshipmen at the Naval Academy has actually grown slightly larger, to 4,100.

During the 1960s the summers that separated one academic year from another were every bit as important as the time spent in class at Annapolis, and there was certainly no lack of ships on which to train. Following their first and third years at the Academy, midshipmen cruised aboard the entire spectrum of our ships at sea, blending in with the crews of the regular Navy. "Youngster Cruise" immediately following plebe year required midshipmen to work with and live among enlisted sailors throughout the fleet, an immensely valuable learning experience that allowed them to understand the demanding routines and the cramped living conditions aboard most ships. Following their third year at the Academy, midshipmen went on first-class cruise, living aboard ship in Officers' Country, dining as junior officers in the wardroom, and shadowing different officers as they performed their military responsibilities.

The day after plebe year ended I packed my sea bag and boarded a military aircraft along with hundreds of my classmates, heading to Long Beach, California, where I served first aboard the USS *Hornet*, CVS-12, and then on the USS *Princeton*, LPH-5. Long Beach in the mid-1960s was a huge Navy town, and the pier sides and wharves along America's West Coast were busy in the summer of 1965.

The entire U.S. military had shifted into high gear for the war that had just begun in what the sailors liked to call simply "West Pac." Only three months earlier, President Johnson had ordered Marine combat units ashore in the outskirts of Da Nang, South Vietnam's second-largest city. More Marines were on their way, aboard troopships and military flights, as were Army soldiers, some of them combat units moving into Vietnam from South Korea. Carrier battle groups, including cruisers, destroyers, and frigates, were already rotating regularly on the gun lines of Yankee Station in the north and Dixie Station off Vietnam's southern coast. Along with a host of resupply vessels such as ammunition ships, refrigerator ships, and oilers, the Navy had already established a continuous logistical train that stretched from East Asia back to Hawaii and to key ports in California. The Air Force was flying into Vietnam from bases in Guam, the Philippines, and Thailand, as well as operating from bases inside the country itself.

The energy of this surge was palpable along the pier at Long Beach as we off-loaded from the buses and reported to the *Hornet*. Throwing our sea bags over our shoulders and walking up the ship's brow, we stared all around us at long rows of grey, heavy-gunned combatants. The wharf area was bustling with vehicles and thickly netted cargo. The air was dank and musky, filled with a mix of odors from the ships and from the sea. Fire-hose-like "shit sleeves" dangled along the sides of many of the ships, discharging sewage from the innards of the vessels into the brown waters of the harbor.

Most tellingly, the groups of sailors who walked past us in their working dungarees or in their more formal service dress whites were giving us bullet-like, measuring stares. The "middies" had arrived, and the sailors of the Fleet were ready for us, in more ways than one.

Aboard the *Hornet* I and five other midshipmen were assigned to a cramped compartment where we bunked among perhaps three dozen "snipes," the hard-toiling, usually grease-covered boilermen and machinist's mates who worked well belowdecks to fire the eight boilers and propel the ship's four steam-powered turbines. Nearly a thousand feet long, with a crew of 3,000 officers and sailors, even at its rather advanced age the *Hornet* was capable of steaming steadily at thirty-three knots. The six of us lived and worked with the snipes, packing our gear in the same four-by-four-foot steel lockers that they were forced to use for months and sometimes years at a time, sleeping above them and below them on the thin mattresses of the same stacked bunks, wearing the same dunga-rees and black "boondocker" brogans, keeping the same hours through a long workday and then a four-hour watch in the middle of every night at sea.

In the living spaces and the work areas, the snipes tolerated and sometimes harassed us while at the same time acutely measuring our reactions. Each one of us was being quietly judged. Every one of them knew full well that in a few years one of us might be their officer. Predict-ably and understandably, they had saved up some of the dirtiest jobs down in the boiler rooms in order to test the humility of middies who someday just might return and, at least in titular fashion, be in charge.

The coffee-swilling, cigarette-smoking, traditionally potbellied chief petty officers ran the boiler rooms, most of them having worked their way up over as long as twenty years for that privilege and responsibility. Along with the first-class petty officers, all of them aspiring chiefs, they ran us in the Fleet's little version of plebe year. Just to make sure we understood the power of a chief as compared to the legal authority of a commissioned officer, we spent the first few days at sea cleaning greasy metal deck plates around the boilers with wire brushes and cans of syrupy lemon juice, and then wading again and again into the muck of the bilges.

The only difference in our shipboard uniforms was the blue ring at the top of our Dixie Cup "white hats." In port the sailors loved to warn women who approached pier side that this was "The VD Ring," and that they should stay away from the men with the blue ring on their white hats, since they were ostensibly recovering from venereal disease.

One night as we steamed at sea after a couple of weeks aboard the *Hornet*, the senior first-class petty officer in our living spaces called me over to a privileged four-by-four-foot locker. A half-dozen other sailors had gathered on nearby cots or were sitting cross-legged on the deck itself. The first-class petty officer, a veteran of ten years at sea, gave a little speech informing me that they had decided I was not the typical asshole that they had come to expect from the annual onslaught of middies. And in a ritual that involved giving me the combination to the locker that held their rather exotic (and erotic) "Hong Kong library," as well as passing around a bottle of contraband whiskey mixed in with a can of apple juice liberated from a nearby supply room, they accepted me as one of them.

I gladly took both. Like infantrymen in the Marine Corps, the snipes were the "grunts" of the seagoing Navy. I have never forgotten how hard they worked, so frequently out of sight, monitoring the steam pressure in the tubes and firing up the oven-hot boilers. They rarely saw sunshine while the ship was hard at sea. In fact most snipes considered it a luxury just to stand in the open air of the ship's fantail for a few minutes, catching sundown and a cigarette in the late afternoon breeze. Pallid and greasy, they deserved to take great pleasure while watching the white foam of the wake behind the ship. As with so many other realities in life, amid the bustle of operating an aircraft carrier from the exalted heights of the bridge it was easy to forget that if it were not for the snipes down in the boiler rooms above the bilges, the four churning propellers just below the water line would have been motionless and silent.

When I was Secretary of the Navy, on every ship that I visited, big or small, I always insisted on taking the ladders down the steep metal steps from the breezy vistas of the bridge and the captain's cabin high up in Officers' Country, deep below the water line to the bowels of the boiler rooms and the engineering spaces. Holding on to the hot metal railings as I made my way down toward the bilges, I would pay my regards to those who worked in the stifling heat and the whirring forgotten engine rooms. When greeted by the master chief, I would always give him a wink and ask how often the ship's commanding officer came down to visit his snipes.

"Well, sir," the chief would often reply, winking mischievously back, "the captain's got a lot of things to take care of, up there on the bridge."

Both the *Hornet* and the *Princeton* had begun service as straight-deck Essex-class aircraft carriers during World War II. Following the war, as larger and more sophisticated "supercarriers" joined the Fleet, both had been converted to other uses during what was known as the Fleet Rehabilitation and Modernization Program, also known as FRAM. The *Hornet* was reengineered with an angled flight deck and became a CVS, a carrier devoted to antisubmarine operations. The *Princeton* kept its straight deck and was configured as an early version of the LPH, which stood for "landing platform, helicopter." The principal function of the *Princeton* was to carry Marines to the littoral edge of a battle zone and to serve as a launching platform for helicopter-borne attacks, embodying a tactical concept then known as "vertical envelopment."

The *Hornet* had a memorable history during World War II. The ship's crew had spent sixteen continuous months in combat in the Pacific, winning nine battle stars in support of numerous sea engagements and amphibious operations, including the battles of Saipan, Tinian, Guam, the Philippine Sea, Leyte Gulf, Okinawa, and Iwo Jima. She would be decommissioned in 1970. Due in large part to her contributions in the war, in 1991 the *Hornet* would be was designated a National Historic Landmark, and in 1998 the ship would be opened to the public as a museum in Alameda, California.

Aboard the *Hornet* we steamed the waters of the Pacific during maneuvers off the West Coast of the continental United States, making liberty stops in Seattle, San Francisco, and San Diego before heading back to the ship's home port in Long Beach. Halfway through the summer our midshipman contingent boarded the *Princeton*, which was on-loading a battalion of infantry Marines as well as a full complement of helicopters. We would off-load the Marines in Hawaii, where in the near future they would soon board another troopship and head to Vietnam.

And so I had finally made it to Hawaii, the place I had so longingly dreamed of during those cold Nebraska winters as I pored through stacks of magazines in the attic of The Ranch and devoured the novels of James Michener. Honoring a long-held tradition inherited from the Royal Navy, as the *Princeton* left the open sea and headed into port, thousands of sailors and midshipmen stood at quarters in our dress whites, at parade rest all along the railings of the ship. Heading toward Pearl Harbor, the *Princeton* steamed just off the coastline of Oahu. Manning the railings, we stared in awe at the majesty of Diamond Head and the beaches of Waikiki.

A good friend who had grown up in California and had been with me at Southern Cal before we both left for the Academy stood next to me as we paralleled the tantalizing beaches. "I always thought California was God's Country," he said softly as we stared out at the turquoise water and the distant beaches. "Forget it, man. Look at that! This is truly God's Country."

The ship navigated the channel past Ford Island and Battlefield Row, into Pearl Harbor itself. For anyone who has ever worn the uniform of the Navy or Marine Corps, these waterways where so much carnage and destruction had been inflicted during the Japanese attack on December 7, 1941, will always be a hallowed sanctuary. Nearing pier side we slowly passed the sobering sight of the USS *Arizona*, still barely underwater and still leaking steady pools of oil nearly twenty-four years after Japanese dive bombers had sunk it, killing 1,100 sailors in a single attack.

We finally docked, off-loading the Marines, who eventually would board another troopship on a long journey that would end with them debarking into combat in the vicious environs of Vietnam's Quang Tin and Quang Nam Provinces. Little did I know that less than four years later I would find myself serving as a rifle platoon and company commander in that same area.

The *Princeton* idled for eight days in Pearl Harbor before returning to California, and every day we were allowed "Cinderella liberty," riding a military shuttle bus to Waikiki in the morning and returning to the ship by midnight. It had been four years since Michener's novels had set my mind aflame with the determination to go to Hawaii and to visit all of Asia. The images and cultural histories from his books, particularly the novel *Hawaii*, constantly reverberated in my mind as I walked the beaches and toured the island in a rental car with three of my midshipman friends. Michener had not led me astray during those cold Nebraska winters when I tried to eat the mango that I had bought with my pocket full of tips from a long day's work in what now seemed to be an eternity ago.

I ate plenty of mangoes in Oahu, and even more pineapples. I swam and surfed every day along the beaches of Waikiki and farther south in the rough waters that bordered the naval station at Barber's Point. I tried to imagine what it would have been like to have come to Hawaii as an unburdened, surf-loving civilian, knowing with a tinge of envy that it would be years, and possibly decades, before that luxury would even be thinkable, much less attainable. But still, I had made it to Hawaii. And I already knew that soon I would become a child of Asia, although the price of my admission would be an airplane ticket to a year of combat on one of the bloodiest battlefields of Vietnam.

The ship finally steamed slowly out of Pearl Harbor, heading back toward the mainland. I had only 15 cents in my pocket to get me to the next payday, which was just enough to purchase one pack of Herbert Tareyton cigarettes in the ship's tax-free store. I was broke, but there was nothing to spend money on aboard a ship in the open sea anyway. And I had just consummated a lifelong love affair with Hawaii.

First-class cruise was different, moving from the history of past wars and a peek into my Marine Corps future in Vietnam to a raw, explosive panorama that demonstrated the vital role our Navy plays in sudden global confrontations.

Following my third year at the Academy, I served with the Navy's Sixth Fleet in the Mediterranean Sea aboard the USS *Saratoga*, a Forrestal-class supercarrier with a thousand-foot flight deck and a crew of more than 5,100 officers and sailors. With the suddenness that so often seems to attend crises in the Middle East, I and the other midshipmen who reported to the USS *Saratoga* Battle Group had stumbled into a fascinating and memorable period in American and regional history.

On June 5, 1967, the Arab-Israeli War began, bringing explosive violence to the region as Israel fought military forces from Syria, Egypt, and Jordan, with the ferocity of the ground battles immediately spilling out into the surrounding waters of the Mediterranean. In Annapolis two days later, as the brief, intense series of battles continued in the Middle East, the Academy's Class of 1967 graduated. The next morning a contingent of new first-class midshipmen boarded a military transport plane at McGuire Air Force Base in New Jersey and flew to Rota, Spain. From there a number of us continued on to Souda Bay, Crete, where we were to report to the ships of the USS *Saratoga* Battle Group. While we were in the air, in an engagement that remains contentious to this day, the USS *Liberty*, a communications ship, was attacked by elements of the Israeli Defense Forces, leaving thirty-four American sailors dead and another 171 wounded. The *Saratoga* had been diverted to the battle scene in order to medevac the *Liberty*'s casualties before proceeding to Souda Bay to pick us up.

The entire Middle East was twitching nervously with aftershocks from the vicious six-day war. Its implications were also going global. In unprecedented numbers and strength, the Soviet Navy was now pouring into the Mediterranean. The skeletal NATO base above Souda Bay had just been reinforced. Our aircraft landed on a remote runway well above the bay. One by one we climbed out of the aircraft and peered out at a dry, weed-filled vista that seemed little changed from the preceding decades or even centuries.

A few military shuttle buses carried us down narrow winding roads from the runway to the small harbor. Farmers walked lazily alongside tiny, burdened burros on their way to town. Nearing the harbor we passed cluttered little markets where armies of flies slowly buzzed around the fresh meat of recently skinned goats that hung from tenterhooks in the store windows, waiting to be bought and eaten. In the harbor itself clusters of fishermen mended their nets in the midday heat, heedless of why we had just landed at the nearby airstrip and talking with each other. Now and then they stared curiously at these young, khaki-clad Americans who piled out of the buses and into the waiting skiffs that would take them out to the huge ships that were moored, death-like, in their normally quiet and unthreatening bay.

We stared unabashedly back, most of us equally mindless of the routine of their daily lives. True to America's tradition of sending its Fighting Tourists all around the world, we took lots of pictures, causing some of the fishermen to gesture toward us with the universal hand salute. Ever curious, I found myself wishing whimsically that I could have stayed behind, at least for a day or two, to explore the harbor and absorb the daily life of these people for whom the mayhem in the Middle East and the power struggles between the United States and the Soviet Union were little more than irrelevant, far-removed curiosities. But that was not in the contract I had signed three years earlier, when I had sworn away at least nine years of my life. Nor was it part of the profession of arms that I had now decided to pursue.

The *Saratoga* was a mythical vision as we approached it aboard the small ship's boats, riding high in the water where it was anchored in the bay. Powerful and foreboding, the supercarrier loomed above the skyline like a deus ex machina that could have found a literary purpose in an ancient Greek drama that the Cretan fishermen themselves might have studied in their youth. Ominously, for them at least, its flight deck was chock-full of warplanes. Making our way along the royal-blue waters of the bay, we reached the side elevator of the ship. Without orders we made a human chain up the steps of the elevator from the ship's barge all the way to the hangar deck and tossed our sea bags one after another until they were stacked in a pile just inside the hangar deck.

The hangar deck was protected by a perimeter of armed Marines. On the other side of their human barrier the aircraft carrier's cavernous inner deck was littered with the quiet, shell-shocked casualties from the USS *Liberty*, who had received initial medical treatment aboard the ship. Stepping off the elevator I gazed intently at them as they sat or lay on their makeshift cots. We quickly learned that staring was not allowed. The Marine guards told us curtly to pick up our sea bags and move on.

Later that day the anchors came up and the *Saratoga* again put out to sea. Within hours the casualties from the *Liberty* were cross-decked to the USS *America*, which took them into Athens for further evacuation. And the *Saratoga* Battle Group kept moving, patrolling the unpredictable waters just off the coastline of the Middle East.

As we cruised in the open sea an A-4 Skyhawk aircraft sat permanently on the front right catapult of the *Saratoga*, guarded by Marine Corps sentries and ready for launch at a moment's notice. The word among the ship's crew, difficult to verify but also hard to refute, was that the A-4 was loaded with a nuclear weapon.

The other three catapults of the *Saratoga* remained in motion day and night, launching all variations of naval aircraft, as did the tail hook traps along the angle deck, on which each plane would land after completing its mission. My living quarters were in a small stateroom in Officers' Country, just below the forward left catapult. Day after day, night after night, the stateroom would vibrate from the loud roar above my bunk as the ship conducted round-the-clock flight operations. The jets would rev their engines at full throttle, preparing to launch, followed by the hard clunk of the catapult's hook as it separated from the aircraft, smacking into the flight deck, having slung it like a slingshot into the sky above the blackened sea.

The *Saratoga*'s ship complement included nearly a hundred aircraft, twice what the old Essex-class carriers such as the *Hornet* could have held. A squadron of UH-2 Seasprite helicopters was responsible for the ship's search-and-rescue missions. *Saratoga* also boasted contingents of multicapable F-4 Phantom fighters; precision bombing A-4 Skyhawk attack planes; the dual-propeller-driven S-2F Tracker antisubmarine craft; the single-propeller A-1 SPAD, a durable close-support aircraft that could carry more than its own weight in ordnance; and the huge RA-5 Vigilante reconnaissance planes, in those days the largest and fastest aircraft ever to operate off an aircraft carrier.

Some evenings after dinner I would climb a series of ladders from the hangar deck up to the flight deck. Sitting on the open deck near the "island" superstructure, I would then watch the repetitive launches as if I were a spectator at an opera or a football game. For the sailors of the *Saratoga* the scene was little more than a normal day at sea, but for an outsider the entire flight deck was filled with drama and no-nonsense expertise. The deck crews managed every phase of these launches and recoveries largely without words, which was a good thing, since the noise that attended their duties was often overwhelming.

The multicolored jerseys that every deckhand wore contributed to their efficiency and eliminated the need for talk. The supervisory aircraft-handling officers and petty officers wore yellow. The all-important plane captains wore brown. The deck handling crews such as chock men and elevator operators wore blue. The maintenance crews wore green. Those involved in ordnancè, crash, and salvage functions wore red. The fuel crews wore purple. The "neutrals," such as combat cargo specialists, safety and medical crews, and photographers, wore white.

I myself wore khakis. I was not supposed to be on the flight deck at all. But since no one ever told me to leave, I pulled up a deck plate, sat back against a grey-painted steel bulkhead, took out my camera, and enjoyed the show. Quite a show it was, and most important, it was taking place with serious implications. The real-world turbulence of the Middle East was at the turning point of almost every flight that had been launched from the roaring catapults.

The U.S. Navy had invented aircraft carrier technology and modern sea combat doctrine. The kind of expertise demonstrated every day on the flight deck of the *Saratoga*, seemingly as normal as driving one's car to work back at home, was the product of decades of trial and error, plus the hands-on tutorials that are the end result of world-class leadership.

And, it must be said, with the retrospective that time allows. Although every launch and recovery was an adventure, when it came to the huge and heavy RA-5, it always seemed nothing short of a minor miracle that these leviathans did not repeatedly end up at the bottom of the sea rather than up in the air. The aviators and their flight deck crews made it look simple, but it was no small task to launch a plane that weighed more than three Greyhound buses up into the sky within half the distance of a football field. Without exception every RA-5 that was launched briefly dipped like a struggling, squawking goose toward the water line as it separated from the catapult and roared off the flight deck of the *Saratoga*. And it was not unusual to see the RA-5s tug and veer as their tail hooks caught the recovery cable upon landing, until their noses were precariously hanging above the sheer, ninety-five-foot drop between the flight deck and the sea.

Thus a cruise originally designed to be a relatively tranquil visit of the historic cities along the Mediterranean coastline became instead a tension-filled period of continuous operations in the open sea. Members of the Class of 1968 had dispersed throughout the globe for first-class cruise, including many who served aboard ships that were steaming the gun lines of Yankee and Dixie Stations just offshore from Vietnam. I had signed up for the Mediterranean because I knew that hard ground combat in Vietnam awaited me in a year anyway, and that as a Marine, I would spend most of my military career in Asia. Serving aboard a ship in the Sixth Fleet would offer a rare chance to visit the exotic, legendary locales of that historic region.

During its six-month deployment to the Med the *Saratoga* was scheduled to make port calls at such places as Barcelona, Mallorca,

Toulon, Malta, Istanbul, Athens, and Naples. The ship would indeed visit many of these ports in the final months of its deployment, after the other midshipmen and I returned home and the region regained a semblance of stability. But in the weeks following the Six-Day War, the *Saratoga* Battle Group remained mostly at sea. Other than a brief visit to Naples, we saw only—and from a distance—the raw mountainous beauty of Crete, where the Battle Group often anchored in Souda Bay and where, due to the sparse local population, only 4 percent of the crews were allowed to go ashore on any given day.

Returning to Souda Bay from a long sea patrol, the entire Battle Group again was anchored offshore. On the other end of Crete, ships from the Soviet Navy did the same. Unable to let their men go ashore and precluded for diplomatic reasons from visiting the more exotic ports of the region, the Battle Group's commanding officers searched for a diversion that might boost the morale of their bored and restless sailors and Marines. As happened frequently in the Navy of that era, they decided to hold a task force boxing smoker, bringing the best fighters from the Battle Group for a night of fights on the hangar deck of the *Saratoga*.

The officer in charge of putting together the smoker had been a boxer at the Naval Academy. Calling a meeting of the forty-eight midshipmen aboard the *Saratoga*, he told us that he wanted the Academy to be represented in the fights. Our contingent included many top-ranked athletes, including a nationally recognized football player and the captain of the Navy basketball team. But when it came to fighting, all eyes immediately turned to me. I protested, explaining to the lieutenant commander that I was now cruising as a junior officer and that as a future Marine I had strong feelings about an officer ever publicly striking any enlisted sailor or Marine. He took my concern for false modesty, which it was not. Then he chuckled and ordered me to report to a compartment in the ship's forecastle that afternoon.

Along with perhaps thirty enlisted sailors who wished to try out for the fights, I reported to the gym space near the ship's forecastle.

I spent the afternoon in a series of box-offs against more than a half-dozen sailors in my weight class. Watching me fight and learning of my win-loss record and years in the ring, the officer in charge of the smoker matched me with a Marine corporal who was stationed on the cruiser USS *Galveston*. The Marine, who turned out to be a rock-hard Native American, had enlisted in the Corps after winning the welterweight division of the Northwest Golden Gloves. With a posted record of 29-0, the corporal had never lost a fight. The officer explained that we would meet in the "semi-windup" fight, which was in reality the main event. Tradition demanded that the formal windup fight of the night feature two heavyweights, he said. But the records that I and my Marine opponent shared were rare for a boxing smoker in the fleet.

Personally, I was not inspired. I had not come to Souda Bay to box; I had signed up for a cruise in the Mediterranean to see Barcelona, Mallorca, and Toulon. I held with the long tradition of the Marine Corps that an officer should never strike an enlisted Marine. But there we had it. I had received military orders to step into the ring and fight, and fight I would.

The date for the boxing smoker arrived. Night descended upon the waters of Souda Bay. The carrier's hangar deck filled with sailors and Marines. The gloves went on. The fights began. The bells rang in the rounds. The cheers from the crowd rose and fell. And despite myself, I began to feel the blood boiling inside my veins.

A raised boxing ring had been erected in the middle of the hangar deck, which by the time the fights began was packed with at least a thousand sailors and Marines. The fights were also being televised on closed-circuit TV throughout the ships in the Battle Group. I waited, wanting to be done with this, and then waited some more, paying little heed to the fights that preceded my own. Finally the twelfth and next-to-last fight was announced. I walked from the darkness toward the brightly lit arena. My opponent and I climbed the wooden blocks and stepped into the ring.

Surprisingly, as we did so the ship's band began playing the Marines' Hymn.

Nearby, a section of the crowd that was filled with dozens of Marines began wildly cheering, their fists in the air. And as I waited for the bell to ring, a chilling realization overwhelmed me. They obviously were not cheering for me. In fact, with all the strength they could muster, they were cheering against me. They wanted to see me go down, for the pride of the very Corps to which I had already sworn my allegiance. Even worse, if I did go down, in a year or so I might be standing before one of them, maybe even my opponent, while serving as their platoon commander in combat. And the word would quickly go out that their new lieutenant had already gotten his ass beaten by an infantry corporal.

This could not happen, no matter how good my opponent might be—and he was good. No, I decided. This would not happen. Even if I did go down, I had to do my best to take him down with me. More important than anything else to me at that moment, I had to at least mark him so that every one of his fellow Marines would look at him tomorrow morning and know that he had been in a real fight.

The bell rang. Ten seconds into the fight he hit me as hard as I have ever been hit, before or since, with a right-hand lead that literally popped my right eye, closing it with a sudden gush of blood. For the rest of the fight I could not see out of it. I fought back, with more determination than in any other fight in my life. Under the glaring lights of the ring at that moment, he and I were not merely engaging in a sport, as with the boxing programs at the Naval Academy. Nor were we wearing the cumbersome twelve-ounce gloves used at the Academy. Forget the Naval Academy and the tiresome coach who lectured to us day after day that we were indulging in a team sport and that we were supposed to be focusing on "points, boys, points, not knockdowns." We were wearing the smooth-fisted, eight-ounce gloves that I had cut my teeth on in the dank gyms of Omaha with the legendary likes of Whitey Lohmeier and Harley Cooper. And we both had years of experience.

This was not a boxing match. It was a blood brawl, between two people who could not afford to lose. He could not bear losing because he had never lost and did not intend to. And I could not bear the thought of losing to someone who in little more than a year might be serving under my command.

And beyond all that, we both loved the U.S. Marine Corps, and we both believed in oddly different ways that we were fighting for its honor.

We pounded each other, dancing, attacking, counterattacking, working the ring ropes, sending sharp bursts of punches to the body and the head. And finally, in the third round I dropped him, stepping below the same right-cross lead that had popped my eye at the beginning of the fight, throwing a hard left into his solar plexus followed by a right hook to the side of his chin. Down he went. He was a terrific fighter. Anyone else would have been out for the count. Astoundingly he climbed slowly back to his feet. I attacked him again and again until the bell rang, trying to knock him out, but he was still facing me with his hands up and his chin down when the fight ended.

We both looked like pulverized meat. I had two black eyes. His nose was smashed and bloodied.

The next morning the ship's newspaper led with a story about the thirteen fights of the night before, focusing mainly on our brawl. Ironically the writer did not mention that my opponent was a Marine, nor did he say that I was a midshipman. "Easily the most action-packed bout of the evening was the contest between J. H. Webb of the SARATOGA and C. P. Colburn of GALVESTON. Both boxers displayed their wares handily in an all-out effort to dispose of their competitor. Both boxers exhausted themselves in an effort for a knock-out. As it turned out Webb won a unanimous decision from Colburn in one of the best matches in SARATOGA history."

In eight years of fighting, win or lose, I never fought a tougher opponent than this Marine, who, for military rather than mere athletic reasons, I simply could not allow to beat me.

• • •

First-class cruise ended. We were given twenty-six days of leave. Returning to the Academy, the Class of 1968 assumed command of the brigade striper organization and prepared for graduation. My academic grades had varied wildly from nearly straight A's in my courses in English, history, and government, to the Dismal D's in courses such as Electrical Engineering, Fluid Dynamics, and (my all-time least favorite) Thermodynamic Properties of Steam. But my leadership evaluations were consistently at the top. I was among the final six interviewees for the position of brigade commander and was assigned as a four-striper on the brigade staff, with only four midshipmen in the brigade ranking above me.

Every day from our return to the Academy in the autumn of 1967 until our graduation on June 5, 1968, was a military and societal rollercoaster ride. In October a massive march on the Pentagon, later memorialized in Norman Mailer's Pulitzer Prize–winning book *Armies of the Night*, signaled the growing influence of the antiwar movement, not only on college campuses but also among the elites of our national media. Soon thereafter the North Vietnamese Army's division-scale attacks at Dak To in the Central Highlands and especially the siege of the Marine Corps outpost at Khe Sanh raised the specter that the United States might be falling into the same trap that had resulted in the landmark French defeat by the Viet Minh at Dien Bien Phu in 1954. Civil rights agitators such as H. "Rap" Brown and Stokely Carmichael were urging violence on a scale that threatened to marginalize more principled and constructive leaders such as Martin Luther King. And more personally for all of us who had now spent three years preparing to serve and to lead, the To Those Who Went Before Us boards in the rotunda of Bancroft Hall were filling up with the names and photos of people we had known and grown to respect.

This was a time of conscription and of a war that became so costly and unpopular that the stigmas regarding military service among our parents' generation eventually were turned on their head. Military service was venerated among the Greatest Generation that fought World War II. In our parents' era, those who did not serve were often spoken of contemptuously as "draft dodgers." Among the elites of the Vietnam generation, avoiding the draft became something of an art form, sparing a talented, well-educated, and ambitious individual the time-robbing nuisance and inherent dangers of military service. As I wrote in a flashback scene regarding one character in my Vietnam War novel *Fields of Fire*, "Mark went to Canada. Goodrich went to Vietnam. Everybody else went to grad school."

The war and the stark class divisions in our age group among those who fought it, opposed it, or simply wanted to avoid it sometimes visited us in unexpected ways. In one of the great ironies of the loophole-filled policies regarding conscription during the Vietnam War, a draft-eligible male could be excused from military service if he was teaching inside the Department of Defense public school system, whether at a high school on a military base in places like Guam or Germany or, as it turned out, as a professor at the Naval Academy. As one might have expected, this policy brought about an almost hilarious, Monty Python–like anomaly. More than a few of those who were teaching the sons and daughters of our military professionals overseas were young men who found this to be a great way of avoiding military service.

This anomaly did not exist at West Point or at the Air Force Academy, since their entire faculties were required to be active-duty military officers. Nor did it often occur at the Naval Academy, where, although half of the faculty was made up of civilians, the academic credentials necessary to secure a teaching position were so stringent that a person of draft-eligible age seldom made the cut. But toward the end of my time at the Academy one of my professors, a self-described intellectual all of twenty-six years old, had done so. And he frequently made a point of mentioning his draft-deferred status to the midshipmen in his class.

One morning during his usual five-minute warm-up comments at the beginning of class the young professor read to us an article from that day's *Wall Street Journal*. The basis of the article was a survey purportedly showing that when career military officers left the service they tended to seek nonchallenging jobs, safe within a bureaucracy, even if the jobs brought them less pay. The professor smirked as he finished the article, looking out at a class filled with young men who within the next year or so would be risking their lives all over the world while he remained behind in the protected cocoon of the Academy. "This validates what I have always believed about career military people," he said. "They are basically second-rate players."

After all the tribulations that my family and so many others had endured, I could not contain myself. In my view the survey was debatable and the data probably skewed. The professor may indeed have been a certified "intellectual," but his comments were unwarranted. He had insulted my father, whose deployments and whose journey to obtain a college degree had spanned a period greater than his entire lifetime. And he had insulted a lot of other people as well. My brother, Gary, would soon join the Marines, serving more than five years as a helicopter pilot. My older sister, Pat, was married to a career Air Force NCO who was then stationed in the Philippines. My younger sister, Tama, would soon marry one of my roommates, John McKee, whose uncle had been killed in a sea battle during World War II and whose father, a career naval officer, had lost his life only a few months before when the helicopter in which he was riding went down at sea, taking all of its passengers with it. My fiancée, Barbara DuCote, whom I would marry two days after graduation, had also grown up in the military; we had met in high school when our fathers were stationed in Nebraska. Her father had served in Korea and now, at the age of forty-seven, was flying dangerous missions in Vietnam, piloting the C-7 Caribou aircraft into remote Green Beret and Montagnard outposts. Her uncle had been killed in World War II, flying as a fighter pilot in Burma. Her brother had served as an Army soldier with the 101st Airborne Division in Korea.

Any price I might pay by arguing with a professor could never match the enormity of the sacrifices that needed to be defended. I could not sit quietly as if I were accepting the validity of the professor's remarks. I raised my hand, well aware that I was embarking on an academic suicide mission. I took a minute or so to summarize my father's bottom-up career, including his brilliance in the missile program and the long years he had spent away from our family. Then I matched the professor's smirk.

"Actually, no offense, sir, but if you're looking for a nonchallenging job, safe inside a bureaucracy, I think you ought to just go be a college professor."

He stared blankly at me. I smiled back. No one else said a word. In defense of my silent classmates, some of them thought I was unnecessarily picking a fight, while the remainder felt that there was nothing else left to say. Predictably my grade in this young professor's class took a hit, but I had already assumed that this would happen. In fact it fit neatly with my lifetime pattern of incompatibility with structured academia.

At a dress parade just before graduation I was one of eighteen midshipmen to receive a special letter of commendation from the superintendent for leadership contributions during our time at the Academy. My father bought my granny an airplane ticket so that she could travel from Riverside, California, where Aunt Carolyn had bought her a tiny house just up the street from her own, to be at the parade and at my graduation. As my name was called I stepped forward on the parade ground of Worden Field to receive the letter of commendation. With a glance I caught a look on Granny's face from where she sat in a special row in front of the entire Brigade of Midshipmen. A rush of feelings suddenly coursed through me. For a moment I was a little kid again, wanting desperately to know when my father was coming home from Germany, and she was taking my hand, speaking calmly in her slow Arkansas drawl, guiding me down the creaking wooden steps behind the kitchen, taking me to the backyard and showing me where we were going to plant some corn.

At the age of seventy-five, Granny had just taken her first airplane ride. She had not liked it. For the entire week of her stay, she could not stop talking about how uncomfortable she felt, way up in the sky with the clouds and the buildings and the mountains so far below her. When it came time for her to return to California, she took the bus.

Most surprising of all, no one had more mixed feelings about my choosing to enter the Marine Corps than my own father. He was a professional who understood the risks and costs of military service. He agreed that America needed to stay strategically engaged in East Asia. But he also had made a logical calculation that the danger to our national security posed by Vietnam was not worth his son's life on that ever more confusing battlefield. This was not sentimental drivel; in fact it became a point of argument between us, as if it were a removed, sterile debate. More than anything else, my father's hesitations were motivated by the arrogance and incompetence of Secretary of Defense Robert McNamara and his much-ballyhooed bunch of civilian Whiz Kids whose data-based "systems analysis" approach to fighting our wars had diminished the historic role of military leadership.

My father's conclusions had been formed during two years spent in the Pentagon, working in the Air Force's legislative liaison office, dealing daily with the Whiz Kids on the one hand and Congress on the other. As I began my first-class year at the Academy he had been assigned to Air Force Systems Command at Andrews Air Force Base, Maryland, where I later learned he was responsible for the development of a satellite linkup between the battlefield and the White House, a program euphemistically called Spy in the Sky.

When I went home for sporadic weekend visits and on Christmas break during my first-class year, my entering the Marine Corps became a recurring argument at the kitchen table of my parents' quarters at Andrews Air Force Base. Due to the restrictions placed on him by his ultra–Top Secret security clearances, my father knew more than he could say and thus was able to communicate with me only in guarded code.

Shaking his head as we talked about the war, he would roll his eyes in disgust. More than a thousand Americans were dying every month, and the prospect that these numbers would change was dim. "What are your Marines doing out there in the middle of nowhere?" he would ask, partially as a taunt and partially as a hint that he knew what they were doing but that even he could not figure out why they were doing it. "Who's the enemy? Who's shooting at you? And how do you know who to shoot back at?"

"Typical Air Force ignorance," I would answer, teasing back.

As the arguments dwindled one by one into stalemate, my father would fall back on his sarcastic, mountain-boy sense of humor. "Listen to me, Sonny Boy. Do not go into the Marine Corps. Do you hear me? This isn't the battle of Iwo Jima. Go into the Navy. Find yourself a nice ship, way out in the ocean. Stay on the ship. Visit Hong Kong. Go to Tokyo. Watch the movies. Eat ice cream."

As graduation day neared he became more visibly troubled. His warnings were as direct as they could be without revealing the classified nature of the programs he was working on. "Do you realize that Lyndon Johnson is going to know you're wounded even before your division commander does?" On this point he may have been technically correct, but he was politically wrong. By the time I was wounded, Johnson had headed home to Texas and Richard Nixon was president.

Yet I could not dismiss either the urgency or the sincerity of my father's arguments. At bottom he was above all a military professional. He had given the Air Force every ounce of his energy and loyalty for twenty-six years. He had enormous respect for the Marine Corps; his animus was reserved for the way it was being used. In later years no one was prouder to point out that although he had served in the Air Force, he had given the Marine Corps both of his sons. But shortly after I graduated from the Naval Academy my father put in his papers to retire from the Air Force. His reasons for retiring, like all such decisions, were filled with complexities and competing emotions. But one of those reasons was abundantly clear. He was working every day to perfect a satellite program that was going to be taking rolling, real-time snapshots of the Vietnam battlefields, which in his view might end up harming the well-being of his son. If the worst-case scenario happened and he was standing at a grave site in Arlington Cemetery, he did not want to feel personally accountable as the bugle played "Taps" and he watched my young remains being lowered into the pit. A generation later I would face my own conundrum as my son shipped out with a Marine Corps infantry battalion for the vicious urban warfare of Ramadi, Iraq, a bad place in a bad war whose strategy I believed from the outset was absurd.

"I just can't bear to watch this while I'm still wearing a military uniform," he finally said. And as I reported to the Marine Officer's Basic School at Quantico, Virginia, my parents prepared to leave the Air Force and move to the retirement haven of Florida.

★   ★   ★

My parents' final home during my father's military career was an old farmhouse near the back gate of Andrews Air Force Base in Maryland. Located ten miles southeast of Washington, the base was built on lands claimed by the government through eminent domain in the early days of World War II. A vast system of runways and hangars had been constructed on what once were farm fields but which now comprised the center of the base. Military aircraft of every imaginable sort and from all the services flew in and out of Andrews, including helicopters, jets, propeller-driven planes, and jumbo-size transports. More relevant to the day-to-day lives of most Americans, beginning shortly after World War II and continuing over the decades even to this day Andrews Air Force Base has been the home of Air Force One, the president's personal aircraft.

The area that eventually made up Andrews Air Force Base was hardly the empty wilderness from which Vandenberg Air Force Base had been fashioned along the desolate coast of central California. This was flat, usable farmland surrounded by small communities, fortuitously located a stone's throw from our nation's capital. At the direction of

President Franklin D. Roosevelt during a period of national emergency, roughly four thousand acres had been taken from longtime family farmers, whether the inhabitants liked it or not. Predictably included in such acreage were a number of small, quaint farm dwellings which the government decided to refurbish and turn into military housing.

Despite their military heritage, on the issue of confiscation my parents probably would have empathized strongly with those farmers who were forced to give up their homesteads. Additionally, for personal reasons, they certainly were not eager to move to Maryland. The farmhouse at Andrews was sedate and somewhat charming, but it was socially isolated. Surrounded by military fields and buildings, the house was only a few blocks from a series of ugly hangars and warehouses that made up the more cluttered side of the base's runways. Neighborhood amenities did not exist; in fact neighbors did not exist. And they were leaving my mother's all-time favorite home at Lake Barcroft in Falls Church, Virginia, where they had lived during my father's tenure at the Pentagon.

Lake Barcroft, six miles up the Columbia Pike from the Pentagon, was something of an idyllic oasis, a community built around a 125-acre lake in the middle of an ever-growing urban sprawl. In addition to the discomfort of his job at the Pentagon, my father hated the slow crawl of traffic during morning and evening rush hours, but like my mother he had come to love their home at 6311 Aqua Terrace, with its ultramodern kitchen, spacious recreation-room basement, and boat access to the placid lake just down the hill. Being able to rent the house at Aqua Terrace had been a lucky windfall for them. Military pay scales in the 1960s were infinitesimal compared to modern-day compensation. As a full colonel at the height of his military career, my father's basic pay plus his housing allowance was around $16,000 a year, less than half of what a colonel makes in today's military, even factoring in the change in the value of the dollar. Ever the talented hands-on electrician, he had reached an agreement with the owner to renovate and repair the house's electrical and mechanical infrastructure in return for a markedly reduced rent of $240 a month.

Thus my parents, along with Tama and Gary, were able to reside on a choice piece of property within eyesight of the lake itself. My mother found a special bliss in Lake Barcroft's community activities. For the first time in her life she was able to participate in social interactions such as the bridge club and the duckpin bowling league, where she mingled with the wives of high-ranking civil servants, lawyers, and corporate executives. Tama finished high school at nearby JEB Stuart in Falls Church, working summers as a waitress in the local Hot Shoppes restaurant, dating and soon falling in love with my roommate. Following high school she worked at the Bureau of Indian Affairs in nearby Washington.

After all the years of family relocations Gary was particularly disappointed with the move to Andrews. A talented athlete who played football, wrestled, and rowed crew at JEB Stuart, Gary also played lead and bass guitar in a local band. In order to finish high school at JEB Stuart he was forced to make a brutal commute from Maryland to Virginia during weekday rush-hour traffic, often staying overnight with friends in Virginia. Since he was finishing school in Virginia and thus not registered in the Maryland school system, the local draft board attempted (eventually unsuccessfully) to conscript him into the Army as soon as he turned eighteen, erroneously flagging him as a high school dropout.

But there was no way around it for my parents. In the late spring of 1967, when my father was assigned from the Pentagon to his sensitive post at Air Force Systems Command, a move to Maryland became obligatory. Packing up once again and reluctantly leaving her treasured coterie of friends at Lake Barcroft, my mother reckoned that she had now moved more than thirty times for my father since their marriage twenty-four years before. Despite good intentions, few people outside the military are able to comprehend the price that military families so often pay through such constant relocations, including spouses for whom a professional career during those years was nearly impossible. We had come to accept these realities as the unavoidable consequences of the needs of the service, but for my mother and my siblings, each move carried with it its own unavoidable emotional, professional, and educational costs.

No matter. The old white-frame farmhouse at 3552 Pennsylvania Avenue had become our family's latest definition of a home. The house was not unlivable; in fact its age and mysterious history emanated a somewhat welcoming comfort. We knew that not so very long ago it had been the center of a tranquil working farm, on lands that now were covered by concrete, where military aircraft hummed and roared. The property had a nice yard and a decent little outbuilding that had been turned into a garage. Amid the shade trees next to the garage was a fenced dog run for Snoopy, a spirited English pointer my brother had liberated from a frustrated customer at the base service station, where he pumped gas part-time during the school year and full-time in the summer.

Reminiscent of our earlier days at The Ranch in Nebraska, I teased my brother that it was now his turn to clear the mousetraps in the basement every morning. Typical of his offbeat creativity and dry sense of humor, Gary gave the task his own little twist, meeting the age-old challenge of building a better mousetrap, although the world was not following through in beating a path to his door. Puttering in the basement one evening, Gary rigged a soup can to one end of a rat trap and fixed its lid on the spring-fed hammer at the other. Soon he was catching mice alive inside the can, just for the fun of it.

But the long years of Webb family moves were finally over. A lifetime of never-ending relocations had taken us from one end of America to the other, as well as to the historical and lovely countryside of England. Our living quarters had varied from the squalid $5-a-night motel apartment in Pismo Beach to the grandeur of The Cedars. And so, without predictability or logic, the old farmhouse at Andrews was simply where the roller coaster stopped. In January 1969 my lifelong journey as a military brat ended at this unfamiliar home near a busy military runway. And it was there that I said good-bye to my parents, a few short weeks before I myself departed for the battlefields of Vietnam.

The year 1968 had just faded into history, clocking over into the New Year, although for our beleaguered and embattled country, 1969 would be almost as contentious. As I would learn firsthand, 1969 became the second-worst year for American casualties in Vietnam, made famous for the Battle of Hamburger Hill and the *Life* magazine cover story showing the pictures of 242 Americans who had died in one typical week of fighting, between May 28 and June 3. April through mid-May had been much worse, often bringing more than 400 dead per week. But those of us then fighting on the battlefields were not keeping aggregate scores. We knew that 1968, especially during the Tet Offensive, had been more costly, and that 1967's numbers had been about the same. Indeed if Vietnam casualties were placed on a bell curve, those three years were at the peak.

By early 1969 the political and emotional mood at home had begun to shift, and by the end of the year it had changed altogether. Nationally any optimism about a reasonably quick and positive outcome in Vietnam was gone. Antiwar protests escalated dramatically. 1969 would become known more for the festival at Woodstock in August, the Vietnam Moratorium in November, and the continuing revelations about the horrors of an American Army unit that had killed scores of civilians in a little village called My Lai. The fighting in Vietnam continued full-bore, but unlike in the earlier years of the war, for the opinion makers back home news of the war had become passé. The success or failure of our combat operations had reached an odd stasis, becoming almost irrelevant to media reporting, political debate, and academic discussions about the war.

As a result 1969 would turn out to be a very odd year to be spent in combat. Peace symbols, antiwar protests, and the drugs, sex, and rock and roll of Woodstock Nation were becoming more emblematic of our generational peers than military service. And yet 12,000 Americans would die on the battlefields in that one year, twice as many as would be lost in Iraq and Afghanistan combined over the entire span of both wars between 2002 and 2013.

This is more understandable in retrospect than it was at the time. I was a Marine, not a professor or a politician. I had no control over the direction or the debate of the war in which I was about to fight. And so, as I reached my parents' house on a cold morning in early January, none of that was on my mind. I had driven from Quantico to Andrews Air Force Base so that I and my parents might jointly say good-bye. Intellectual debates were for another time. A completely different set of circumstances was facing the members of the Webb family.

I would soon be shipping out for combat, while my parents would even sooner be leaving the military altogether. For us the alpha and the omega of military service were sadly and rather nervously intertwining, inside a house whose very unfamiliarity signified the power of family and individual duty over any notion of grand politics or geographic place. The war was not going to change over the next year, whatever my political theories. On the personal front, due to my father's military career we no longer belonged to a civilian community, anyway. After all the years of relocations and new assignments our local loyalties were not defined by a neighborhood or a town but by the larger concept of the military itself. And among members of the military such things as deployments and retirements were seldom belabored. We all went through these transitions; in fact it was unseemly to complain. One of the darker put-downs in the Marine Corps was "Shut up and die like a man."

A brittle sun masked the windswept cold as I parked in the driveway of the old farmhouse. Barbara was with me. She knew the drill; her father had returned from Vietnam a few months before and was now stationed at Air Force, Pacific headquarters in Hawaii. We left the car and walked inside. The door was not locked. My parents greeted us in the kitchen. We made small talk, pouring fresh cups of coffee, and then made our way to the living room, where we sat on sagging, familiar couches that dated back to my high school days in Nebraska.

It seems a fact of life that the more truly momentous an occasion, the less there really is to say about it. How could any of us put into words the long years of turmoil and preparation that had made both of our transitions so inevitable?

My parents seemed subdued and preoccupied. Their quiet angst was understandable. My coming months of combat were laden with the certainty of violence and the possibility of physical wounds or death. At the same time, their imminent departure from the military would bring with it a transition so enormous that it could be characterized in emotional terms as the death of their very way of life, with no way to predict what might replace it. And to make it worse, both of these two realities were happening at the same time.

Sitting on the comfortable old couches that brought back memories of my teenage years, it occurred to me that my parents were fully alone for the first time I could ever recall. Everything was changing for all of us, not only because of the social and political upheavals inside the country and not only with my orders into combat in Vietnam or the reality of their impending retirement. On top of all that, over the space of less than a year our family had permanently headed into separate unknowns. As the next three decades passed it would be rare when all six of us would be able to gather for anything that resembled a true family reunion.

This permanent dispersion was our inevitable legacy, the unintended wages of the life my father had so passionately embraced. My siblings and I were, quite simply, the children of our country's military. All four of us were now carrying on the traditions of military service into the unknown turmoil that followed the coming of our own adulthood. The four kids who once had sat cramped together in the backseat of our latest car as we crisscrossed America, reading Burma Shave signs and torturing each other as we piled up seven hundred painful miles a day, all the while ducking and wincing under the threat of my dad's infamous "three shutups rule," were now off on our own unpredictable journeys. Each of us had become like a little moon, spun off from a larger planet into our own orbit. We did not yet understand it, but as the years went by we would largely be orbiting little more than a shell made up of the memories that had shaped us and the painful emptiness of what had been left behind.

My mom, who by the age of twenty-four had borne four children, had become a grandmother at age thirty-nine. Since 1965 she had been a strong force in helping my sister Pat raise three young children born within the space of less than three years (Pat would eventually become the mother of seven), first at Vandenberg and more recently in Maryland while Pat's husband, George, was deployed overseas. Pat herself had just spun off into another new orbit. At this moment she was on her way to join George at his Air Force assignment in the Philippines. Only a few weeks before, at the age of twenty, Tama had married my former roommate John McKee and moved with him to Pensacola, Florida, and then to Meridian, Mississippi, where he would receive advanced flight training, thereafter reporting for duty in San Diego on his way to becoming a naval aviator. Gary was in his freshman year at Northeast Missouri State, where after graduation he would become a Marine. And within days my parents themselves would be moving to the unknown world of retirement in central Florida, with no home to move to and no clear employment prospects to pursue.

As my siblings were scattering across the globe and my parents were so suddenly left alone, I still could not fully grasp the notion that my father was heading for retirement. Of all the professions, military retirement in the days before the gargantuan growth (and soft economic landing) of the military-industrial complex was a brutal and abrupt transformation, often severing talented leaders from their life's calling at the very peak of their careers. At a relatively young age, within a matter of weeks a military officer with enviable acumen and extensive leadership experience would be relegated from a position of power and influence into the unchallenging oblivion of complete professional inactivity.

More personally, throughout my young life my dad had been the very symbol of all that I had come to understand and respect about leadership, integrity, and moral courage. Retirement, for my dad? Why? I still could not believe that this was happening.

The four of us sat in the dimly lit front living room. A small radio blared from a buffet in the nearby dining room, set to the local country music station. I sipped my coffee, trying to absorb the reality of what was about to happen to my parents. The floor around the couches was cluttered with cardboard boxes that my father and mother had been packing. In our military apartment in Quantico, Barbara and I were also packing. As we made chitchat and pretended to enjoy our coffee, my eyes lingered on the haunting, half-packed boxes. Once packed, taped, labeled, and shipped, the boxes would not be reopened until my parents finally found a place to live in Florida. By then I would have arrived at some yet-to-be-determined place in Vietnam, and Barbara would be unpacking a small collection of boxes in California.

It occurred to me that the half-packed boxes symbolized our entire family journey. We were always packing and unpacking. We always liked to look nostalgically backward at where we had been. We liked to make small talk about the new places where we might be going. But from the days just after I was born, the realities of the here and now had always seemed too challenging and too turbulent to simply sit back and enjoy.

Within weeks I would deploy to Vietnam, that endlessly debated but little-understood war that for the Marine Corps would bring three times the number of dead as were killed in Korea and more total killed and wounded than in any other war, including World War II. This ever-expanding war had now consumed my personal and professional preparations for more than three years. As the country struggled to resolve what had originally been considered nothing more than a "dirty little war," its impact on those of us who were serving, and on our loved ones, was persistent and overwhelming. The lieutenant who had been our next-door neighbor when we first moved into quarters at Quantico had deployed to Vietnam only two months before. I now owned his dog. And he was already dead.

But the transition facing my parents spoke of a completeness that for the moment overwhelmed my own trepidations about combat in Vietnam. My father had just turned fifty-one; my mother was not yet forty-four. All of the Webb kids were suddenly and permanently gone. My father's military career, the defining force of my entire young life, was over. My mother's very existence since the age of eighteen had been dedicated to raising a young family and adjusting to the constant moves which, over the span of my life, had averaged a new house every eight months. Where would this brilliant but rough-hewn and socially awkward man who had been such a role model direct his leadership and intellectual energies? And with both of them having overcome such difficult circumstances in their early lives, in what capacity would they be able to reenter the so-called civilian world? It scared me, looking at them. What would they do, now that the most challenging journey of their lives was over?

Unsurprisingly my father had other thoughts on his mind. He had lost in his attempt to convince me to go into the Navy. He was leaving the Air Force, wanting to be away from the satellite link-up programs while I was on the battlefield. I suppose he was enjoying the fact that Robert McNamara and Lyndon Johnson were gone too, neither of them well-remembered for the war they had left behind, although neither of us mentioned that reality, since it was irrelevant to what he and I both faced.

My father spoke quietly, asking me the age-old question for which throughout history there never has been a really good answer: "Are you ready for it?"

As much as anyone could say such words without having yet been shot at, I knew what my answer would be and I meant it. In terms of fulfilling its assigned mission, The Basic School at Quantico was the best school I had ever attended. "I'm ready," I said.

The vicious battlegrounds and constant combat of the Vietnam War had shaken the stable, formal disciplines that defined daily operations in the post-Korea, pre-Vietnam Marine Corps. It was one thing to ask for unquestioning obedience when ordering a Marine to undergo a "Junk on the Bunk" inspection inside a peacetime barracks. It was quite another to expect it when ordering a Marine to charge through a rice paddy toward a ridge line while carefully hidden enemy soldiers were shooting at him in the middle of a battle. The operational tempo was exhausting our elite Corps, and the greatest burden was falling upon its youngest and newest members.

Beginning in 1966, in a little more than two years the Corps had expanded from 190,000 to 307,000 Marines in order to adjust to the combat load it was carrying in the northernmost provinces of South Vietnam. Two of the Marine Corps' three divisions, the First and the Third, were fully deployed in combat. The Second Marine Division was operating at reduced strength out of Camp Lejeune, North Carolina. Even those battalions were heavily made up of Marines who had just returned from Vietnam combat, now frequently rotating aboard ship on six-month deployments in the Mediterranean and the Caribbean. As the war intensified even further, in late 1967 two regiments from the Fifth Marine Division, inactive since World War II, were rebuilt from scratch at Camp Pendleton, California, and soon sent to some of the fiercest battlegrounds of Vietnam.

For the Marines, combat and overseas deployments were unending. The greatest burden fell on the privates and lance corporals fresh from Boot Camp who populated the lower ranks of the rifle platoons and the lieutenants just out of The Basic School who commanded them. The Basic School, which we called TBS, was now starting a new class of 250 lieutenants every three weeks. In pre-Vietnam days, TBS had taken thirty weeks to complete. As Vietnam accelerated, the time a new lieutenant spent at TBS was reduced to twenty-six weeks, and then to twenty-one. But true to the traditions and long-held disciplines of the Corps, this reduction took place not by cutting the quality or the content of the curriculum but rather by lengthening the number of hours spent in class and in the field during every workweek. Gone were the pre-Vietnam

Wednesday afternoons reserved for one's favorite athletic activity, and gone were the five-day workweeks. Indeed, although a few courses on military drill and ceremony were eliminated, a course on the 60-millimeter mortar had been added to the TBS schedule, since the weapon had been reintroduced as a valuable component in the Marine rifle companies in the bush of Vietnam, where so many of us were going to end up.

Almost every week the TBS companies worked late into Saturday evening. They spent a high percentage of their time in the field, and a large percentage of that time was dedicated to night maneuvers and bivouacs. Our company was given the day off on Christmas, working late into the evening of December 24 and assembling on the tarmac for a field activity at 6:30 in the morning of December 26. We were given the day off on New Year's, then again assembled on the tarmac before dawn on January 2. Within a month after finishing TBS, the infantry lieutenants among us would be boarding military flights at Travis Air Force Base, California, to report immediately for thirteen-month tours in Vietnam as individual replacements in infantry battalions that were already engaged in sustained heavy combat.

Not surprisingly the intensity of this training schedule created special lifetime bonds among many of the young lieutenants, deeper in many cases than long friendships that had developed in college or over four years at the Naval Academy. And in this observer's view at least, the life-or-death circumstances that soon awaited us accentuated the learning process of the curriculum itself.

There was serious reason to pay attention. Those of us who would be leading rifle platoons in the infantry had frequently been reminded that the odds of our being killed or wounded were better than 50 percent. Knowing beyond a doubt that many among us would soon be killed or wounded brought with it an unexplainable but very real feeling of trust and mutual respect. During a time of national turmoil, when so many in our age group were avoiding military service altogether, every member of our TBS company had sought out and accepted the special rigors and dangers that had always defined the Corps.

Beyond the physical risks awaiting us in Vietnam was the inevitability of what was called the burden of command. Every one of us was aware that we would soon be making decisions whose results could determine whether other Marines would live or die. This was not the pretentious rhetoric of some blow-dried politician speaking to an annual dinner at a hometown gathering in the American Legion banquet hall. Barely old enough to vote, we would soon be commanding battle-hardened troops who needed a new lieutenant, often because our immediate predecessor had been killed or wounded.

Haunting many of us in one form or another was the sentiment expressed in a timeless letter written home in 1942 from Marine lieutenant Anthony Tortoras in the days before he was killed in action during the battle of Guadalcanal. Lieutenant Tortoras's admonition had become a "famous naval saying," which every Naval Academy midshipman was required to memorize: "Always pray, not that I shall come back, but that I will have the courage to do my duty."

Not that any of us wanted to die. "Pay attention, lieutenants" was a constant warning from our combat-hardened instructors. "This can save your life."

The Basic School's learning approach was to teach a weapon or a concept in the classroom, then give the lieutenants a walk-through, and finally to "go live," either firing the weapon or carrying out the concept. Tactics were taught at the squad, platoon, and company level. Every form of patrolling was taught, among them reconnaissance patrols, raids, ambushes, and search-and-destroy missions. As with other courses, much of the patrolling package took place at night, in the rolling, wooded hills of Quantico. The capabilities of every weapon in an infantry battalion were taught in the classroom, then the weapon was disassembled and assembled in the field, and after that fired on a range, including the .45-caliber pistol, the M-14 rifle, the M-16 rifle, the M-60 machine gun, the 60-millimeter and 81-millimeter mortars, the 3.5-inch rocket launcher, the Mark 26 grenade (as well as a variety of smoke and tear gas grenades), the M-79 grenade launcher, the LAAW antitank rocket, the flamethrower, and even such arcane weapons as the old Browning automatic rifle and the .45-caliber "burp gun." We learned how to fuse and detonate C-4 explosives, as well as how to place into position and blow a "shape charge" and a Claymore mine. We learned how to call for indirect fire on enemy targets and how to adjust mortars, artillery, and close-air support.

Every lieutenant who finished TBS during that era was given an 0301 infantry qualification, although many would go on to other specialties, such as aviation, artillery, motor transport, and supply. But only after serving competently in an actual infantry unit would a lieutenant receive the coveted 0302 qualification that recognized him as a fully qualified infantry officer.

As in every other area of the Marine Corps, gallows humor prevailed at TBS. Off-loading the buses in O'Bannon Hall's parking lot in the dead of night, climbing the stairways to our company area, our faces streaked and darkened from camouflage paint and our M-14 rifles slung over our shoulders, dozens of young lieutenants would join in a loud, defiant chorus, sung to the tune of "Jesus Loves the Little Children":

> *Fuck, fuck, fuck this TBS shit*
> *Six more weeks and we'll be home*
> *Then it's off to Vietnam*
> *Lose a leg or lose an arm*
> *And be pensioned by the Corps forevermore.*

Little did we know how right we were.

And so as I sat on the worn, soon-to-be-shipped couch in the unfamiliar farmhouse at Andrews Air Force Base on that cold winter morning in January 1969, the answer to my father's question was yes, I was indeed ready.

Quite frankly, after a lifetime in the military and all the years of preparation at the Naval Academy, I could not have been more ready. It had just been announced that as a result of my combined scores in academics, leadership, and military skills I would be recognized as the Honor Graduate of our TBS class. I would also receive the Military Skills Award for excellence in such areas as physical fitness, marksmanship, land navigation, and military instruction. Few moments of recognition in my life have held more meaning to me than receiving these two awards at the graduation ceremony for our company of nearly 250 "highly dedicated, highly agitated" young Marines who had volunteered for the battlefield during such a moment in our country's history.

My parents were unable to attend the TBS graduation ceremony, as I was unable to attend my father's formal retirement ceremony when he left the Air Force. Between the two of us there had been a special, almost secret irony in that ceremony at Andrews Air Force Base. In a real-life example that might have been a passage from Joseph Heller's World War II masterpiece, *Catch-22*, my father had been awarded the prestigious Legion of Merit for his work on the same satellite link-up programs that had caused him to decide to retire.

I would soon drive west, heading for California, where Barbara would rent a house across the street from my granny and I would catch a flight to Vietnam. My parents would clear their quarters at Andrews Air Force Base and then head south, to stay for a while with my dad's longtime friend Bud Colwell as they adjusted to the unknowns of retirement that awaited them in Florida. Alpha had just begun. Omega was, not so happily, done. In less than twenty years our lives had traveled full circle. I was now the one who was leaving. My dad was the one being left behind.

There was nothing left to be said. It was time to go. We rose from the years-worn couches and began to say our final, deliberately understated good-byes. As we slowly made our way toward the front door of the farmhouse, the radio in the dining room began playing "Danny Boy," sung by Johnny Cash. I am not sure that anyone other than God himself could have arranged the sweet sorrow of that moment. Johnny Cash was my favorite singer. "Danny Boy," emblematic of our long-held Scots-Irish heritage of military service, is perhaps the greatest song ever written about the painful anguish of a father watching helplessly as his son marches off to war.

Oh, Danny Boy, the pipes, the pipes are calling
From glen to glen and down the mountain side
The summer's gone and all the roses falling
'Tis you, 'tis you, must go and I must bide.
But come ye back when summer's in the meadow
Or when the valley's hushed and white with snow
'Tis I'll be here, in sunshine or in shadow
Oh, Danny Boy, oh, Danny Boy I love you so.

It was the only time I ever saw my father cry.

Chapter Ten

HELL IN A VERY SMALL PLACE

Hope you got your things together
Hope you are quite prepared to die.

Creedence Clearwater Revival, "Bad Moon Rising"

Unseen, ominous, and unpredictable, the Arc Light was heading our way. It would hit without warning, just across the river. Hundreds of bombs would explode in a curling crescendo of smoke and dust. The earth itself would seem to belch and erupt with all the rumbling ferocity of the bombing mission's well-known moniker, Rolling Thunder.

A flight of three heavily laden B-52 bombers had been dispatched, most likely from Andersen Air Force Base, more than two thousand miles away on the island of Guam, although some were launched from U Tapao, a base in Thailand. Coming in from the South China Sea to our east, the bombers would go "feet dry" as they entered the airspace over Vietnam. Traversing the serene and cloudless blue sky, they would pass miles and miles above us. We would never actually see them. If we watched carefully we might be able to make out the almost invisible little white Y-shaped triangle of their vapor trails. Nor would we ever hear them. The bombers and the airmen who flew them were so far removed from our dingy, disease-infested battlefield that not even a whisper from their massive engines would reach us.

It was not merely their altitude that marked their remoteness from us. If the vagaries of military service were put onto a bell curve, the aircrews would have been on one end and we would have been on the other. Their responsibilities carried with them a precision and a sterility that we would never know. Their five-man crews were flying aircraft that weighed 130 tons when fully loaded with fuel and bombs, each plane half as long as a football field, with a wingspan greater than the length of the plane itself. Guam called for a round-trip of five thousand miles, often in close formation at a cruising speed of 525 miles an hour. From those heights and at that speed they would then drop a monstrous pay-load onto a target that was only a remote dot on their radar screen. And there was scant room for error, particularly since many Marine infantry units were in position nearby, including our own rifle company, which was now about a mile away from their target, at the very edge of what was called the casualty radius.

We couldn't do their job. And few among the B-52 aircrews would have wanted to trade places with the Marines who were on the ground near that remote dot, nestled among the sand and weeds of Go Noi Island. Bored yet anxious, we crouched underneath umbrella-like pon-cho hootches in order to avoid the baking sun. We were tanned and gaunt from months spent in the heat and deprivations of the Bush. We stared intermittently up into the sky and then across the river. We were waiting for the planes to pass overhead and for their bombs to land. To paraphrase a popular Tom Petty song, the waiting was the hardest part—except for the spectacle of the landing of their ordnance, which the aircrews would miss.

They would never actually see their bombs go off. They would never feel the ground shake them like rag dolls from the wrenching explosions.

And most tellingly, they would never be required to personally examine the devastation left in the wake of their passing. It was their job to drop the bombs. It was our job, among other things, to keep score, although the true results were difficult to measure in other than subjective terms, making the score rather hard to keep.

The B-52s would unleash their payloads and then veer seaward back toward Guam or westward for a layover at U Tapao. The bombs would explode. Like an earthquake complete with aftershocks, the ground would jerk and tremble. A long, recuperative moment would pass. Everything would go quiet. Then the "grunts" on the battlefield would emerge like a trail of ants from behind the dunes and the paddy dikes or from their hastily dug fighting holes. Done with the vicious dramatics of the B-52s, the infantry Marines would labor forth in their practiced, unhurried strides, rifles in hand, seeking to find the enemy, to fix his position, and to root him out and kill him. Their flak jackets would be heavy and stained with sweat. Three and sometimes four bandoliers of ammunition would be strapped at their waists and diagonally across their shoulders, as would LAAW recoilless rockets. Their flak jacket pockets would be filled with grenades. Their packs would be pulling backward at them as if they were mules harnessed onto unseen wagons. Their canteens would be hooked loosely at their belts, bouncing rhythmically against their asses as they walked.

That night the B-52 bomber crews would sleep in their homes on Guam or in the quiet peace of U Tapao. The Marines in the rifle companies on Go Noi Island would catnap in the vermin-filled, sandy villages for an hour or two at a time as they manned their fighting holes or sat in ambush along the nearby trails. And many of them would not sleep at all.

Some of the Marine platoons would be assigned to survey the destruction in what was clinically termed the "BDA," for Bomb Damage Assessment. Slowly, carefully, they would patrol through the moonscape left by the Arc Light. Their eyes would be constantly scanning the reed beds and the bomb craters for enemy ambushes. Entire sections of villages would have disappeared. The earth would be so torn that it would be impossible to count how many people, including civilians, had actually been killed. But it would be their mission to somehow quantify the carnage and to report it in measurable terms for the benefit of the bean counters in the Pentagon and the numbers keepers who kept score in the air-conditioned headquarters bunkers in Da Nang.

Other units such as our own would simply resume their patrols and ambushes, carrying out the ceaseless and often costly activities that characterized everyday life in the Bush. As we waited, the members of Delta Company, First Battalion, Fifth Marine Regiment were spread in a wide perimeter along a crumbling bluff, high above the sand banks of the Thu Bon River. We looked north, cynical and bored, smoking cigarettes and trading bitter jokes. Marines knew how to laugh in the face of catastrophe—the words penned onto their helmets and flak jackets often conveyed a rebellious, biting humor: *If I die bury me upside down so the whole world can kiss my ass.*

As an Army friend once succinctly put it, Marines knew how to die. An Arc Light was about to hit, but what were any of us supposed to do or think about that, anyway? You couldn't change it. You couldn't argue about it. It wasn't going to kill you, or at least if it did it had to land on top of you, and we were more than a mile away from the planned impact area. In the cold gallows humor for which Marines are famous, the logic of the oven-hot afternoon went something like this: *All those bombs are definitely going to ruin somebody's entire day, but unless those Air Force weenies totally screw something up it won't be us. And if it does turn out to be us, we can't change that either. The bombs will hit us and that will be that. So there's no sense bitching about it. Just shut up until we get the whole thing over with. Tomorrow we'll still be out here, playing the next round of Russian roulette. Lay Chilly, Man! There are lots of ways to die in Quang Nam Province.*

From the day of my arrival as a platoon commander with "Dying

Delta" we had been engaged in continuous combat operations, inten-sified in recent weeks by a series of unpredictable, vicious firefights. Despite a steady flow of individual replacements, the numerical field strength of our rifle company had been reduced by about half over the past three months. This was an equal-opportunity battlefield. We had lost Marines through every possibility that infantry combat offered, including gunshot wounds from several different-caliber weapons and all kinds of shrapnel: large-caliber rockets, rocket-propelled grenades (RPGs), different sorts of hand grenades, 61- and 82-millimeter mortar fire, recoilless rifles, plus land mines of every size, from a grenade to large-caliber artillery shells.

The rifle platoons were largely made up of the very young, both of-ficers and enlisted. By 1969 the vaunted ranks of career staff NCOs who had historically been the backbone of the Marine Corps were showing the effects of four years of heavy combat. In the infantry battalions that impact was both visible and profound. Within a few days my platoon sergeant, the fourth Marine to hold this key position in the past three months, would leave us, a severe case of ringworm covering his torso, including his entire crotch area, front and back. My first platoon sergeant had been hit by a booby trap while maneuvering one segment of our platoon onto a ridge line during an extensive firefight, suffering shrapnel wounds in his hands and arms and stomach area, blowing off pieces of his fingers and slicing his bladder. The second platoon sergeant had served with us for a couple of weeks and then was sent by the company commander to another unit. The third had picked up his third Purple Heart after being hit by an RPG and had thus been rotated out of Viet-nam. The fifth, on his second Vietnam tour, became sick of the constant combat and suddenly decided to leave the Marine Corps (and our rifle company) when his enlistment expired toward the end of this very operation.

In practical terms this turbulence intensified the relationships between the platoon commanders and the squad leaders as daily life-and-death tactical decisions needed to be made. In these relationships I often ended up being the oldest and most wizened voice at the age of twenty-three. The day-to-day war in Quang Nam Province was fought largely at the platoon and company level, with periodic eruptions that could include several rifle companies or now and then our entire battalion. But these small-unit engagements added up. Records show that of the 14,499 Marines who died in the five northernmost provinces of South Vietnam, 6,480 lost their lives in Quang Nam Province. Another 5,399 died in Quang Tri, the location of the siege of Khe Sanh and numerous larger-scale battles along the infamous Demilitarized Zone; 1,242 died in Thua Thien, remembered for the battle for Hue City and the operations in the A Shau Valley; 829 died in Quang Tin, historically (and now again) a part of Quang Nam Province; and 549 died in Quang Ngai.

I was now on my fourth platoon radio operator, who within weeks would be shot through his elbow, ending his days in the Marine Corps. Two months before, in April, I had lost two radio operators in one day. The first was shot through the hand by an enemy sniper as he held the receiver of our PRC-25 radio in the middle of a firefight. Luckily for our platoon, if not for him, his hand had partially shielded the radio's handset, which had survived the bullet; otherwise we would have been isolated, surrounded by hundreds of mobile and highly adept enemy soldiers. On combat patrols that ranged far away from our company headquarters, the tactical radio was our sole means of communicating our position and to call in artillery support and medevacs. This, of course, was why the enemy loved to shoot at it. An hour later the second radio operator had been blown off his feet, hit below the knees in both legs by a booby trap as we assaulted a ridge. Radio operators did not have much luck in my platoon. By the time I left the platoon I had gone through six.

Two of my original three squad leaders had been killed, one by an enemy rocket and the other from a gunshot wound to the chest. The third had been shot through the lung and in the liver during the onset of an enemy ambush. Although grievously wounded, he had survived the firefight and was later medevaced to a Navy hospital ship.

And so it had been for the officers who had initially staffed our rifle company. The first platoon commander had been killed three weeks before. The second platoon commander had been lightly wounded less than two weeks before and within the next few weeks would suffer a serious gunshot wound in his upper thigh, the bullet narrowly missing an artery. I had been lightly wounded and would be more seriously wounded a month later.

In mid-May our company commander had been hit in the back of the head by shrapnel from an RPG. Rather than accepting a helicopter medevac that would have brought him to the cool blue sheets of an air-conditioned hospital bed in Da Nang, Captain Mike Wyly had led a squad-size patrol through more than a mile of enemy-controlled terrain into the battalion's rear area at an outpost called Liberty Bridge, where he was treated by our battalion surgeons. A gritty, understated leader who years later, after his retirement from the Marine Corps, would become the director of a well-regarded ballet company, Captain Wyly, then on his second combat tour, had returned to the Bush. Underneath his helmet was a large X-shaped bandage that covered the back of his head, where the doctors had shaved and treated his shrapnel wound, making a perfect sniper's bull's-eye every time he removed his helmet during daylight hours.

Among the Marines of Dying Delta, the joke became that anyone who stayed in the Bush after being hit in the head by shrapnel must be crazy. Thus Captain Wyly became known fondly as Captain Crazy. But in truth his tenacity and courage in remaining was far more the norm than the exception, despite the oft-told tales of people looking for a way out of combat. One Delta Company Marine, a mortar man who was the son of a World War II infantry Marine, had been shot between the eyes, the bullet entering just off the bridge of his nose and exiting below his jaw. Every morning when this corporal looked into the mirror to shave, he could see the dime-size hole just off his nose where an enemy sniper had scored a bull's-eye, and where, if his head had been tilted just a bit in a different direction, he would have immediately perished. But he had somehow, miraculously, survived. After three months of hospital time, beginning with an extended stay at the Naval Hospital in Yokosuka, Japan, he had returned to our company.

From outside eyes, Dying Delta may have looked like a ragged and combat-weary bunch, and I suppose we were. But the tactical proficiency of these Bush Marines was beyond question. More to the point, it would be redundant to say that I would trust my life to these Marines, because I already had, day upon day, time and time again, for months. Like all combat units throughout history, we had our laggards and complainers, but in the aggregate these men were the finest people I have ever served with, in any professional endeavor. Most of them had not yet reached the age of twenty. In the best sense of citizen-soldiering, they had left farmlands and cities all across America, typically as soon as they finished high school, volunteering to spend a year in hell before returning to whatever calling their later life would bring.

That hell was now called Go Noi Island. Quietly and expertly, once our rifle company neared the river, our squads and platoons had immediately formed a thin, hasty perimeter inside the sunbaked ruins of what used to be a village. The morning passed. The afternoon wore on. The Marines dug into the perimeter, making fighting holes, and then raised umbrella-like hootches as protection from the scorching sun. They drank bad, musky water from their canteens and smoked cigarette after cigarette. They nursed random and painful jungle sores that had grown into watery ulcers where their skin was opened in the saw-toothed reed beds and the stench-filled thatch of the abandoned hamlets. They casually tossed fiery white-hot corners of C-4 explosives inside punctured tin cans in order to cook up a meal or two from the repetitive twelve meal options that came in every case of C rations.

The Arc Light was late. This was becoming personal. The Air Force needed to get this over with. Captain Wyly and our platoon commanders were growing edgy about how we might defend ourselves against a possible attack during the long night that was approaching. Sundown in the tropics came fast, and the rules changed immediately with the darkness. There was no electricity anywhere in the Bush, including the villages. The entire region would be swallowed in darkness, except for occasional illumination flares shot in front of the lines by our mortar men. Inside our lines a flashlight or a match could draw immediate sniper fire. Likewise an oil lamp lit in a village outside the lines would quickly draw rifle fire from our Marine perimeter, to prevent the enemy from using lights as signals.

We knew that when the Arc Light did hit, in a matter of a few minutes more than 300 bombs would thoroughly convolute and rend the earth. If the loadmasters at Andersen Air Force Base had done their jobs, the three B-52 bombers would typically drop 324 bombs, 108 from each aircraft. Not that we would be able to count them. These were huge bombs, dropped in rapid succession from the bellies and wings of the B-52s. Each bomb weighed in at either 500 or 750 pounds. One B-52 aircraft was able to carry the payload of four of the famed B-29 Superfortress bombers that my father had flown during World War II, and to do so more accurately, although the targets themselves were, quite frankly, less strategically useful.

The end result of these massive bombardments was what the commentators liked to term, correctly, "carpet bombing." But this was not World War II. The Arc Light would soon obliterate little more than a section of scraggly villages, manioc fields, and sand dunes at the southern edge of an area the Marines called Dodge City. And somewhere in those villages and sand dunes were, according to intelligence reports, a lot of enemy soldiers.

Dodge City filled the horizon to our front. On our side of the river were the blood-soaked, infamous battlefields known as the An Hoa

Basin, where I now was in the fourth month of a year of unremitting combat. The Basin extended southward into the Que Son Mountains, eastward toward the South China Sea, and westward through a hard-fought region known as the Arizona Valley, ending abruptly with another series of mountains that stretched from there for perhaps twenty miles into Laos.

The Basin was one of the most heavily contested areas in Vietnam, its torn, cratered earth offering every sort of wartime possibility. In the mountains to the west, not far from the Ho Chi Minh Trail, the North Vietnamese Army operated an infantry division from a jungle-covered redoubt called Base Area 112. In the valleys of the Basin, main-force Viet Cong battalions whose ranks were 80 percent North Vietnamese Army regulars moved against the Americans every day. Local Viet Cong units sniped and harassed, gathered intelligence on our daily movements, and laid mines along our routes.

The ridge lines and the trails along the paddy dikes were laced with sophisticated booby traps of every size, from a hand grenade to a 250-pound bomb. The villages sat in the rice paddies and tree lines like individual fortresses, crisscrossed with trenches and spider holes, their homes sporting bunkers capable of surviving direct hits from large-caliber artillery shells. The Viet Cong political infrastructure was intricate and permeating. Except for the old and the very young, those villagers who opposed the communists had either been killed or driven out to the government-controlled enclaves near Da Nang.

In the rifle companies we spent endless months patrolling ridge lines and villages and mountains, far away from tents, barbed wire, hot food, or electricity. Luxuries were limited to what would fit inside one's pack, which after a few "humps" usually boiled down to letter-writing material, towel, soap, toothbrush, poncho liner, and a small transistor radio. Due to casualties and disease, during this period in the war relatively few Marines would actually survive a full thirteen-month tour as members of the rifle companies in the Bush of the An Hoa Basin.

We moved through the boiling heat carrying sixty pounds of weapons and gear, causing a typical Marine to drop 20 percent of his body weight while in the Bush. When we stopped we dug chest-deep fighting holes and slit trenches for toilets. We slept on the ground under makeshift poncho hootches, and when it rained we usually took down our hootches because wet ponchos shone under illumination flares, making great targets. Sleep itself was fitful, never more than an hour or two at a stretch for months at a time, as we mixed daytime patrolling with nighttime ambushes, listening posts, foxhole duty, and radio watches. Ringworm, hookworm, malaria, and dysentery were common, as was trench foot—which in Vietnam was called immersion foot—when the monsoons came. Respite was rotating back to the mud-filled regimental combat base at An Hoa for four or five days, where rocket and mortar attacks were frequent and our troops manned defensive bunkers at night.

Underneath a waxing moon toward the end of May our company had been assigned to lead the Third Battalion, Fifth Marines, known colloquially as "Three-Five," on a four-mile night move from the barbedwire perimeter of Liberty Bridge into the no-man's-land of Go Noi Island. My platoon led the company. As always, during night moves I walked fourth man in the platoon, behind the point man, his backup, and the squad leader, in this case an unerring Mexican-born corporal named Anastacio Castro. The company had taken more than a dozen casualties as we maneuvered in the darkness through the choked trails and the ashy, smoke-filled villages of the Cu Bans and the Le Bacs. At the tip of a spear that itself was the tip of a spear, most of the casualties had come from my platoon.

In the stench-filled darkness we had medevaced our most grievous casualties from a landing zone shaped out of a small clearing just off the trail from the edge of a blown-out village. Crouched in the middle of the LZ a Marine used a strobe light set inside a helmet to make sure our flashing signals went upward toward the inbound helicopters rather than outward toward the enemy. The CH-46 medevac chopper descended tightly into our quickly improvised LZ. As the rotor wash whipped into us we carried our dead and most seriously wounded up its rear ramp, tossing their weapons and packs inside the helicopter with them. Back on the trail we picked up our own gear and moved on. There was no time for reflective thought, or even to say good-bye to good Marines who now were bleeding on the floors of the ascending helicopter as it lifted off, heading back toward a landing zone in Da Nang.

We walked all night. Not unlike the years I had spent under the lights as a boxer, we did not control the clock; the clock controlled us. Just after dawn our company waded across a thin, leech-infested strip of water that would fill up and become a stream when the monsoon rains washed over the region. To our right, half submerged in the murk and sand, was the bullet-ridden hulk of a Marine amphibious vehicle that had been destroyed in an earlier battle. We climbed up a ridge of sand and weeds, officially leaving the Le Bacs and entering Go Noi Island, crossing what the Marine Corps planners at division headquarters in Da Nang had marked off on their maps as Phase Line Green. We had thus fulfilled our tactical obligation, stepping over a random line drawn with a grease pencil on our maps. We had made it to the geographical starting point of the operation.

The morning sun beat down on us. Inside a tall reed bed at the top of the ridge line we finally were permitted to stop for an hour in order to eat a C-ration meal and to catch our breath. In the boiling morning heat I pulled off my boots, seeking to dry my socks, and then placed my helmet and M-16 rifle next to them. Reaching into my pack, I grabbed my camera from a plastic bag and took a picture of the boots. They once had been black, but after months of continuous patrolling they had become so scuffed and bleached that they were as blond as the sand. I swore that if I made it back from this war, I would keep that picture as a permanent reminder never to glamorize the brutality of the hellhole of the An Hoa Basin.

The orders came to saddle up. I quickly pulled my boots back on and repacked my camera. My socks were still wet. We had walked all night, but it was morning on Go Noi Island. A new operation had begun.

That was ten days ago.

A flat plain of sand dunes, reed beds, ghostly fields, and largely empty villages extended for miles in every direction on our side of the river, behind us and around us, bordered by bald, rocky ridge lines. Farther behind us were the steep, jungle-canopied slopes of the Que Son Mountains, a long finger emanating from the vast Annamite mountain range that extended all the way to Laos. Their canopied trails formed an important avenue that began in the intricately constructed Ho Chi Minh Trail, which was feeding legions of North Vietnamese soldiers to and from the battlefields against the American and South Vietnamese outposts around Da Nang.

In strategic terms, Da Nang was the reason we were at this moment sitting in a treeless, oven-hot perimeter, staring across the Thu Bon River at Dodge City, waiting for the Arc Light that like Godot seemed destined never to arrive. Go Noi Island was a major connecting route between Da Nang and the Que Sons. Da Nang, relatively luxurious with its complement of actual roads, cars, and electricity, was perhaps ten miles on the far side of Dodge City. With a huge, recently expanded airport, a deep-water seaport, large population, and rich cultural history that stretched back hundreds of years to the days of Portuguese merchant ships, in this war Da Nang was second only to Saigon in its strategic and political importance. The Que Son Mountains pointed like a spear toward Go Noi Island and Dodge City in the direction of Da Nang itself. The Arc Light would emphasize that reality, landing halfway between the Que Son Mountains and Da Nang.

And now there was a new, unexpected problem.

Our company commander received a coded message from higher headquarters. Given the unpredictability of high-altitude bombing, it had been decided that our company perimeter was too near the impact area. The unseen planners in the three-star headquarters at Da Nang or maybe on the four-star staffs in Saigon had taken a second look at our position reports and suddenly decided that we were set up too close, even though the river separated us from the villages and tree lines where the bombs were supposed to fall. They had put us here, but now they were moving us.

We had to move quickly. The Arc Light would soon hit. There was no time to break down our little perimeter of poncho hootches or to pack up our scant supplies. We knew that leaving our gear behind entailed serious risks. The Arc Light could be delayed yet again, stranding us overnight. The enemy might scavenge among our gear or booby-trap it, or they might ambush us, knowing that we would soon return. But in truth they did have other things to worry about, and when the Arc Light hit they would have a lot more things to worry about.

The order had come down, clear and precise: *Get the hell out of Dodge. Fast.* We grabbed our ammunition and our canteens, leaving behind the little tent city and most of our supplies. We could curse the starched, spit-shined planners at higher headquarters, but none among us would argue in favor of remaining too close to a bombing run that would soon drop more than 150,000 pounds of steel and high explosives onto the battlefield.

Almost every Marine who has ever fought in close combat can relay stories of short rounds, stray rounds, misdirected shots, accidental discharges, and other chaos resulting from friendly fire. Mortars, artillery, and air strikes can easily wander from their intended targets, sometimes due to "map error" and at other times because of human error. Historically, friendly fire incidents during mobile, close-combat operations make up about 10 percent of casualties. "Intramural firefights" can break out among friendly units that misidentify their fellow infantrymen, particularly while moving through enemy terrain at night. The death of the famed Confederate general Stonewall Jackson in 1863 after being shot by one of his own sentries during the battle of Chancellorsville comes immediately to mind, as does the tragic death of former NFL football star Pat Tillman, who was shot by fellow Army Rangers during a confused night patrol in Afghanistan in 2004.

The Fifth Marine Regiment in Vietnam lived in a world of night movement and hands-on close combat. We routinely walked our own artillery and mortars almost to the edge of our lines. We had run the whirling streams of Gatling-gun Spooky gunships closer than that. For close air support we had a rule of thumb: a meter a pound. If you were running 250-pound bombs from the bellies of A-4s or F-4s it was best to be at least 250 meters away. For an A-6 Beacon Hop capable of dropping twenty-eight 500-pound bombs within a few seconds, the safety zone expanded, usually to a "click," meaning 1,000 meters.

Things could go wrong, and often did. Even the seemingly generous rules of thumb did not always hold. Only three weeks before, while running F-4 Phantom strikes against a North Vietnamese Army unit entrenched in a tree line 400 meters away, one of the aircraft misread our position and dropped a 250-pound bomb that landed squarely in the middle of our company lines. Following normal procedures, the F-4 had made a dry run over the enemy position, roaring past us above the tree lines and the brick-hard rice paddies to our front. But on its second run it came in too fast and too low, centering on our tree line rather than the enemy's. Luckily for us, the bomb had bounced just outside our lines, breaking off the tail of the "Snake," causing it to be a dud. Not knowing that, we shared a moment of stark terror as the bomb twirled through the air and thudded in among us, landing on the pack of one of the company commander's tactical radio operators. If the bomb had gone off, our entire company command element would have been killed or badly wounded.

And that was just one bomb. We were not arguing. Distance mattered. We hurriedly moved a thousand meters to our west, making a new perimeter inside a scraggly little hamlet called Bao An Tay. Sweating from the haste of our sudden move, dismissing for the moment the peril of leaving our gear behind, as we waited for the Arc Light we stood in the torn earth of Bao An Tay and began talking obsessively about—

Food.

None of us had any. What little C rations that remained from yesterday's resupply were in the perimeter we had left behind, along with our packs. And we were dreaming of water—pure, clean water. We had filled our canteens from a murky collection of nearly dry wells and bomb craters that had become small ponds. Finally one Marine coughed up a couple packets of powdered C-ration coffee from inside his flak jacket pocket, which at least masked the sewer-like color of the water from our canteens as we shared a drink from a metal canteen cup. Then our corpsman pulled out the afternoon's surprise: a "B-2" C-ration tin containing a half-dozen crackers and a smaller tin filled with caraway-flavored cheese spread. We carefully and democratically broke apart the crackers and dipped them into the tin of cheese.

Without warning, the Arc Light hit on the far side of the river. The ground trembled and shook uncontrollably. Few of us watched the bombs. I threw myself belly-first into the dirt. The earth below me, noxious on my boots a few minutes before, was now my friend. I hugged it, my arms and legs outstretched like Spider-Man. It moved in every direction. And yet even at that moment I could not shake the thought of how lucky I was to be on this side of the river, drinking putrid water and nibbling on a cracker, rather than on the other side, curled into a fetal ball and wishing for a life-saving miracle as this massive bombardment rolled steadily toward my bunker.

Then it was over. The Arc Light was history. We stood, shaking off the dirt of Bao An Tay, and hurriedly formed into a company column, making our way back toward the river. We knew that Marines on the far side of the river were already moving into the impact area and that the bomb damage assessment had begun. We had our own tasks to attend to. The bombs had been dropped. Artillery missions inside this zone were shut down. The resupply helicopters would now be cleared to fly through the tactical airspace from Da Nang. Our Marines would need to refurbish and eat before it became too dark to start a cooking fire and too dangerous to walk freely through the perimeter. Nighttime listening posts and ambushes needed to be assigned and briefed, their map positions sent by radio to higher commands so that other friendly units would not mistake their movements for the enemy and start an intramural firefight.

We reached the banks above the river, falling back onto our gear, glad to discover that it had not been disturbed. In what seemed like only a few minutes we heard the welcome thumping sound of helicopters coming toward us from Da Nang. There was no sweeter sound in the lonely, isolated environs of the Bush. Soon we could see a CH-46 resupply helicopter laboring in the hot and sultry air. An external net dangled below its frame, holding ammunition and C rations, for some reason always reminding me of an eagle flying with a field mouse clutched in its talons. Darkness was approaching. During the daytime we signaled our position with bright cloth air panels or smoke grenades, but due to the impending darkness we were using a strobe light placed inside a juice can, flashing upward into the dusky sky.

The CH-46 helicopter approached the perimeter, ready to drop our day's load. Two Huey gunships circled overhead, flying cover for the highly vulnerable resupply helicopter, which soon would be hovering above the battlefield and slowly descending into the small dirt clearing we had scraped out to make a landing zone. At the center of our perimeter the strobe light flashed, showing the pilot where to land. But circling in the weed beds, one of the gunships mistook the strobe light for the tracer bullets of an enemy machine gun.

The Huey immediately powered toward us in a low attack line that came in just above our heads, strafing our weary, beleaguered perimeter, its machine guns spitting out hundreds of 7.62-millimeter bullets. I had just climbed a small sand dune to urinate at an empty spot away from the poncho hootches and radios of my platoon command post. The Huey's machine guns sprayed back and forth inside our lines, kicking up a trail of dust spots just below my feet as I stood in the open. After one pass the Huey was finally waved away, back into its circling defensive laps around our perimeter. Exposed as we were, it seemed a miracle that only one Marine, a radio operator near the strobe light in our company command post, was hit, taking a bullet in the stomach.

The resupply helicopter hovered, the net carrying its external load of supplies gently descending until it almost sighed into the landing zone. Holding steady just above us as Marines unhooked and unloaded the re-supply, the twin horizontal rotors of the CH-46 drove hurricanes of loose sand into the air. We lay flat in the sand and weeds, trying to keep our gear from swirling away like autumn leaves. The net was unhooked. The day's resupply packages were unloaded. Then the helicopter reclaimed the net, picked up our belly-shot Marine, and powered off into the black-ening sky.

It grew sullenly quiet. Along with the resupply rations came a few red mailbags. There was a letter from my sister Tama, dated June 5, which was the one-year anniversary of my graduation from the Naval Academy. I had lost track of the weeks and months as they were calcu-lated back in what we called The World, other than the impact that each day might have on my thirteen-month combat tour. Tama wrote that her husband, my former roommate John, had just been promoted to lieuten-ant (junior grade), the Marine Corps equivalent of first lieutenant. I was still a "brown bar" second lieutenant and would be for another three months.

I shrugged it off. Promotions always came faster in the Navy than they did in the Marine Corps. Putting the letter inside a sandy cat-hole and flicking my Zippo lighter, I quickly burned it, a requirement for all our mail in the Bush lest the addresses on the envelopes somehow end up in enemy hands. Darkness was coming. I had things to do. It was time to send out the ambushes and the listening posts. And yet my sister's letter had for some reason left me feeling dislocated from everything but Vietnam, floating outside their orbit. Here on Go Noi Island I was neither old nor young. More to the point, whether I liked it or not, I was no longer like her and John and the others I had left behind, and I never would be again. What was age, anyway? Time, after all, was a relative phenomenon, no matter that for practical purposes human beings had agreed to measure it through the arbiter of a calendar and a clock.

But had it been only a year since Granny had so proudly watched me on the parade deck of Worden Field, and Robert Kennedy had been shot, and all of those midshipman graduation caps had been tossed so happily into the air?

★   ★   ★

Many years have passed. I am older, but the memories do not dim. Sitting at my desk in the quiet of a Virginia evening, I struggle with how I might put the emotional tangle of what we called the Bush into simple words. I find myself contemplating a gauzy Kodak Instamatic photo of a family hootch taken in the Arizona Valley during the hard fights of May 1969. The hootch sits at the very edge of a tree-choked, cluttered village. In reality it is nothing more than a raised dirt-floor porch marked at its corners by bamboo posts, themselves covered with a roof and walls patched with thatch. The most important feature of this hootch is not the porch itself but the round, chin-high mound of earth that adjoins it, for no villager in the An Hoa Basin could have survived the fierce combat of this war without the protection of their family bunker.

The dual-entrance shelters, built like large rabbit hutches, were a common sight to every Marine who patrolled the An Hoa Basin, although nowadays they are little more than quizzical pieces of photographic history to those who did not. Village life in the Basin revolved around the quick safety provided by these bunkers. The villagers would retreat into them every night without fail, staying inside from sundown to sunup, sleeping on wooden benches that lined the bunker's walls. The bunkers were also their refuge during daylight, when frequent firefights would erupt between our side and theirs and they might quickly scurry from their work in the rice paddies or their chores in the villages. Day or night, when the battles flared, they would rush to the bunkers and cringe inside the cave-like darkness while bullets, mortars, and artillery crackled and crunched ferociously above them. Left out in the open, they might be caught in the vicious crossfire, and sometimes they were. But the thick earth of the bunkers kept them safe, even from the direct impact of our most lethal artillery. Inside the family bunkers they could light their flickering lamps, smoke long twists of tobacco, chew the red betel nut that stained their teeth, and talk longingly of when this all might end.

We did not teach the villagers of the An Hoa Basin how to design and build a family bunker. The Viet Cong did, years before we arrived. Nor did we teach them how to dig deep, thin trench lines just inside the pathways that marked the outer perimeter of their villages and atop the crests of their highest ridges. On the other hand, neither did we try to keep them inside these brutal, populated battlefields rather than allowing them to move to more secure locations outside the Basin. It was not for us that they grew the rice and paid part of it as a tax to the Viet Cong political agents and the soldiers who would come down from the mountains at night to refurbish and to probe, sometimes guiding large North Vietnamese units to positions of attack. And if any of their family members announced that they wanted to leave, the local Viet Cong infrastructure could make things even more complicated.

In this valley the choices of the villagers ranged from horrible to hopeless, while our own seemed to range only from miserable to horrible. The difference, of course, was that after thirteen months, and often sooner, we would go home, although many of us did so inside body bags or with grievous wounds, while this battleground was their home, with few ways to make things better and fewer still to leave.

In my little Instamatic picture a wide rice field appears on the far side of a worn trail that passes next to the family hootch. The field is broken into individual paddies, interlaced with squares of deceptively quaint, wall-like paddy dikes. In addition to holding in the water from the rains to irrigate the fields, the paddy dikes made instant revetments for patrolling Marines who might be trapped in the flat open fields by sudden bursts of enemy fire. On the horizon beyond the rice paddies is a tree-filled ridge line. You might see rocks and trees on this ridge line; I would see sniper nests and points of attack. There the photo ends, but not my memories. I know with certainty that on the far side of that ridge there was yet another rice field, and more paddy dikes, and still another village, and after that another, as if the valley itself were a vast piece of wide-ribbed corduroy, until this portion of the valley rose up into a high, bald finger of earth we called Razorback Ridge. Two miles to the north and west, Razorback Ridge merged into the rising mountains where the North Vietnamese kept their base camps inside a thick canopy of jungle and steep slopes that eventually extended all the way to Laos.

I spent long months as a rifle platoon and company commander in the infamous Arizona Valley. I walked every square kilometer of those ridges and rice fields. I fought in many of those villages. I was wounded there. I still know the crevices and streambeds with an intimacy normally reserved for one's family neighborhood. In fact I know them so intricately that from the first moment I returned to the Arizona Valley in the early 1990s I was able to find my way quickly to every remembered location without the help of local hosts.

More tellingly, I still know and feel the rhythms and nuance of every weed and crust of earth inside this photograph that I now contemplate, although it was taken so very long ago. And here is where I and my fellow combat veterans stand on one side of a great, impassable divide, with the rest of the world on the other. Most who did not fight in Vietnam will see in this photograph a piece of crude but instructional art. Some may even visit this very spot and embrace its emotional and historical surroundings. But those of us who fought in places such as the Arizona Valley inevitably find ourselves searching such a photo for small intricacies and little hints of danger that would be impossible for others to understand or even detect. Because every one of us knows that if our luck had run out, or if someone among us had made one inadvertent mistake, we could have died there.

The truth is even deeper than that. As I stare at the blown-out thatch hootch and the curving edge of an even more blown-out village, I can still smell it. Wispy, smoky strands of morning air rise above the thatch, mixed heavily with the murk of nearby ponds. The ash from yesterday's cook fires surrounds me, as does the musk of rotting vegetation and the stench from a nearby water buffalo pen. A tin can filled with water and decaying fish heads sits near the bunker's entrance, emitting noxious fumes as it ferments a sauce called *nuoc mam*. I can even smell myself, not having fully washed for weeks. And I remember other, more unforgettable odors that speak to me of death and loss.

I have heard it said with scientific certainty that one cannot actually remember a smell. It is said that one might intellectually describe the characteristics of an odor, and that one can then identify a smell when confronted with it, but that it is impossible to remember a smell in the same way that one remembers, say, a catchy tune that stays forever inside your head. Whoever said that has never been overwhelmed by the mix of high explosives and quarts of blood, where the explosion has been immediate and only inches away from the body it has ripped apart. There is a sickening richness to this mixture, particularly when the blood is as new to the air as fresh whole milk at the moment it has been squeezed into the bucket from a cow's teat.

There is no particular human value in knowing that smell. But after all these years, let me be your witness: I can remember it.

Forget the glorified helicopter scenes in such movies as *Apocalypse Now*. The battalions of the Fifth Marine Regiment were constantly on the move, and most often they moved on foot. In early May, weeks before our rifle company led the night move into Go Noi Island, we made a midnight crossing of the neck-high waters of the Vu Gia River into the Arizona Valley. Already weary and yet crack-high on adrenaline, we waded slowly across the turgid river in the darkness like burdened mules, laden with packs and gear, our weapons carried high above our heads. On the other side we walked all night across the loose sand of a dry riverbed, turning north into the weed-choked trails and positioning ourselves as part of a predawn multi-battalion maneuver called a sweep and block.

That night the enemy had been on the move as well. In the open paddies and thin tree lines the sweep and block trapped well more than a thousand enemy soldiers who were in the middle of a regiment-size descent from the mountains into the valley. As the old joke goes, the barking dog had caught the fire truck. Our rifle companies spent eight days largely in the attack, trudging up and down a wide swath of torn villages and endless rice paddies across the eastern Arizona, in constant contact with large-scale North Vietnamese units, chasing them down and often digging them out of the trenches and the spider holes. Well-disciplined and with no immediate exit, the North Vietnamese curled back from our assault and counterattacked our most exposed units before finally breaking out, having suffered heavy losses.

The larger, regiment-size battle waned, but sharp fights continued throughout the valley. We made an early-morning attack across a sand bar through a village called Giang Hoa and ending at the edge of the Thu Bon River. As we finished our sweep, a rifle company that had begun in tandem with us was bogged down inside a thickly fortified village a few hundred meters to our west, swallowed up inside a large-scale enemy ambush. That hand-to-hand ambush went on for hours, the gunfire often so intense that our own Marines were forced to lie flat behind a series of paddy dikes as the bullets cracked just above our heads. Then, surprisingly, we were ordered to leave our position and head eastward, out of the Arizona Valley.

We walked toward the Vu Gia River, under intermittent enemy fire, wading back across the river at the same crossing point we had used to enter the Arizona Valley at the beginning of the operation. In an odd, almost surreal interlude we were allowed to catch our breath for an hour or so at the Liberty Bridge compound, where in the mess hall they handed each Marine a sandwich and a carton of milk. Then we continued for several more miles, walking well into the night, in a state of collective exhaustion as we reached our objective, a dry clearing near the villages of Cu Ban and Le Nam.

We had no way of knowing, and politics were irrelevant anyway, but we were in the middle of a countrywide spike in fighting. In retrospect it is clear that the enemy was paying a conscious price in order to drive American casualty figures upward as President Nixon flew to Guam to discuss the course of the war with South Vietnamese president Nguyen Van Thieu, a meeting that would end with the famous announcement to "Vietnamize" the war effort. In the A Shau Valley of Thua Thien Province just to our north, the well-remembered battle of Hamburger Hill had begun just after we entered the Arizona Valley and would end a few days after we left it. We had our own problems. We did not know about Hamburger Hill, and it would not have changed anything if we did. On May 19 we spent Ho Chi Minh's birthday under night attack from three sides in a village called An Tam. After that attack we returned to the Liberty Bridge compound, where we linked up with the point elements of Three-Five and led them into the desolate sand and reed beds of Go Noi Island.

Earlier, in late March and throughout the month of April, we had operated from a scraped, bald dirt perimeter that we called Henderson Hill. The Hill was a favorite place, not exactly comfortable but as good as it could get in the An Hoa Basin. The fields of fire around its perimeter were well cleared and clean, making night attacks rare. Many of the villagers were openly friendly, a stark contrast to the bitter, stoic faces of Go Noi Island and the Arizona Valley. Local children gathered outside the perimeter during the day, inventing errands such as filling our canteens in local wells in exchange for candy, cigarettes, and food. Daytime firefights with the enemy were frequent as we patrolled a hotly contested and booby-trap-infested section of villages with names like La Thap, Phu Lac, My Loc, and Phu Nhuan. On every third day each rifle platoon in the company rotated onto a series of small outposts that protected a vital road that connected the An Hoa Basin to Da Nang.

Henderson Hill sat above a little hamlet called My Loc (2), which bordered this ribbon-like red clay road. The convoy road was the Basin's most important lifeline to Da Nang. Every day in the early morning and in the late afternoon a long, dust-spewing convoy of trucks and jeeps churned to and from the First Marine Division's logistical gathering points near what was called Freedom Hill in Da Nang, protected on both ends by tanks and amphibious tractors. Heading south, the convoy would cross the Thu Bon River, thus entering the deadly terrain of the An Hoa Basin. No motorized vehicle dared to drive this road unless it was protected by the heavy guns and collective firepower of a convoy.

The convoy road was the only land entrance into the An Hoa Basin. Important for the infantry Marines on this side, it connected our battalion's command element to our regimental headquarters. The battalion's command center sat inside the green, sandbagged bunkers and barbed wire of the Liberty Bridge compound. Regimental headquarters was located in a sprawling, militarily quizzical collection of tents and bunkers inside the combat base of An Hoa, eight miles farther south. The Liberty Bridge compound and the regimental headquarters at An Hoa were the only Marine positions inside the Basin where one could sleep on a cot inside a tent, seek cover from enemy fire inside a bunker, benefit from generator-driven electricity, eat in a mess hall, and be protected at night by fields of concertina and barbed wire around its outer edges. Elsewhere the continually operating rifle platoons, companies, and battalions lived in the open of the Bush, sleeping in the dirt, eating C rations for every meal, washing at and drinking from nearby wells or streams, and relocating their defensive positions in the villages, ridge lines, and mountains almost daily.

The Liberty Bridge compound sat on top of a J-shaped ridge line a mile to the north of Henderson Hill, overlooking the intersection of the Thu Bon and Vu Gia rivers. Below the compound were actually two Liberty Bridges. A wooden one built many years ago was now an unusable, charred remains, having been blown up and burned by the enemy. The new one, a low, concrete structure, had just been built by American Seabees. Better than the barges that had been tediously ferrying the convoys across the river, the new bridge was so low that it often went underwater when the rains came.

An Hoa was, literally, at the very end of the road. A former outpost of the French military, the base was nestled uncomfortably in a valley surrounded on three sides by dense mountains. In its red-clay mud was a thousand-meter airstrip where helicopters and small fixed-wing aircraft made frequent runs from Da Nang. At the site of this old French position the Marine Corps had erected a large artillery base and a regimental headquarters. The base included a logistical operations center for processing the supply runs from the convoys and from the aircraft that flew into and out of the base. The sounds of outgoing fire from all sorts of artillery and heavy mortars were as common as breathing, as the guns in An Hoa supported infantry troops deployed throughout the regiment's area of operations. Incoming rocket and mortar fire was also a daily, and nightly, expectation.

The airstrip was just long enough to land a C-130 cargo plane, which was a mixed blessing. Numerous enemy rocket and mortar positions flanked the combat base from hidden, mobile locations, all hard to detect but still within easy range. In order to take off on the airstrip's short tarmac a C-130 needed to taxi to one end and then pause, fully revving its engines to gain the power to lift off by the time it reached the other end. Once a C-130 landed at An Hoa it became a proverbial "target of opportunity," almost certain to draw heavy enemy fire. And whenever a C-130 began taxiing slowly toward its takeoff position, the Marines of An Hoa knowingly headed for their bunkers.

There was good reason that a sign was posted at the outer edges of its many sectors of barbed wire and concertina:

"Welcome to An Hoa. Little Dien Bien Phu."

Notionally the South Vietnamese government held political jurisdiction over the entire An Hoa Basin. In reality any official from the Saigon government who dared to enter the Basin alone and unprotected would be lucky to survive until sundown. Many in the American media took this as a sign that the South Vietnamese government was inherently corrupt and that the rural population strongly supported the communists. True, there was indeed corruption in the South Vietnamese government. And true, in the most highly contested rural areas such as the An Hoa Basin it would have been rare, if not unprecedented, to see a villager waving a flag in support of the South Vietnamese government. But the reality was much fuzzier, on both sides of the political equation. Corruption, while counterproductive and regrettable, is a common trait among Mandarin hierarchical systems. It was not unique to the South Vietnamese regime, as anyone who has tried to do business in Vietnam since the communist takeover in 1975 has quickly learned. And in the villages, open support of the South Vietnamese government could bring serious personal consequences.

But something else was going on. It stemmed from the reality that on any given day, three different wars were being fought in the An Hoa Basin.

The first war involved conventional combat against North Vietnamese Army regulars and main-force Viet Cong soldiers. Despite the tribulations of placing our military thousands of miles away onto terrain that the enemy knew well, there is no question that we won this war overwhelmingly. Woefully misunderstood by contemporary historians, the best American units, both Army and Marine, excelled at ground combat and fought with a tenacity that their countrymen may never fully understand. In 1995, twenty years after the fall of Saigon, the communist government in Hanoi admitted that it had lost 1.4 million soldiers, compared to 58,000 Americans and roughly 245,000 South Vietnamese. For those who claimed that the American body count during the war was grossly inflated, Hanoi had just confirmed its accuracy, twenty years after the fall of Saigon.

The second war was the daily challenge of an insurgency, dominated by a long-term war of attrition aimed at driving American public opinion and troop morale against our involvement in Vietnam. At the beginning of what became known as the American War, communist leader Ho Chi Minh had famously predicted, "For every one of you we kill you will kill ten of us. But in the end it is you who will grow tired." Those of us who fought on the battlefields understood the dynamic of insurgency warfare, and as our involvement grew we adapted and learned. Its principles were passed down from daily experience among the continuously deployed combat units and refined until they became highly effective, normal operating procedures. By 1969 our salty, sometimes wise-ass Marines took small precautions and countermeasures every day that were not even in the mind-set of those who had been on the battlefield four years before. But by 1969 the impact of a war of attrition was indeed being felt hard at home, as well as among many Americans who were being conscripted into military service.

In sum, as Ho Chi Minh had predicted, even as our skills in fighting counterinsurgency warfare increased, the years-long war of attrition was wearing down the morale of our country. Thus winning this war of attrition required that we eventually pass on our combat role to the South Vietnamese Army, which, despite criticism, was growing a new generation of combat leaders who were doing quite well on the battlefield. This battlefield transition was possible. The communist forces were taking horrendous casualties, and despite media prognostications, they were not preordained to prevail. But it also required that we, and the South

Vietnamese government, comprehend and neutralize the third form of warfare that was taking place every day in such contested areas as the An Hoa Basin.

Here we failed. And in this failure, we eventually lost everything.

This third war was a focused and precise form of domestic terrorism. At this point in our history America's top leadership had yet to fully grasp the power and impact of a type of terrorism that went well beyond traditional notions of military insurgency. Nor did the South Vietnamese government ever find a way to completely counter it. A largely invisible war of terror and seduction was taking place daily among the rural populace, designed to discredit the South Vietnamese government and to drive a murderous wedge between the people and that government. Amid all the other violence, this third way of war was little understood by most Americans. Its political motives were rarely commented on, even among the brightest and most experienced minds in the media. And as the undeniably accurate reports of Vietnamese civilian casualties at the hands of the American military became known, the methods and the price of this form of deliberate terrorism were never fully grasped by the American people.

The French author Bernard Fall remains one of the preeminent and most accurate chroniclers of the French and American experiences in Vietnam. He was also one of the most courageous. In 1966 Fall published *Hell in a Very Small Place*, a military classic describing the siege of Dien Bien Phu which in 1954 had caused the defeated French to withdraw from Vietnam. In 1967 Fall was killed by a land mine while on patrol with the U.S. Marines along the infamous "Street Without Joy," a road located between the cities of Da Nang and Hue.

In 1963, four years before his death and more than two years before President Johnson sent the first contingent of combat Marines into Da Nang, Fall published *The Two Vietnams*. The book was a historical and political examination of the communist and noncommunist adversaries in Vietnam's journey from French colonialism to national independence.

Its middle chapters should have been read, reread, earmarked, and digested by every military officer being sent to combat, especially by everyone holding the rank of colonel or above—and just as important, by every major journalist who covered the war. Regrettably they were rarely read at all.

In the book Fall explained the necessity of understanding the mission and makeup of the Vietnamese communist forces that were carrying out this third way of war. He warned that the Dich Van, or "moral intervention" cadres, were "the most interesting and the least understood component of the [communist military's] control apparatus—and by far, the most dangerous." These units, he observed, carried out "psychological warfare but with an added 'punch' that is implied in the polite phrase 'armed propaganda' . . . through means ranging from friendly persuasion to murder."

> It is the Dich Van operations which create havoc in South Vietnam and which, for obvious reasons, neither American helicopters nor U.S. Special Forces can cope with; the DV's make themselves felt at a specifically "Vietnamese" level of fighting upon which the foreigner simply has no effect. . . . It is that type of operation—*the violent act for psychological rather than military reasons*—which is the source of the success of the Viet Minh. . . . The Dich Van will simply go on murdering village chiefs, youth leaders, teachers, and antimalarial teams—thus isolating the Saigon government from the countryside. And in a revolutionary war, that is precisely what separates victory from defeat: the control of the rural population.

Fall's observation was precise, knowing, and crucial. It is important to remember what he said, and also what he did not say. He was not maintaining that victory and defeat would be determined by the "support" of the rural population, a notion that was often characterized by the rather pitifully naive American slogan that our forces needed to "win the hearts and minds" of the Vietnamese countryside. Aptly for the vicious environment of the most hotly contested areas, Bernard Fall was speaking about control, as opposed to support. The communists, through a mix of persuasion and intimidation, had built their war effort around this distinction. And even the lowest-ranking infantrymen who fought in the An Hoa Basin viscerally understood it. However crudely it might have been put, and despite how quickly it might have been misused by left-leaning intellectuals and even by the ever-cynical Marines themselves, the communist strategy was embodied in a slogan that often appeared on Marine helmets and flak jackets:

If you have them by the balls, their hearts and minds will follow.

Later in his book, Bernard Fall commented on President John Kennedy's decision in late 1961 to escalate America's advisory involvement in Vietnam. In his speech announcing that decision, Kennedy had mentioned that communist terror squads were assassinating an average of eleven South Vietnamese government officials every day.

"Losses of South Vietnamese village officials were extremely heavy before anyone in a position to know was willing to admit how desperate the situation had really become . . . 4,000 low-level officials were killed between May 1960 and May 1961 . . . perhaps 13,000 small officials have been killed in South Vietnam (from 1957 to 1963)." Favorite targets were village leaders, including local police, schoolteachers who "form young minds and educate them to love their country and its system of government," and social workers and medical personnel, "because their activities create good will for the government."

What Fall warned about in 1963 was doubly apparent by 1969. On the battlefield, it had been made worse by the heavy toll of civilian casualties as a result of the randomness and intense use of American artillery and air strikes while operating in populated areas. And it had been made worse at home because few knew that communist assassination teams were killing people with deliberate precision as a central instrument of their policy, while it was common knowledge that Americans tended to do so negligently, recklessly, and on some disgusting occasions personally, to the detriment of our mission and our effectiveness.

In the An Hoa Basin we lived inside these complex realities every day.

In April, while our rifle company was operating from Henderson Hill, our higher leadership arranged a visit to the Basin by the South Vietnamese government's district chief. The district chief, who resided in a villa in Da Nang, had been criticized for living in such remote splendor, far away from his war-ravaged constituents. It was decided that he needed to spend more time meeting with his people and that his people needed to learn more about the concept of representative democracy. After meetings with our company commander, thirty delegates were chosen by elders from the nearby hamlets to come and meet with him. The district chief and his personal assistant would ride down from Da Nang on the morning convoy, which would drop them off near our perimeter. Escorted by the Marines, he would then meet with the chosen delegates inside the thatch roof and dirt floor of one villager's home just down a trail from the bottom of Henderson Hill. Under the umbrella of our protection, in the bright light of midmorning, they would have their meeting. And a few hours later the district chief and his assistant would be picked up by the convoy as it made its way back from An Hoa to Da Nang.

It would not be a long visit. The political message of his coming would outweigh the length of time he spent inside the An Hoa Basin.

The day arrived. My rifle platoon was on an early-morning combat patrol. Across an expanse of paddies, from the tangled tree lines and dirt paths of a nearby village we could see a trail of red dust rising on the valley's floor. We knew that the convoy had crossed the river and was churning southward from Liberty Bridge toward An Hoa. We passed the final checkpoint of our patrol. My radio operator called in our position to the company command post:

"Delta Six, this is Delta Three. Be advised we have now passed checkpoint five."

"Roger that, Delta Three, understand checkpoint five. Six out."

I relaxed a bit, knowing from experience that our patrol would not be ambushed. When the rice paddies were empty and when the villagers were hiding inside their bunkers my skin would crawl with apprehension and even as we walked I would start anticipating the methodology of an attack, a defense, and then a counterattack. But now the villagers were on their porches, squatting lazily in front of their morning cook fires. Water buffalo roamed in the nearby rice fields, many of them mounted by local children, who rode them playfully as if they were sleepy elephants. We would soon be inside the welcoming perimeter of Henderson Hill.

We passed the outer edge of My Loc (2), our long column of Marines funneling into a narrow, overgrown trail and heading in the direction of Henderson Hill. The trail was tunnel-like, thick with overhanging bushes and banana trees. We were only minutes from the end of the patrol. We relaxed further, knowing there were Marines rather than enemy on the other side of the vegetation to our front. The tactically dispersed column of our combat patrol tightened up like a compressing accordion until our Marines were only a few meters apart. The tension eased from the grips on their M-16 rifles. The wise-ass jokes began, breaking the previous tactical silence. One Marine pulled out a cigarette, readying to light it once we came within eyesight of the perimeter. Henderson Hill was just on the other side of the trees.

There was no warning. From around that unseen bend the air suddenly belched and erupted, quick explosions piercing our ears and reverberating like an unseen blast of wind. My adrenaline surged. I counted three quick bursts of rifle fire and then the whump of three grenades. The entire platoon became animated, tense, picking up the pace to a jog as we strode toward the noise. Within a few heartbeats a young Vietnamese, wild-eyed and gasping for breath, collided on the trail with the point man of the platoon. Instinctively the Marine tackled the young man and held him on the ground. We did not know it yet, but there had been two others. After its attack, the assassination squad had split apart.

We would not capture the other two. More regrettably, we would not be able to kill them.

The district chief's meeting had not lasted very long.

We were the first Marines to reach the hootch. I quickly deployed my platoon in defensive positions around it, in case there was a second attack. Then I stepped inside the shadowed, blood-soaked room. My platoon corpsman and my radio operator came with me. Within minutes our company's chief corpsman stepped inside, having jogged down from the command post on Henderson Hill. Their Unit One medical bags would soon be empty of battle dressings and tourniquets. Together we began the ugly business of triage, separating the dead from the near-dead, and the near-dead from those who might be medically saved.

And yes, I do remember the smell.

In 1992 I revisited My Loc (2) during a longer trip to Vietnam, one of dozens I have made over the years. By chance I stumbled into a lengthy conversation with a group of villagers who had been children during the war. We talked almost nostalgically about the Marines on Henderson Hill who used to give them soap, cigarettes, and chocolate, trading old phrases of pidgin slang that we once used. "Hey, Honcho, check it out, you number one, maybe number ten, I washy-washy you, you souvenir me boo-coo chop-chop, most ricky-tick!"

We laughed together. In those early years I was the first American they had seen since the war. They were surprised not only that I showed up but that I could speak Vietnamese as well as the long-ago pidgin. After a while I asked if they remembered the attack in April 1969 that had killed so many villagers. They all did.

"Right over there," one of them exclaimed, pointing down the trail. "Seventeen people, all dead at once."

"No, not seventeen," I said, remembering. "Nineteen. You forgot the district chief and his assistant."

Indeed, nineteen were dead, out of thirty-two inside the hootch. And none of the others was unscathed.

Inside the hootch my hands, arms, trousers, and boots had quickly become covered with blood. We pulled the dead outside, lining them up in a field as if they were already under markers in a cemetery, then covering them so that the feasting flies might find some other place to linger. We had a problem with flies on this battlefield. They buzzed everywhere, into our food and onto our open sores. On an earlier morning I had counted more than a dozen floating inside my canteen cup as I heated a mix of water and C-ration hot chocolate. Foolishly I had bitten into them, thinking they were chunks of chocolate.

We carried out the wounded. On the dirt floor of the hootch we had found them wriggling and turning like worms among each other as they sought to escape the ankle-deep syrup of blood and innards. I noticed the district chief's young deputy, who stood out from the others due to his fancy clothes. Blown backward into a family altar by the blast, he was frozen in death with one arm raised in the air as if he were trying to catch the grenade that had killed him. That hand was gone. Nothing but the top of a forearm remained, its white tendons sticking out randomly like unspliced electrical wires. I approached an old woman who was leaning back against a mud wall with a stunned look on her face. Her jaw had dropped and her eyes stared unbelievingly at nothing. I had thought she was merely in shock. I pulled her arm and immediately recognized the lack of muscular response of the dead. I looked closer and saw that she had taken a square, nickel-size piece of shrapnel in the middle of her forehead, just above her eyes.

And so on. As I waded in the muck it did not get any better.

This was the war we were losing, perfectly summarizing Bernard Fall's observation. On this morning the Viet Cong were not asking for anyone's support; they were asserting their control. For all of the bombs we dropped, many of them so randomly that they killed the very people we were trying to help, and for all of the enemy soldiers we killed, our leaders did not understand the cold, focused violence perpetrated by the other side. On this day the enemy had killed people who, if pushed to decide, were probably their supporters, including, quite possibly, the friends and relatives of enemy soldiers who were fighting against us. As Fall had succinctly warned us six years earlier, there would be no compromise for any villager who in any way cooperated with the Saigon government. They had deliberately killed a room full of their own people, a "violent act for psychological rather than military reasons," as a warning to everyone in the An Hoa Basin that it was a crime, punishable by death, to even attend a political meeting hosted by the other side.

For all the carnage, our senior leaders in Da Nang and Saigon lacked the acumen even to issue a press release about the incident in My Loc (2). Within two days, as the villagers came family by family to claim the bodies of those who had been killed, this little moment disappeared, just one bitter day in a long and bitter war.

To paraphrase the philosophers, war may indeed be defined as the continuation of politics by other means, but those other means are often vastly different. As the ever-cynical "grunts" liked to snicker while the politicians and rear-echelon pontificators preached, "War is hell. But combat is a bitch." Infantry combat remains the most apolitical environment I have ever known. To steal from another platitude, just as there are few atheists in a foxhole, there are even fewer preaching politicians. In the infantry, winning was killing and losing was dying. But as on that bleak day at the bottom of Henderson Hill, every now and then there came moments of clarification. Some of them were tragedies and some became opportunities. And not all of them shone glowingly on our side.

From Go Noi Island we trudged south and then into the steep, canopied jungle trails of the Que Son Mountains, and in late June we returned to the Arizona Valley, leaving a continuous trickle of Marine Corps casualties in our wake. During the first days of July a listening post picked up enemy movement toward our night defenses in a hamlet called Phu Phong (4). The enemy patrol was coming in from the west, along a trail that led through another hamlet closer to the mountains in an area called the Phu Ans. Our perimeter was larger and more heavily defended than usual, including Marines from another rifle company. Our bolstered defenses allowed portions of my platoon to be pulled from a section of the defensive lines in order to hit the enemy patrol before they could mount a mortar barrage or a full-scale assault. Racing in the darkness down a trail atop a narrow ridge, we formed a quick assault line and opened fire, pushing into the sky-silhouetted village. A wild splattering of gunfire, rockets, and grenades echoed through the porches and the water buffalo pens. Dogs yelped. Hogs squealed. The villagers as usual were hiding, down inside their family bunkers.

We had bitten the bear before the bear bit us. Discovered and unorganized, as was their custom the enemy broke contact and quickly retreated, disappearing into the night-black paddies and down the distant trails. We had preempted a larger attack on our perimeter. For the other side, there was always another day, or another week, or another year. Wisely they usually did not fight unless trapped or in the assault. But our melee had wreaked havoc on the porches and in the side yards of the village.

At first light the next morning I led a patrol back into the village, accompanied by our Vietnamese interpreter, a rather scholarly fellow named Sergeant Tuan, to seek information about the enemy that had been there the night before. As was our practice, we formed a wide assault line, carefully and methodically sweeping through the village. Our Marines did this expertly every day, and sometimes several times a day. Our squads and fire teams cleared every family bunker as we moved to the forward edge of the village where it opened up into the rice paddies. At each bunker Marines would call three times for the occupants to come out, then throwing a grenade into the bunker after the villagers crawled out in order to ensure no enemy soldiers would fire at us from behind after we passed. After that, the Marines would crawl inside the bunker and search it, just to be sure. Once we had secured the village we began searching every hootch and shed and questioning its inhabitants.

Within minutes I was surrounded by a cacophony of wailing, desperate complainants. The wispy-bearded old men shrewdly watched us with hollow, piercing stares, shaking their heads and mumbling, making movements with their arms that depicted bombs falling from the sky. The women wailed and cried, their teeth stained from betel nut and their hair pulled back tightly into buns, chattering rapidly and pointing in various directions, many of them holding up cooking pots now pierced and useless from the bullets of the night before. The smallest children stared at us numbly, clutching their mothers' filthy black silk trousers. Many of them were naked from the waist down, the rural Vietnamese version of potty training, their heads shaved except for small tufts at the front to keep the vermin from nesting in their hair.

Clinically Sergeant Tuan simultaneously translated their complaints as they spoke. *Why do you shoot our village? These soldiers are not from here. Now we have no cook pots to feed our children. We did nothing to you. How can we draw water from our wells? Our children cannot go to school. When we work in the rice paddies you drop bombs on our village. We do not know these soldiers. Why do you do this to us?*

I empathized with their hopelessness, but by now I also had grown inured to many of the histrionics and the oft-repeated stories, especially in the Arizona Valley. They were right, but they were only half-right, and the other half could kill us. I nodded toward the small children and then looked around at the collection of villagers, none of whom was a young man.

"Where are your husbands?" I asked.

"Gone," the women all said, glancing quickly at one another.

We all knew what that really meant: gone for soldiers, gone to the mountains, already dead, or maybe hiding from nervous, trigger-happy Marine patrols that might shoot them on sight and ask questions later, with the assumption that every one of them was an enemy combatant.

Gone, watching us from high up in the trees or covered with thatch down in the ditches, gone for a little while, gone for a long while, but, almost certainly and also understandably, not on our side.

Gamely I decided to challenge them with the ultimate question. "This whole valley is Viet Cong. If you don't want to be in the middle of the war, why don't you leave?"

A fortyish woman with piercingly intelligent eyes looked at the others and then stepped forward, each of her arms clutching a prepubescent child. "How do we leave?"

"The resettlement village," I said, pointing southward toward An Hoa, less than three miles away, on the other side of the Thu Bon River. A resettlement camp had indeed been built on the outskirts of the combat base, near the South Vietnamese district headquarters compound of Duc Duc. We had passed the camp on several occasions as we headed toward a shallow river crossing that we regularly took into and out of the Arizona Valley. To put it mildly, the camp had not appeared to be a beehive of activity.

"We already tried," the woman said, gaining nods from her fellow villagers as Sergeant Tuan took the time to translate her response. "Viet Cong soldiers patrol the banks next to the river. They won't let us cross."

I scrutinized her, measuring her words. "Would you really go?"

Collective nods joined her affirmation as Sergeant Tuan translated my challenge. "Yes! We would go, but we can't!"

I answered, filled with all the certainty and unvarnished naiveté of a twenty-three-year-old Marine who knew a lot about combat but very little about duplicity. "Then follow me. I will get you there."

In the baking hot July morning an entire village followed my platoon down a ridge line and across the dikes of a wide, sweeping series of rice fields. They chattered excitedly to one another, their faces electric with anticipation. Baskets filled with pots and pans and clothes were balanced carefully on the heads of many of the women. Children clung to their hands or walked behind them like rows of waddling ducklings following a mother duck from pond to pond. I walked triumphantly in front of them, daring to feel that we might just win the battle of the Arizona after all. I was already imagining the leaflets that might be dropped on other villages, describing the hope embodied in what had just happened.

No Vietnamese civilians were allowed inside any Marine perimeter in the An Hoa Basin, so I left them in the rice paddy just below Phu Phong (4). At our company command post I explained this opportunity to our company commander and requested a helicopter pickup, or lacking that, permission to escort the village across the river to the refugee camp. He radioed battalion. They radioed regiment. They called the political operatives at Duc Duc. They called whoever it was that needed to be called for the right clearances. Within a half-hour the word came back: there was no room at the resettlement village; it was full.

Angrily I disputed the report. I had seen the camp, at least from the outside. It seemed impossible that it was full. An entire village was waiting for me at the bottom of the hill. Didn't the authorities understand the impact that their relocation might have in the vitally important battle for public support? We tried again. The second response was no different: there was no room. The camp was full.

Comprehending the reason for my vitriol, Sergeant Tuan pulled me aside. The military was not his calling; somewhere in his civilian life he had been a professor. He did not want to get into trouble with the political authorities, perhaps ending his tenure as an interpreter and causing him to be sent somewhere else, even into the regular Army as an infantry private. "Please do not tell anyone I said this," he said delicately.."But you are my friend, so let me explain. The official in charge of relocations receives rations for each refugee. So the camp is full, but it is not full. Do you understand? It is full on paper. He cannot change his story. He would lose face, and maybe his job. He has already said the camp is full. They send him the rations. And then he sells the extra rations on the black market."

One of the great Vietnamese songs from those war years was a ballad called "Ba Me Phu Sa," written by legendary songwriter Pham Duy, a northerner who had become disillusioned with the communists and then came south only to become disenchanted with the whole course of the war. The song told the story of an old woman living in a remote village who had two sons, one of them an ARVN soldier and the other a Viet Cong soldier. When the Viet Cong soldiers came to her village, Ba Me Phu Sa hid the ARVN son under her bed. When the ARVN soldiers came, she hid the Viet Cong son under her bed. And when the Americans came, she hid both of her sons under the bed.

Ba Me Phu Sa could well have lived in the Arizona Valley, although on this bitterly contested battleground it did no good to hide anybody under the bed. In the Arizona Valley, sooner or later the bombs were going to blow up the bed.

There was no howling from the villagers at the bottom of the hill when I gave them the news that the resettlement camp was full. Knowingly and tired, they put their bundles back on top of their heads, grabbed the hands of their children, and returned to the howling dogs and hungry water buffalo of Phu An.

★　　★　　★

My mother, usually a late sleeper, woke early on the morning of July 10, 1969. Troubled by a dream, she made her way from the bedroom into the kitchen and joined my father, mixing herself a strong cup of their favorite Taster's Choice instant coffee.

She and my father were staying in Ocala, Florida, at the home of my father's lifelong friend Bud Colwell and his wife, Anna. It had been six months since my dad's retirement from the Air Force, but they had not yet found a permanent home in Florida. In no real hurry, my dad had been looking around Florida's central coast for a house and possibly a new occupation. He had also caught a lot of fish. Over the past couple of months he had sent me several letters with Polaroid pictures of him and my brother, Gary, home on college break, with their stringers of bass at the lakeside house my parents were renting. I had sardonically replied that even if I were required to sleep in the doghouse in the backyard, it would be an upgrade from the soft-soil manioc patches of the Arizona Valley. His letters were also filled with some of the stupidest jokes I had ever read, many of them leaving me laughing simply because they were so bad.

Not completely idle, my dad was also working as a consultant at the fuller's earth plant that Uncle Bud now partly owned just outside of Ocala. The major moneymaker from the plant was the lucrative production of kitty litter, which was largely made up of the super-absorbent fuller's earth. New environmental laws had just been passed requiring stricter controls over smokestack emissions, which was a major problem for Uncle Bud's plant. Ever piddling and brilliantly innovative, my dad had designed an electrostatic precipitator that shot a current across the top of the smokestack, ionizing the particles of fuller's earth emissions. This caused them to become microscopic little balls that would roll like marbles into a collector pan, not only cutting the emissions from the plant by 99 percent but also creating a byproduct that was later sold for use in satellite filters in the aerospace industry.

I knew nothing about fuller's earth either, but I did understand my dad's raw intellect. I never saw a mechanical problem that he could not fix. Despite my degree in engineering from the Naval Academy I would not have recognized an electrostatic precipitator if it were sitting by itself in a field with a large label on it, and if I had seen one in a village in the An Hoa Basin I probably would have become suspicious and blown it up.

As was her way, my mother had internalized the perils of the months I was spending in combat. Ever-quiet and accepting of the dangers I had consciously sought from childhood, years before when I had begun fighting under the lights it was she and not my father who had signed the medical waivers required before most fights. And so it had been with the Marine Corps and with war. Viscerally rather than intellectually, my mother understood each of her children with a completeness that could neither be taught nor explained. And as with my granny, she carried inside her the toughness of the Scots-Irish pioneer women who had been the backbone of our culture for generations.

While I was at war, as a point of pride and loyalty my mother refused to publicly discuss the perils that I faced or the unthinkable possibilities that could become realities at any moment when hundreds of Americans were dying every week. Without discussion, I understood her reasons. The odds for and against my survival were not an appropriate topic to be chattered about when people met for bridge games and cocktail parties. She had nurtured me inside her and given me life. If something happened to me, a part of her would die. The only visible sign of the thoughts that never left her mind was a subtle one: in a long-held tradition among women of the South that dated back at least to the Civil War, my mother had not cut her hair since I deployed to Vietnam, and would not cut it until I returned from the war.

But on that morning she was addled and distracted. Sitting in the kitchen, she looked worriedly at my father and at Bud and Anna. "I had a bad dream. Young Jim was in the jungle, trapped inside a bamboo cage."

Call me superstitious, but I am a believer in the uncharted powers of the human brain, including the ability to transcend physical boundaries, particularly when it comes to intense relationships, such as the bond that connects so many mothers to their children. When my mother went to bed in Ocala the night before, it was morning in Vietnam. And as the night grew longer in Florida it became afternoon in the Arizona Valley. While my mother slept and so fitfully dreamed, I was hit by two enemy grenades while clearing a series of well-camouflaged bunkers. The bunkers were built inside a bamboo thicket, at the edge of a murky streambed.

The first grenade peppered me lightly on the face and shoulders. The second detonated behind me just after I shot the man who threw it and a second soldier who was inside the same bunker. I was hit in the head, back, arm, and leg. The grenade's concussion lifted me into the air and threw me down a hill into the stream. I still carry shrapnel at the base of my skull and in one kidney from the blast. But the square, quarter-size piece that scored the inside of my left knee joint and lodged against the bone of my lower leg would eventually change the direction of my life.

Having for months repeatedly seen far worse among many of my Marines, I did not pay a great deal of attention to my wounds. Medevaced into An Hoa, I was treated for several days at the Battalion Aid Station. Some of the shrapnel in my head, back, and arm was removed, and some was left to work its way out naturally as my skin healed over time, the scars pushing the shrapnel out onto the surface. On an operating table at the Aid Station, the surgeon pushed platinum probing rods deep into a puncture hole in my lower back, finally informing me that the dime-size shrapnel was somewhere inside my kidney and was unreachable unless they cut the kidney open, which he thought was unwise. The shrapnel, he said, would either encapsulate over time or be passed through my system in the same manner as a large kidney stone. I was then sent to Da Nang, where another doctor scrubbed and further sliced my leg, finally removing the square piece of shrapnel that had lodged against the joint and was not working its way out. He then cleared me for a brief R and R in Hawaii, telling me the saltwater of the ocean would do the leg as much good as the daily scrubs in the hospital.

I returned to the Bush as soon as possible. But the leg wound went deep into the joint and had not completely healed. In the muck of the rice paddies and the filth of the An Hoa Basin's villes, it soon became infected. I did not know it at the time, but the infection was moving into the bone, causing permanent septic damage. The wound refused to close over my skin. I was given penicillin by the battalion surgeon, which temporarily closed the wound but did not kill off the infection, which stayed for months. The damage to the joint was further complicated by a razor-sharp piece of shrapnel from the same grenade that over time migrated into its open spaces and chewed on the cartilage whenever I walked or ran.

There were other things to worry about. The rains had begun, and soon the monsoon season would be upon us. The Bush was a place of constant ringworm, hookworm, diarrhea, and open sores. When the monsoon hit I developed bronchitis and extensive ringworm that covered both my legs from hip to ankle. I would not learn the full extent of the damage to my leg until after I completed my tour and returned to the United States. There would follow two years of repeated surgeries and plaster dressings, rehabilitative therapy, and finally a medical retirement from the Marine Corps.

In August our company executive officer called me on the tactical net from the company rear area in An Hoa. A billet had opened up with the Force Service Regiment on Okinawa, a large supply point responsible for processing logistical requirements for the Marine Corps units inside Vietnam. With two Purple Hearts and extensive combat, I was being recommended for the billet. What the executive officer was saying in sterile, military language was less important than what the offer meant in terms of the life-and-death mathematics of pure survival. If I accepted the assignment, for me the Vietnam War could be over within a few weeks. And an assignment on the quaint and gorgeous island of Okinawa would give me several months to decompress from battlefield combat before I returned home.

Life's gambles are sometimes settled in mere moments, weighed against years of previous thought and decades on the other side, where one might reflect on the wisdom involved in a sudden decision. I listened to the executive officer and fought inside myself, pressing the radio handset against my face as I leaned against an old grave in the middle of a desolate village. Those few seconds became, as they like to say in the Marine Corps, a teachable moment.

But I could not say yes. After all the years of preparation and the months of hardships that I had endured with one infantry battalion in this small but violent section of a seemingly never-ending war, I could not simply walk away. Bonds formed on the battlefield are often as unbreakable as the strongest family ties. In a word, I felt obligated. Like my father, service to country defined my self-respect. More to the point, I loved leading infantry Marines. With a gritty élan, they faced the gravest dangers. They took the greatest risks. They absorbed the highest casualties. They had the fewest creature comforts. But they also stood face-to-face and toe-to-toe with the enemy, every day. And they answered in their honor to no one.

Taking a deep breath, I finally said no, and stayed in the Bush. In September I was given command of Dying Delta. In the muck and drenching rains of the monsoon season we operated almost constantly in the Arizona Valley. The helicopters were sometimes grounded. The rains fell heavily, by one count in Phu Bai north of Da Nang measuring sixty-eight inches in one week. We kept our company perimeters in the valley, lacking even the protection of cots or tents, our Marines constantly drenched and the rice fields overflowing. On the safer side of the river the resupply convoys into An Hoa were shut down when the low lanes of Liberty Bridge went underwater, the angry, rising river at one point taking an observation tower downstream with it and drowning the Marines inside it. The C-130 missions into the An Hoa airstrip became more important as the convoys dwindled and the regimental headquarters itself became more isolated. Artillery support for the infantry units from An Hoa's many guns was reduced, due to lack of ammunition.

When the helicopters were slowed by the rains and the resupply missions became less certain our battalion was ordered to make a tactical withdrawal from the Arizona Valley, forming a shrinking perimeter along the edges of the swollen Thu Bon River. As the chalky current pushed against us we crossed to the An Hoa side by pulling ourselves hand over hand along a cable that had been strung across the river from tree to tree with the help of local Vietnamese fishing skiffs. But after a week at the combat base and in the mountains just to its south, we were sent back into the Arizona Valley, making its ridges and villages our monsoon home. And there we stayed.

Bullets win battles, but infection and disease can often lose them, robbing military units of their field strength. During the months of the monsoon we were never dry and we rarely fully disrobed. Ringworm and immersion foot were a constant challenge. When one's feet stay continuously wet for longer than a day or so, they tingle and burn for a while and then they grow numb. And when a Marine's feet went numb he tended to forget about them. Then the flesh would swell and the skin would die. After another couple of days the Marine would pull off his boot, only to leave a good portion of the skin of his foot inside it. We had a hard-and-fast rule in the First Battalion, Fifth Marines: Every Marine took off his boots every day for ten minutes, to massage his feet and allow them to be inspected by our company corpsmen. It worked.

In other ways the weather favored us. We shifted to the offensive despite the mud and rain. The terrain features shrank. Enemy patrols from the nearby mountains became easier to ambush, as many of the trails crossing the Valley went underwater, narrowing the enemy's movement and thus increasing our own chances of success against them.

At the end of November our regimental commander pulled me into An Hoa from the field. Since arriving in the Bush I had now served under four different battalion commanders and three regimental commanders. Colonel Noble Beck, a garrulous veteran of World War II and Korea, was my third regimental commander. An edict from the First Marine Division headquarters in Da Nang had ordered the regimental commanders to pull any officer with two Purple Hearts out of the rifle companies of the Bush.

Colonel Beck was bringing me back to serve in the operations section of his headquarters. I was nearing the end of my combat tour, and I did not want to come. I reported to him in his small room inside the roach-infested sandbag bunker that comprised the regimental command center. I did not want to be in this bunker, nor did I not want to finish my tour among the muddy roads and sagging tents of An Hoa. Stepping inside the colonel's cramped semblance of a personal office, my first words were a request that I be allowed to return to the Bush.

The colonel laughed. "Lieutenant, you can stand there with tears as big as horse turds in your eyes, but I'm being a little selfish here. The division commander says no officers with two Purple Hearts should be out in the rifle companies. If I kept you out there and you got killed, that would be the end of my career."

In February 1970 I left Vietnam from the port of Da Nang on a Navy cargo ship, the USS *Tulare*, along with a contingent of Marines that included fifty others from the Fifth Marine Regiment whose combat tours had expired. The Americans had begun their long draw-down of troops, and even though we had completed our tours, on paper we had become part of the draw-down. A complicated formula had been dreamed up by the ever-imaginative bean counters. The fifty Marines embarking on the *Tulare* from the Fifth Marine Regiment, which was remaining in Vietnam for now, were being counted as part of the dwindling numbers assigned to the Twenty-sixth Marine Regiment, located far from An Hoa, which had already begun its withdrawal.

Or so they told us. The practical impact was that rather than flying out of Vietnam and going immediately home to The World on one of the celebrated jets known as the "Freedom Birds," we slowly steamed across the Pacific, at sea for three weeks before we finally pulled alongside the pier in San Diego. As the *Tulare* eased into port, a raucous crowd of family and friends of the ship's crew lined the pier, holding "Welcome Home" signs and waving to the crew members. The ship had been gone for six weeks. Our Marine contingent stood quietly in formation on the ship's main deck, murmuring well-directed curses at the sailors, at their histrionic welcoming party, and at the Navy in general. Gone for a year, many of these Marines had been through unrelenting combat, but they had been directly ordered not to invite any friends, relatives, or welcoming parties to the pier in San Diego.

As soon as the ship was docked and moored, our Marines were marched down the brow and loaded onto a line of large, moving van–like cattle cars. Once we were inside, the cattle cars pulled away from the Navy's kiss-and-hug party on the pier and drove us up a busy freeway to nearby Camp Pendleton. There we were processed through a military form of customs, where senior NCOs sifted through our gear and an administrative officer searched through his files in order to hand each of us the official copy of our personal orders.

Welcome back, Marine. Stop feeling special. You're no different from the other 400,000 Marines that preceded you. Now get the hell out of here and go home. On my orders I was given thirty days of leave, after which I would report for duty at the Marine Corps Base in Quantico.

Granny knew I was coming back on a ship, but she did not know when.

The morning after I arrived on the *Tulare* I drove to Riverside. Barbara had lived there while I was overseas, eventually finding a well-paying but emotionally challenging job as a psychiatric social worker in the California state mental institution system. Aunt Carolyn lived down the street in one direction; Granny lived nearby in the other. Barbara had picked me up at Camp Pendleton, and Aunt Carolyn was making dinner. But I needed to see my granny.

I knew the way by heart. Turning off the highway and onto the side streets of Riverside, I soon parked on the road in front of her house. The door was unlocked. I had known it would be. You did not lock your doors in Arkansas, and no matter what the threat, you could not scare or hardly even surprise my granny. I slowly opened it and stepped inside. I could see her standing at the kitchen sink, washing the dishes. Her hair was filled with bobby pins and pulled tightly into a bun. As always she was wearing a long cotton dress that came down nearly to her toes. I walked into the small dining room just next to the kitchen. Casually she turned toward me, her hands still in the sink, and began talking as if I had just come back from driving to the grocery store.

"You know that leak in my ceiling over there?" she said. "Well, your uncle Cyril fixed it. He had to get a ladder and lay tar up there on the roof."

I laughed, remembering that her ceiling had leaked from a heavy rain just before I left for Vietnam. Knowing Granny, it had been frequently on her mind over the past year, a loss of face that needed to be made right.

"Aw, Granny, I didn't even remember that." I could not say anything else. I walked up and hugged her.

"Well, well," she fussed, in her slow, quiet drawl. She allowed herself a half-laugh that always seemed to come to her when she was embarrassed by her own rigidly controlled emotions. "I need to dry my hands, here."

She dried her hands and finally hugged me back. "Did you go see Carolyn yet?"

"Well, I thought I'd drive you over there with me."

"You don't need to drive, Jimmy, you need to walk. I was following it. You've been sitting on a ship for weeks."

"I've done a lot of walking, Granny. But okay, we'll walk."

So began the first day of the rest of my life. One hug from my granny brought things back to normal, more or less. I had just turned twenty-four, but in some ways I had become as wizened as she herself. In her mind this was not a Marine who had just sauntered through her doorway. A part of me was still that little boy, made safe under the protective umbrella of her nighttime stories and her quiet, comforting courage. Another part of me had changed, but in life's journeys we all change anyway, and nothing that had changed could truly surprise her. It was just another page in the never-ending story; that was all. Whatever the cost, I had upheld the long traditions of our family. I was the latest son who had gone off to fight a war he didn't start. I was her quietly cherished treasure, the soldier who had finally come home, the man who was young in his face, scarred here and there on his body, and yet old in his heart. I was as complicated as she herself was, a part of me fiercely proud of my service and another part wistfully longing for the carefree, Tom Sawyer inside me to return.

She knew all that. She had been through it in so many ways, far too many times. It is always possible to cure the infection in a wound, but there is no magical medication that can allow you to recapture your innocence. It's an old story, unless you've never lived it. My granny could not change it, but as with so many other things, her tight hug told me that she understood.

Chapter Eleven

FIGHTING WITH MY BRAIN

Absolution? Sentence?
No matter. The thing itself is in that.

—*James Dickey, "The Firebombing"*

I had spent my young life preparing for war but I had not really planned for the peace that would follow. The next few years would bring their share of surprises and unanticipated change. And as the months went by the ultimate question only seemed to grow: What next? How should I spend the rest of my life?

Behavioral scientists point out that facts can be learned, forgotten, and relearned rather easily, but that once an attitude is shaped, it is difficult and sometimes impossible to change it. Thus it was with the patterns set in motion in the Bush of Vietnam. I was on full-time adrenaline overload. Relaxation was no longer in my makeup, if it ever had been. Pushing myself to the very edge every day was not a decision; it was an irreversible and not altogether regrettable fate.

The operational and personal dimensions of combat, and especially of command responsibility, had taken me beyond any physical and mental limits I ever imagined I could endure. They also hardened my already inborn cynicism. Daily decisions in combat were high-risk, morally blurred, and intensely subjective, making many debates back home seem naive and romanticized even as they raged more loudly. Bold theories were fine at a congressional hearing or in a graduate seminar or on a newspaper's editorial page. But words were cheap when somebody was trying to kill you. In combat, philosophical babbling was the worst alternative of all. Inaction under fire killed people. Decisions had to be made. And who would make those decisions?

Combat had taught me the importance of decisiveness and of accepting personal responsibility. When the risks were high and the answers were unclear, the simple phrase "I accept responsibility" had magically unlocked uncountable doors, whether I was requesting artillery support when fighting in a populated area or cajoling a medevac helicopter into the dangers of a hot landing zone or explaining why battle plans needed to be adjusted due to realities that senior officers could not see from far away.

"I accept responsibility" became the most important phrase in my young life. It meant I was duty-bound to clarify and sometimes question orders, even under fire. Leadership requires knowledge, courage, integrity, vision, and loyalty. But loyalty is all-encompassing, despite the temptation to define it simply as carrying out orders from above. The daily struggle to remain loyal to those above me and accountable to those below me hardened a self-reliance that has informed every difficult decision I have since made.

What did you do in the war, Daddy?
I learned how to accept responsibility.

Like so many war veterans throughout history I came home hypercharged, animated, and restless. Assigned to the Officer Candidates School in Quantico, Virginia, my new role as a peacetime Marine contradicted every parameter in my psychological makeup. It was as if I were being forced to drive thirty miles an hour in a car that was used to cruising at eighty-five. With the simple turning of a page, the intensity that had permeated every second of my life had vanished. Most of my young thoughts and preparations now seemed spent and largely useless. Done with combat, the emptiness of having survived was somehow unnerving. I was staring down an emotional cliff into the vast unknown of peace, in a country that was tearing itself apart because of the war in which I had fought.

In Marine Corps parlance I had become a hard-bitten old salt, although in every other way I was still a kid, not yet two years out of college. It was as if one part of me had prematurely aged, growing wise, reflective, and old, while the rest of me had suddenly awakened, innocent and naive, staring out at the chaotic world of Woodstock, LSD, and Kent State like a twenty-four-year-old version of Rip Van Winkle.

These days just after my return from Vietnam were spent teaching tactics and individual weapons, then working as a platoon commander alongside Marine Corps drill instructors as we trained and evaluated the next echelon of aspiring officers. In the woods of Quantico, a wad of Red Man chewing tobacco constantly bulging in one cheek, I taught the intricacies of fire and maneuver, night infiltrations, and the basic tenets of leadership. But my mind was now exploding with new and different thoughts. As we bivouacked and trained in the remote forests, others in our age group were engaged in their own form of turmoil on college campuses and, most visibly, only thirty miles up the road from us in Washington, DC.

What was happening to my country?

Postcombat adrenaline filled the air among just-returned Marines at Quantico, like ozone after a bad electrical storm. Some Marines transitioned without a hiccup, putting this energy to good use, moving on to highly successful careers in law, business, and government. Some had a more chaotic journey, driving too fast, drinking too much, brawling in bars or howling at the moon, or going through women at such a frenetic pace that, in the words of one friend, having breakfast the next morning became the definition of a long-term relationship. For me, this surplus of emotional energy turned on the lights inside my brain, giving me an appetite for philosophical and historical knowledge and a determination to understand the political disruptions in our society.

This new endeavor was different and adventurous. Always a voracious reader, I had stumbled upon the larger potential of how to use my intellect beyond the enjoyment of a novel or the necessities of learning a professional skill. In my spare time at Quantico I was either reading or prowling through the thin stacks of the on-base Breckenridge Library looking for something new to read. I joined the Book-of-the-Month Club, the Literary Guild, the Military Book Club, and every other mail-order method of finding things to read. I did not care whether they were good or bad, right-wing or left-wing, truth or nonsense, scripture or comic book. I needed to read.

Among other authors in a long and expanding list, I devoured the writings of Plato, Aristotle, Tacitus, Herodotus, Sun Tzu, Will Durant, Reinhold Niebuhr, Winston Churchill, Vernon Louis Parrington, Eric Hoffer, the famed British strategist B. H. Liddell Hart, and historians Bernard Fall, John Toland, William Manchester, and Barbara Tuchman, plus a slew of catchy, little-remembered books that were considered must-reads in an era when every prevailing cultural and political orthodoxy was being dissected and questioned. I read, reread, and made personal notes on those who were considered the literary greats: Hemingway, Steinbeck, Faulkner, Sinclair Lewis, Graham Greene, Robert Graves, the British and Irish poets (as well as the Welshman Dylan Thomas), plus the fact-based fiction of such notables as World War II novelists Leon Uris, Herman Wouk, and Anton Myrer, whose book *Once an Eagle* remains, in my mind, one of the most underappreciated classics of the American military experience. Along the way, Albert Camus sneaked into my consciousness, as did André Malraux and a slew of other French thinkers.

I started writing soliloquies in the margins of the books I read, questioning great minds who would never see my notes. I was catching up with them. I had spent years devoting my energies to more basic pursuits. I had never experienced the luxury of sitting in an outdoor café, killing a bottle of wine, and debating whether there really was a God. On the other hand, I knew what it was like to stare down the barrel of a gun and to pull the trigger on an adversary who was trying to kill me. I could learn those other things.

I began thinking about policy instead of mere tactics. What would the Marine Corps look like in the future? How would it fit in with the still-emerging structure of the Department of Defense? What could we learn from the unfairly denigrated combat experiences of Vietnam, where our adversary lost by their own count 1.4 million soldiers but won the war of public perception with the illusion of battlefield invincibility? How should the United States shape its strategic goals? What should our future presence throughout the world look like, particularly in Asia, which, despite our historical focus on Europe, was emerging as the most dynamic and most challenging sphere of American involvement?

This newfound fascination was accelerated by another turn of events. When I was twenty-five, Headquarters, Marine Corps decided to assign me from Quantico to the Secretary of the Navy's office in the Pentagon. Surgery following my return from Vietnam had revealed damage from the infection in the bone of my left leg, made worse by the piece of shrapnel that had migrated into the loose space of the knee joint, tearing up the softened, articular cartilage like a knife slicing Teflon coating on a frying pan. This required follow-on surgeries, a succession of plaster casts, continual physical therapy, and twice-monthly checkup visits to the hospital. I was put on a medical hold under the supervision of Dr. John Pazell, a pioneering orthopedic surgeon who had been drafted into the Navy from his position as chief orthopedist for the University of Kansas athletic programs.

I did not want to leave the Marine Corps. I had just become one of sixteen first lieutenants out of a pool of more than 2,700 to be promoted a year early to captain. Declining a medical discharge in 1971, I was assigned to the Pentagon while Dr. Pazell put me through a lengthy rehabilitation. It would not succeed. In early 1972, after more surgery, Pazell would note in my formal medical board that he had seen signs of continuing infection in the bone, that the menisci were gone and the articular cartilage was "markedly destroyed," and that while he respected "the motivational factors that have sustained [Captain Webb] as a Marine officer, he has diligently exercised for three years with no improvement; indeed, with worsening."

Meanwhile, at the Pentagon it became my job to research and to write. As a member of the secretary's immediate staff, this included casework, fact sheets, point papers, memoranda, and official correspondence on behalf of the president, the secretary, and various assistant secretaries of the Navy. To an outsider this was heady stuff, but for any infantry Marine during the Vietnam era it was embarrassingly comfortable. After seven years of unending rigor, the predictable, weekends-free job at the Pentagon was like a vacation, giving me ample time to question and to explore. Sitting inside the information capital of the Department of Defense, with "Secretary of the Navy" access to any historical or policy data that I wished, every day and at home at night I researched and I wrote.

Part of this introspection came from the security I found in the cocoon of books on history, government, and the military campaigns of the past. The 1970s were not the best time to be a member of the military in Washington. As unbelievable as it might seem today, the antimilitary atmosphere in the nation's capital had grown so strong that except on rare occasions, military personnel assigned to the Pentagon were not even allowed to wear their uniform to work, for fear of confrontations with those who hated not only the war but also the people who had been sent to fight it.

My shaved head, garish ties, brown leather shoes, and thin-cut sport coats hardly fooled anyone as I made my way to and from "The

Building" in that age of long hair, tie-dyed T-shirts, and hippie beads. My civilian disguise, ordered up by the Secretary of Defense, was especially ineffective, since I always carried a leather briefcase in one hand and usually a book about warfare or history in the other. The stares that I received on the bus or striding down the sidewalk with my loping infantryman's gait confirmed that almost everyone I passed had already figured me out. If I was not a young military officer, then surely I must have been a Mormon missionary or a thoroughly lost Fuller Brush man.

In the late summer of 1971 during my bus commute to and from the Pentagon I was reading B. H. Liddell Hart's grand tome *History of the Second World War*. Gassed on the battlefield while serving as a British officer in World War I, Hart was invalided out of the service, later achieving prominence as a journalist, biographer, and military theoretician. Like others in his generation, Hart had been profoundly affected by the battlefield stagnation in World War I that had descended into four years of hopeless trench warfare, causing millions of casualties on all sides. This bloodletting led Hart to become an early advocate of mechanized warfare and was the basis for his influential book *Strategy: The Indirect Approach*. Tolerated but never fully appreciated by his British peers, between world wars Hart's works were avidly studied by the German military, weighing heavily on its decision to shift its operational doctrine to an emphasis on tanks and maneuver warfare that came to be known as "blitzkrieg" during their swift, early conquests in World War II.

Hart's *History of the Second World War* was his most ambitious and, as it turned out, his final book. He died in early 1970 while still working on it. Difficult for a writer to accomplish during the politically sensitive postwar period, the book focuses only on the military aspects of the war. Leaving politics to others, Hart lays out the metrics of each campaign, particularly in Europe and North Africa, with a completeness that allows students of military history to extrapolate the components of leadership, strategy, and tactics into other war eras.

In the chapters on the North African campaign Hart makes a persuasive case for the battlefield brilliance of German General Erwin Rommel, whose forces were vastly outnumbered and outgunned by the American and British armies. Compensating for his numerical inferiority by adopting what is called the strategy of the interior position, Rommel repeatedly shortened his logistical lines and concentrated his combat power on one army and then the other in order to avoid defeat through the combined size of his opponents. As Hart explains, by seizing the interior position Rommel was able to shift his forces from front to front, often choosing the terrain of his battles in order to further narrow the Allies' points of attack.

These accounts caused me to think about the structure of America's future presence in Asia. It was already clear that once the Vietnam War ended, the U.S. military would be facing budget cuts, reduced procurement of logistics and materiel, and a smaller force structure. I did not know this yet, but the Navy, which had numbered 930 combatant ships when I was commissioned in 1968, would end up being cut in half by 1979, to 479 vessels. America's basing system in Pacific Asia was scattered all over the region, in many cases the result of sheer momentum rather than careful strategy. This structure was clearly in need of change.

I kept a map of East Asia in my office, on which I marked the locations and sizes of American military bases in the region. As I studied it, the small island of Guam began to occupy my thoughts. It was centrally located, and it was a loyal American territory, a major consideration in East Asia, where insurrections and protests threatened the future of many of our bases. One-third of Guam's 210 square miles were already in bases or military retention areas. A large percentage of the B-52 Arc Light bombing missions flown into Vietnam and Laos had originated from Andersen Air Force Base there. The Navy operated extensive port facilities in Apra Harbor, as well as an 8,000-acre ammunition storage area along the central spine of the island. Among other facilities, Guam also housed a well-regarded ship repair facility and a naval air station.

The island of Tinian to its north was largely empty and rarely visited, with an adequate harbor, ample room for training areas, and extensive, high-quality runways left over from World War II that could easily be upgraded.

From my office at the bottom of the Pentagon's totem pole I came to believe that America's future presence in Asia should include a version of what Rommel had accomplished in North Africa: a strategy of the interior position, where we could shorten our logistical lines, concentrate our forces, and still be able to maneuver at will to respond to any crisis or attack in the region. In my view this could be done by consolidating many American ground and Air Force bases throughout the region into a structure focused on Guam and the northern Marianas Islands, buttressed by the presence and maneuverability of a strong and vigorous Navy.

Given my rank and my bland administrative job I was hardly going to get an audience on this issue inside the rigid bureaucracy of the Pentagon. In the military, one's length of service and military rank were jealously guarded, never to be overridden by presumptuous subordinates. By long tradition a junior military professional did not embarrass his seniors, nor did he advance his own ideas in a way that conflicted with the workings of the system. I had been a captain for only a few months, and having been "deep selected" to that rank a year early, I was even at the bottom of the captains seniority list. When it came to policy issues I was not even able to sit in the room as a note taker, much less be at the table. I would be expected to wait my turn for another twenty years or so—if I were lucky enough to climb the promotional ladder to a place where I would be heard at all.

And so I made a rather precarious decision. No one could tell me not to write in the evenings and on the weekends. If I wrote well enough, I could get published. And if I were published, although I would be criticized by some senior officers as a renegade, I could affect policy debates in a way that otherwise would not be possible for decades.

I did not want to wait for decades. I began to write.

While on the Secretary of the Navy's staff I wrote three lengthy articles for military journals. The first was an analysis of the roles and missions assigned to the Marine Corps under the 1947 National Security Act and the little-remembered 1948 Key West Agreements, where Defense Secretary James Forrestal assembled the military chiefs in order to clarify the functions expected of each uniformed service under the new law. Given the task of combining the age-old Department of War and of the Navy and establishing the Air Force as a separate military service, the first-ever secretary of defense had a lot of sorting out to do.

Following World War II there had been a strong push to completely do away with the Marine Corps. Under the new Act the Marine Corps was guaranteed a mission, viewed by some to be a victory, but that mission was limited solely to amphibious warfare, a function also preserved for the Army. Amphibious warfare had been the sole combat role of the Marine Corps only in World War II. The strength of the Marine Corps was its ability to provide a force in readiness to match any emerging threat, which actually had led the Corps to pioneer amphibious warfare doctrine in the first place. This tradition of overall readiness had been demonstrated again and again, including in lengthy ground combat in World War I, Korea, and Vietnam. "The Marine Corps," I wrote, "is a force in readiness with an included amphibious mission. Since WWII, however, we have been known, on paper at least, as an amphibious force with an included mission of readiness."

Subtle as this distinction may have seemed to outsiders, it mattered hugely when it came to interservice competition and budget influence. And my research had turned up an especially damning fact: the commandant of the Marine Corps had not even been invited to the secret, all-important meetings at Key West. As Secretary Forrestal conducted these crucial meetings, the Marine Corps had been represented, as had naval aviators and submariners, by the chief of naval operations—the admiral in charge of the Navy.

Even by 1972 the Marine Corps still lacked full parity with the other services. "The Commandant is still not a full member of the Joint Chiefs," I wrote in my article, "sitting as a member only on matters concerning the Marine Corps. He must 'declare interest' in order to voice his opinions. . . . A proper statement of Marine Corps missions would give the Commandant a rightful full membership on the Joint Chiefs."

Today the commandant sits as a full member of the Joint Chiefs of Staff, and a Marine has now served as Joint Chiefs chairman. But in March 1972 the commandant was not amused to see such a confrontational assertion on the pages of the semiofficial *Marine Corps Gazette*, written by a captain who was expected to be writing about squad tactics or whether Marines should continue to shave their heads. The article caused top Marine Corps leaders no small amount of grief in the secretary of defense's office and in the "tank" of the Joint Chiefs. Summoning a briefing team headed by a two-star general from Quantico to explain the publishing policies of the *Gazette*, Commandant Robert Cushman ordered a rebuttal to be written by two senior officers at the Marine Corps Command and Staff College. Their article was entitled "Roles and Missions: Why Trade a Cadillac for an Edsel?" Ironically, by the time the rebuttal was published I had been medically retired from the Marine Corps, and it was rumored in some places that I had been purged as a result of my writings.

My surprises had only just begun. In July 1972, the month I was retired from the Marine Corps, the Naval Institute's *Proceedings* published my article "Turmoil in Paradise: Micronesia at the Crossroads," examining the strategic importance of Micronesia and particularly the Marianas Islands and recommending that the United States reorient its basing system in Pacific Asia. I outlined the military, cultural, and political history of the region and analyzed the ongoing debates regarding Micronesia's transition from a U.S.-administered United Nations Trust Territory into a permanent political status with the United States. I called for the United States to reposition its military in East Asia into a Guam-Tinian axis, while maintaining a vigorous sea power presence. I also urged that we quickly resolve the future political status of the Trust Territory, maintaining a low-level but permanent relationship in the areas beyond the Marianas Islands to prevent other powers from strategically interdicting American interests, as Japan had done in the years preceding World War II.

The article's publication coincided with a period of personal turmoil and transition as I left the Marine Corps and enrolled in the Georgetown University Law Center. Immersed in my law school studies, I had not followed the debate over the article, and in early October the editors at *Proceedings* informed me that I was the subject of a front-page editorial in the *Pacific Daily News*, a Gannett-owned paper based on Guam with a circulation of 100,000. The above-the-masthead editorial had taken up half of the front page and then a full page inside. Among its comments, the editorial asked (with shades of Ayn Rand's incantation of John Galt in *Atlas Shrugged*), "And who is Captain Webb?"

Unable to believe that the intricately researched analysis could have come from a lowly captain whose office was located in the bowels of the Pentagon, the *Pacific Daily News* editors continued: "Are these his personal opinions or are they in fact the opinions of the Navy Department or the Defense Department? Inasmuch as Capt. Webb has never, that we know of, even been stationed anywhere near Guam or Micronesia, we refuse to believe these are personal opinions. We believe that Capt. Webb, an obviously bright young man, and an obviously talented writer, was given this assignment . . . by the Defense Department. He was fed information about Micronesia, the compacts, the status talks, and more, about Navy strategy for the future. . . . We believe that Capt. Webb's piece is what we call in the newspaper business a 'trial balloon.'" The editors then warned, "When the military moves in there is a natural, normal tendency on their part to control not only the economy but the politics of the place itself."

From my new perch at Georgetown Law, there was a sweet irony in reading this editorial. Having taken a pasting from the commandant of the Marine Corps on my way out the door for being a presumptuous renegade due to my article on roles and missions, the *Pacific Daily News* was now accusing me of being a lackey to the Pentagon's hierarchy.

In a detailed rebuttal to the editors I pointed out that "the basis for a discussion of military realignments does not presuppose a background in Micronesian affairs, as much as in overall military strategy. . . . National strategy and military history have been among my most consuming interests, and the re-disposition that I proposed seems to follow logically from my studies. . . . With respect to your observation that I was provided information . . . in order to launch a 'trial balloon,' nothing could be further from the truth." In fact no one in the Secretary of the Navy's office had even known that I was writing the article. If they had known, they might well have told me to cease and desist, since such observations were indeed above my pay grade and outside my box.

Improbable as it may have seemed little more than a year earlier as I stared at the map of Pacific Asia in my small Pentagon office, as a result of the article, the lengthy editorial, and my response, I now began engaging regularly with key thinkers and leaders in Guam and the rest of Micronesia about America's future military needs in Asia.

★   ★   ★

The year that I spent on the secretary's staff also opened my eyes to the reality that our governmental bureaucracy can be maddeningly opaque. In this microcosm I quickly learned that many of our most deserving citizens lack the sophistication to navigate their way to a place where they can be heard and helped. Working on hundreds of individual cases, I saw this undeniable truth every day. One such case was a letter written in a shaky scrawl from an elderly woman in the rural South. Explaining that her son, a Marine, had been killed as a Marine in World War II, with some embarrassment she pointed out that she had never received his insurance payment from the Veterans Administration. I called the military records center in St. Louis with only three data points: her home address, her son's last name, and the fact that he had been a Marine. Within a day the researchers in St. Louis came back to me: they had found the records of her son, who had died during the battle of Iwo Jima, more than twenty-five years earlier. The impenetrable bureaucracy had failed her. I was not yet born when her son had died. I was overwhelmed to think that she had hesitated this long.

Other issues were legally complex, morally debatable, and often avoided by the common practice of sending form-letter replies. But given my battlefield experience I could not ignore them, and thus I began what would become decades of ruminations on an issue that has haunted humankind since the first days of organized warfare as we attempt to balance self-defense with the sanctity of human life: What is a war crime?

Noncombatants have paid a lamentable price throughout the history of warfare. Nothing illustrates the complexities of this reality more clearly than to consider that America's most justifiable conflict, World War II, was also the war in which the highest number of innocent civilians perished as a result of our military actions. The practice of "total war," as opposed to the "limited wars" in Korea, Vietnam, Iraq, and Afghanistan, went much further than deploying combat forces against an opposing military. Total war meant involvement on a broader scale, including the willingness to destroy not only an adversary's military but also its financial fabric, business districts, residential areas, and national morale. At its core was the decision of national leaders on all sides to acquiesce in the deaths of large numbers of civilians in order to break the spirit and the will of the country they were fighting.

During three days of strikes in February 1945, toward the very end of the European war, allied bombs destroyed the city center of Dresden, Germany, killing at least 30,000 civilians. Three weeks later, on March 9, American bombers dropped thousands of incendiary bombs on downtown Tokyo, setting a sixteen-square-mile area on fire, killing at least 97,000 people and destroying 286,000 buildings and homes. In one night the fire bombs on Tokyo brought a higher casualty number than either atomic bomb would bring to Hiroshima and Nagasaki five months later.

Justifications for these actions and the policies that support them abound. I was not seeking to dismiss them but to understand them. Having fought in a complicated, up-close-and-personal war in Vietnam, I especially had no wish to pass judgment on the soldiers and airmen who honorably carried out their orders. But a nagging moral question lingered, and its very definition was subject to constant debate. What, exactly, was a war crime?

While on the Secretary of the Navy's staff, I was responsible for following and responding to inquiries regarding approximately a dozen cases involving Marine Corps homicides, most of them inside Vietnam. We half-jokingly called these Marines our "problem children," since their cases received intense coverage in the media and frequent requests for updates from Congress. Some were clear-cut examples of unforgivable criminality, but others were complicated, both legally and morally. As with so many other events on the populated battlefields where many of the war's engagements were fought, on the one hand it was impossible to defend the acts for which each Marine had been convicted, while on the other it was difficult to agree with the characterization of every one of them as murder.

Among the incidents involving the Marine Corps, the killing of sixteen civilians in the village of Son Thang in Quang Nam Province during the night of February 19, 1970, was the worst. And yet among all the problem children whose cases I was responsible for learning about and briefing, the conviction of Private Sam Green on fifteen counts of second-degree murder during this incident troubled me the most.

The incident itself was clearly beyond the acceptable parameters of wartime conduct. On a night patrol a five-man "killer team" dispatched from a nearby rifle company had entered the village on a mission to find and kill enemy soldiers. By some accounts the patrol took enemy fire from the far end of the village as they entered it. For lack of a better description, the patrol leader had then gone crazy. He pulled villagers, including children, from their family bunkers, telling the others on the patrol that he had orders from their lieutenant to kill all of them. He also led the shooting. None of the people killed was a soldier. Once ordered to fire, the entire patrol obeyed his orders.

Private Sam Green, eighteen years old and new to Vietnam, was the most inexperienced member of the patrol. Tried by a general court-martial in April 1970, Green was convicted of second-degree murder on fifteen of sixteen counts, receiving a Dishonorable Discharge and a prison sentence of five years. His conviction was based on a finding that his actions aided and abetted the conduct of the patrol leader due to his continued presence at the scene and his obedience to orders that he should have known were "patently illegal." But Green's presence at the scene was dictated by military commanders, and leaving a combat patrol in the middle of the night in the hostile villages of Quang Nam Province was impossible and possibly suicidal. And importantly, whether or not a Marine "should have known" an order was illegal did not mean that he in fact did subjectively know it. If he did not know, then his actions were due to negligence or perhaps stupidity. If he did know, then his actions constituted murder.

Taking civilian lives in a hostile combat environment presents the most complex set of legal issues in which to convict someone of homicide. Soldiers are already armed. They are subject to military disciplinary codes. Criminal culpability cannot be determined simply because a soldier fired his weapon and a civilian died. Instead it is necessary to measure the actual intent behind the actions. The same physical action could be knowingly wrong, purposeful, and malevolent, which is murder. It could be reckless, without considering standards of conduct, or it could be negligent, meaning that a soldier did not fully understand his obligations but should have, each of which meets the standards for manslaughter. Or it could be legally excusable in some form due to the mental state of the perpetrator, who may have believed he had a duty to carry out orders from above.

The disposition of the cases of the five Marines involved in the Son Thang killings shows how difficult it is to establish and follow a simple moral and legal standard. Of the five Marines involved in the night patrol, one turned state's evidence, all charges dropped in exchange for his testimony against the other four. Two others, including the patrol leader, a seasoned combat veteran who had given the orders to shoot the civilians and who had done much of the shooting, were represented by experienced civilian lawyers after residents of their hometowns in Ohio and Oklahoma donated money to pay for their defense. Both were acquitted. The other two members of the patrol, a Marine from rural West Virginia and Private Sam Green, an African American from the inner city of Cleveland, were represented by young military lawyers only recently out of law school. Both were convicted.

In short, these two Marines were convicted of obeying orders that the military court decided they should have known were illegal, while the patrol leader who actually gave the orders and did much of the killing was acquitted.

It was not exactly popular to defend the actions of a convicted "war criminal" on the heels of the My Lai revelations as America was slowly exiting from a vastly unpopular war, but having served in this same geographical area of Vietnam, I was troubled by Green's conviction. His relatively short prison sentence, which was reduced even further after he turned out to be a model prisoner, seemed an indication that the Marine Corps leadership itself was conflicted by the results of the trials.

Green's intellect was marginal. When signing up for the Marine Corps he had low test scores and had even misspelled his middle name, George. He was nonetheless highly motivated, having scored an impressive 4.7/ 4.6 in Proficiency and Conduct on a scale of 5.0 while in boot camp, which, if translated to college grades, would have put him on the Dean's List. He had spent only eleven days in Vietnam, during which his rifle company had been involved in three different actions in which civilians had directly aided the enemy. His patrol leader was highly respected, having recently been recommended for the Silver Star, the third-highest decoration for valor that our country can award. And importantly, during his court-martial Green was asked if he had ever been told that sometimes a Marine had a duty to disobey a direct order. His unsurprising answer was no.

There was no doubt that Green screwed up terribly, as did the other four members of the "killer team" and particularly the patrol leader, who had ordered the killings and spurred on the others to participate. The thought nagged at me. Sam Green had been convicted for encouraging the actions of his patrol leader, yet it was more likely that the patrol leader had spurred the actions of Sam Green—and then had been acquitted for the consequences of his own orders. The killings themselves were sickening, as were a lot of other things that happened, at the behest of both sides, in Quang Nam Province. But was Sam Green a murderer? What should his level of culpability be when the person whose orders he obeyed was found innocent of all charges?

Shortly after beginning law school I asked Commander John Jenkins, the legal advisor to the assistant Secretary of the Navy for manpower, to pull records from the Green case so that I could study it. I had worked with Jenkins daily during my final year in the Marine Corps. A great naval officer who eventually would become the Navy's judge advocate general, Jenkins not only got me the pretrial and court-martial record but also set up a small desk for my use inside his private office.

Thus began a six-year journey. At Georgetown I received the Horan Award for excellence in legal writing based on an article I wrote about the case entitled "Presenting the Case for the Reasonable and Honest War Criminal." As I researched the trial records I learned about Jim Chiara, a lawyer in Cleveland who had been working pro bono to try to help Sam Green. I contacted him and we began working together. The Court of Military Appeals had declined to hear an appeal, thus exhausting Green's legal remedies inside the military system. In an effort to bring the case into the federal court system, in 1974 I wrote a twenty-thousand-word "collateral attack" that Chiara filed in the Northern District of Ohio, asserting grave constitutional error in Green's conviction based on the makeup of his military court-martial, which did not include anyone who had served in the infantry in Vietnam, and on the unavoidable privity of his relationship with the patrol leader whose orders he was obeying and who himself was acquitted of all charges.

A strong defense by a team of federal lawyers wrote a counterbrief. Their well-compensated aggregate effort, compared to the part-time, pro bono attempts by Chiara and me, gave me an indelible example of the awesome powers that the federal government is able to amass against an impecunious defendant who, as the saying goes, must rely on the kindness of strangers. We were nonetheless hopeful. Chiara reported to me that the judge seemed sympathetic. But finally the court decided that our argument in the collateral attack did not rise to the rarely met standard of "grave constitutional error." Despite that narrow legal decision, on his own initiative the judge wrote a personal letter to the Secretary of the Navy asking him to exercise his clemency powers and reverse the findings of the court. The secretary declined, responding with a form letter. Sam Green, whose expectations had been elevated, grew despondent.

But I am getting ahead of myself.

★　　★　　★

Even for those who revel in historical trivia, August 9, 1974, is not a particularly memorable date. In fact most Americans do not remember it at all, and those who do would probably prefer to forget the day that Richard Nixon resigned from the presidency of the United States. On that day I sat like a shipwreck survivor on the tiny island of Saipan in the middle of the Pacific Ocean, grateful that I was having breakfast in the restaurant of the Royal Taga Hotel rather than slaving away as a summer intern in an air-conditioned law office in Washington.

By the summer of 1974 I had been home from Vietnam for more than four years. I would become a frequent visitor to that country after the war, but I had never returned as a combatant. As the months progressed, the metaphorical lights were inexorably being turned off inside South Vietnam. Our country, uncomfortable with failure, was averting its national gaze from what was shaping up to be a disaster of historic proportions. Few wanted to claim ownership of this ugly result, and no matter where anyone stood on the wisdom of the war, most were exhausted by the long years of bitter debate.

Much of our national leadership thus took the option of slowly turning the page, including many who at one time had encouraged the effort that was now ending so disastrously. America was moving on. To this day our elites rarely discuss the final years of a war whose fierceness continued after our withdrawal. Retrospective analyses like to focus on American and South Vietnamese mistakes, both in planning and on the battlefield. Seldom do we see a discussion about the human and societal impact of the communist takeover. Few courses on the war in our major universities mention the vast reeducation camps that swept up a million South Vietnamese soldiers and held 240,000 of them in prison for more than four years, some of them for as long as eighteen years, or the historically unprecedented exodus of more than a million who became known as the boat people, or the strategic tilt toward the Soviet Union that gave the Soviet Navy warm-water ports in the Pacific and ended only when the Soviet Union itself fell apart.

More than anything, the nation's cognoscenti wanted to end the arguments here at home, to stop sending troops to the proverbially doomed land war in Asia, and even to stop appropriating money that helped fund the South Vietnamese effort that we once had so avidly encouraged. The coldness of those final years conjures up the image of a bunch of Wall Street investors who have decided to cut their losses on a bad business deal.

Those South Vietnamese who bet their country and their lives on America's loyalty were not afforded that luxury. As the end approached, there was a saying among some of them: "You brought eggs from the chicken. We brought bacon from the pig. You made a contribution. We made a total commitment." The American chicken would live, finding a few new barnyards in which to strut and peck and lay its eggs, but the South Vietnamese pig would die. Except for embassy duty and a few advisors, the U.S. Marine Corps had left Vietnam by mid-1971. By early 1973 all American units had been withdrawn. But the battlefield itself continued to rage. Shortly after that, even combat air support from remote locations was curtailed, to be followed by the strangulation of direct aid to the South Vietnamese military itself.

The Marine Corps was gone from Vietnam, and I was gone from the Marine Corps. I spent my days inside classrooms located only six blocks from the Capitol grounds in Washington. Looking at me, it might have been hard to tell that I had so recently been a hard-core infantry Marine. My hair was growing into the Celtic version of an Afro. I wore wire-rimmed glasses and bell-bottom trousers. My energies were devoted to briefing legal cases and reciting the intricacies of judicial precedent as I endured the Socratic questions of my professors.

But mentally and emotionally my mind was constantly elsewhere, as it always had been when it came to classrooms, and especially now in the aftermath of my military service. In the summer of 1973, due to my retired status I was able to hitch rides as a space-available passenger on a series of military cargo planes, hopping from base to base, to California and Hawaii and then on to Micronesia. Proving that one could indeed tour Asia on $10 a day, I often slept on the floors of military air terminals or in roach-infested hotels.

One morning as I shaved at the $8-a-night Hotel Micronesia on

Guam, the sewer suddenly burped up into my metal sink, inviting me to rinse my razor in a bowl full of human excrement. I avoided that mistake, but overall I could not complain. I was the only non-islander staying at the hotel. The corridors and restaurant were filled with squat, rough-hewn visitors from places like Yap and Kwajalein and Ponape. Lacking air-conditioning and frayed at the edges, it was still far better than a sand-bag bunker in An Hoa. The sheets were clean, breakfast was included, and nobody was shooting at me. The rain fell harmlessly onto the lush weeds on the other side of rusting screens that covered the windows. A fan turned slowly above the bed, churning the damp air. Gecko lizards barked and flitted along the walls, chasing bugs and slow mosquitoes.

Familiar sounds and damp, fecund odors welcomed me. I felt contented, glad to be away from Watergate Washington and back in Asia.

Upon my return I had written my first book, a blueprint for America's strategic interests in the Pacific, with an emphasis on the potential post-Vietnam military shift from its forward positions into Guam and the Marianas Islands. In the summer before my final year of law school I had been recruited to conduct a detailed study for the governor of Guam, providing a facility-by-facility analysis of what this strategic consolidation might actually look like, especially in Guam, Tinian, and Saipan. I had quickly accepted this offer. In distance and in tone the Marianas Islands were as far away from Washington as one could get, which pleased me greatly, and I was working for myself, which pleased me even more.

Having spent twenty-six years either in uniform or as a member of a military family, no amount of money and no form of seduction were going to rob me of my independence. I had made an inalterable promise to myself: rich or poor, I would never again walk on somebody else's treadmill or allow myself to become a gear in someone else's machine. That was the plan. I would find something I really cared about, and I would do it. And then I would find the next thing that I really cared about, and I would do that. And sooner or later, rather than finding a civilian career, a civilian career would find me. I knew how to lead, and I had come to understand the value of my ability to write. Combining the two, I had found a professional path to follow, even if it did not include the certainty of continuous employment.

I had learned the value of fighting not with my hands or with a weapon but with my brain. Independent thought meant working my way through issues not as an eager-to-please student or as an understudy but to challenge the assumptions of prevailing orthodoxy and offer new solutions. I loved the feeling it gave me, just as I had embraced the surge of adrenaline when stepping inside a brightly lit boxing ring and when leading infantry Marines in combat.

I rose early on that August morning in 1974, becoming one of the first diners in the restaurant of the Royal Taga Hotel. The first major hotel on Saipan, the Royal Taga had been built in 1967 on the island's most beautiful shoreline by the legendary entrepreneur Ken Jones, on a property that had housed Marine Corps headquarters units during and after the 1944 battle of Saipan. A North Carolina native who first went to Guam as a sailor during World War II, Jones returned after the war with a few boxes of beads and costume jewelry, married Elaine Cruz, from a local family, and partnered with his friend Leon Guerrero to open up a store. Back home few Americans knew much about Guam, and it was surprising how many would confuse Saipan with Saigon. But Jones was making serious money here, and he had built a nice little hotel.

Entering the restaurant, I grabbed a copy of the *Pacific Daily News*, making my way to a table near the expansive windows that looked out upon the sea. On Saipan, dawn was my favorite part of the day. As if watching the fade-up opening of a movie or a Broadway play, sitting next to the window I could absorb the rising of the sun, which in minutes would creep balloon-like above the edge of the horizon and illuminate the endless expanse of the Pacific Ocean.

Saipan is 140 miles north of Guam across an open sea that includes the Marianas Trench, which at 38,000 feet is the deepest ocean water

in the world. As dawn broke, history as well as the beauty of the tropics glowed outside the window. Gorgeous starbursts of Pandanus trees
arched above the sand along the beaches, leaning out toward the endless,
empty sea. Many of the trees were rooted near the concrete structures
and firing apertures of a ring of old Japanese bunkers that still lined the
western edge of the island. Only a few hundred yards from where I sat,
the turret of a World War II American tank lurked just above the water-
line, its rusting main gun pointing hopelessly toward a now-forgotten
Japanese target, having been silenced and thus enshrined in the shallow
lagoon since June 1944.

That battle had ended thirty years ago during the ferocious summer
of 1944, taking second place in the national news as the country focused
on the European war and the June 6 D-Day landings at Normandy. But
a month of hand-to-hand combat on Saipan had taken the lives of 3,400
Americans, most of them Marines, as well as more than 30,000 Japanese
soldiers and another 22,000 Japanese civilians who, at the urging of their
emperor, had chosen suicide rather than cooperation with the Americans. Several thousand more Americans had died during that summer in
battles on the nearby islands of Tinian and Guam. In early 1945 many
thousands more would perish farther to the north on the tiny island
of Iwo Jima and then in a protracted campaign on the larger island of
Okinawa, the first battle actually on Japanese soil. And it was from Tinian that the *Enola Gay* was launched in August 1945, dropping the first
atomic bomb on Japan.

A waitress appeared. I ordered a full breakfast of juice, toast, bacon,
and eggs. She poured me a freshly brewed cup of coffee. I took a welcome gulp, leaning back into my chair and unfolding the newspaper.
Looking at the headlines I almost choked. In this age that preceded cell
phones and the Internet and on the islands of Guam and Saipan where
even television access was limited, I seemed always to be a day behind
the news cycle. But how could I have missed the biggest story of the
year?

Like a growing cancer the Watergate scandal had paralyzed our governmental system. Its ever-expanding political and criminal reach had dominated the news for nearly two years, during the entire time I had been a student at the Georgetown University Law Center. And now the resignation of a president, bringing with it a series of constitutional and foreign policy unknowns, was deeply unsettling, even as I sat on this remote island eight thousand miles away, sipping my coffee and watching the rising of the sun.

Richard Nixon had just become the first president in history to resign from office. Gerald Ford, a good-hearted but untested former congressman from Michigan, was now president of the United States. Ford was not only an accidental president; he was also an accidental vice president, appointed as a replacement for the scandal-besieged Spiro Agnew, who himself had resigned from office ten months before. The first president to resign from office would be replaced by an unelected and clearly stunned vice president.

Nixon was a man of many flaws, but despite the ethical and political quicksand of Watergate, except in certain circles he was not exactly a detested pariah. In the 1972 elections he had received an impressive 60.7 percent of the popular vote and 520 of 538 votes in the Electoral College, losing only Massachusetts and the District of Columbia. His popular majority was higher than any presidential candidate in history other than Franklin Roosevelt's infinitesimally higher 60.8 percent in 1936 and Lyndon Johnson's 61 percent in 1964. Ronald Reagan would win his 1984 reelection with 59 percent of the vote, but in recent times no other candidate has come close. Bill Clinton would be the furthest away, winning only 43 percent of the popular vote in 1992 and 49 percent in 1996. Clinton would suffer his own ethical challenges, including an impeachment proceeding, but would remain in office and then prosper, financially and otherwise, upon his retirement. Nixon, facing relentless attacks in the media and from Congress that were not going to go away, had wearied of the two-year fight and finally folded.

The implications of this resignation went beyond the turbulence that the Watergate controversy had brought to the governing councils in Washington. Whatever one thought of Nixon personally, he had played a deft hand in foreign policy, laying out a pragmatic framework called the Nixon Doctrine, opening the door for restoring relations with China, and despite constant battles with Congress, having worked to bring the Vietnam War to a less than cataclysmic end. Among other things, with Nixon's departure and Ford's intrinsic passivity, it was now certain that the United States would completely abandon an already weakened South Vietnamese government, thus ignominiously ending a war that had consumed America for more than a decade.

Indeed in November 1974 a shaken electorate would tilt heavily away from the Republican Party, electing a large number of one-issue, left-leaning Democratic candidates from dozens of congressional districts that traditionally had voted Republican. In its first major vote in January 1975 this new "Watergate Congress" would cut off funding for the struggling South Vietnamese military. In March an all-out North Vietnamese offensive, supported by weapons and funding from the Soviet Union, would overrun the South. And after fifty-five days, during which the United States did nothing to assist its former ally on the battlefield, on April 30, 1975, the South Vietnamese government would cease to exist.

The stability that America's governing institutions had brought to the post–World War II international community was severely shaken. It would take years before American foreign policy and prestige would recover.

In my own small way, I was trying to do my part in restoring that prestige. During breakfast at the Royal Taga Hotel, I sorted through a stack of maps, charts, and carefully researched historical data, including water tables, old troop strengths, and other intricately compiled statistics. I had spent months putting it all together, comparing the troop numbers and force structure on Guam, Tinian, and Saipan not only against the American military presence in World War II but also against the basing system and naval capabilities that existed in Pacific Asia during these final days of the Vietnam War. Over the past two months I had walked, driven, or flown over every existing and potential military area on Guam, Tinian, and Saipan, as well as most of those located on Okinawa. I had met with military leaders and with local environmental and urban planners. Crunching the numbers, I had put theory into practical possibility.

No one could predict exactly what would happen in East Asia over the next decade or so, but I was confident that the matrix I had assembled would become a useful tool for future discussions about Guam's place in America's strategic posture in Asia. Soon I would finish a detailed report showing how the United States could restructure its military presence as I had predicted in my seminal article two years before, shortening our logistical lines, increasing our maneuverability, and reducing our exposure to the political uncertainties of local turbulence where American troops were now based.

Thirty-two years later, when I entered the U.S. Senate, one of the key issues facing the United States and Japan was, rather surprisingly, how to relocate a large portion of the American military presence on Okinawa to facilities on Guam and possibly Tinian. The issue had finally come to an inevitable head. Okinawa lost nearly 150,000 civilians dead during World War II, a huge percentage of the total population and far more than the losses of the American and Japanese military combined. After the war the island became known as a "giant American aircraft carrier" and by 2007 had been hosting an extensive American military presence for more than sixty years. Local leaders were demanding that American bases be removed, some to remote locations on Okinawa but most of them off the island altogether and relocated to Guam. Facing more immediate challenges and addicted to the comfortable accommodations on Okinawa, American military leaders had repeatedly punted the issue downfield to their successors. The Tokyo government, historically viewing the Ryukyu Islanders of Okinawa as less than fully Japanese, had done likewise.

In this highly charged political environment American military leaders had come up with a relocation plan involving both Okinawa and Guam that was either naively or deliberately unworkable. By 2007 the stalemate had entered its tenth year, with no realistic answer in sight. As a member of the Armed Services Committee I pulled out my 1974 report and sent it to the Department of Defense. The report had held up well, given the unpredictable nature of the intervening years, and still does. During my six years in the Senate I made two journeys to Guam, Saipan, and Tinian, and many more to Tokyo and Okinawa, in an effort to break the stalemate.

But without strong national leadership and in the absence of a crisis that would force at least a halfhearted solution, the strategic and political agreements necessary in Washington, Tokyo, Okinawa, and Guam in order to bring about such military relocations will continue to be put on hold. That crisis continues to creep up on us, in the form of public opinion on Okinawa itself. Unlike the rest of Japan, Okinawa has strong historical ties to China as well as to Tokyo. Its people endured horrific casualties during World War II and have long absorbed the highest burden when it comes to the presence of the American military on their soil. Tokyo and Washington ignore these realities at their mutual peril. In the long run the future of the United States in East Asia depends heavily on a viable military presence there, and the future of that military presence will ultimately depend on local harmony, which cannot exist without mutual respect.

All of these concerns were visible in the summer of 1974. Eating breakfast in the shadow of the craggy cliffs at the edge of the endless sea that marked the coastline of this blood-soaked little island, I studied my charts and graphs. At that moment I was not thinking of the Pentagon, which I had left as a Marine two years before and in which I again would serve as a civilian executive ten years later. Nor could I imagine that I would someday be elected to the U.S. Senate. I was contemplating the implications that might visit our country after the unprecedented resignation of a president. I was thinking of the past and of the soldiers and Marines who had died on this island. I was struggling to define the value of their sacrifice, in a breakfast room that was rapidly filling up with chattering, picture-taking Japanese tourists, many of them young honeymooners, for whom the rusting American tank out in the lagoon seemed to be little more than a conversation piece.

I finished my breakfast. The sun sparkled above the turquoise lagoon, but on the far side of the reef the ocean was turgid and dark. It occurred to me that life itself was perilously like that thin line of coral where the tranquil lagoon met the voracious sea. Its certainties were calming and yet ephemeral, while its dangers were impossible to measure. We could eat, walk, wade, and even grow pineapples on Saipan without ever comprehending that in reality we were standing on a tiny nipple of earth at the top of a vast underwater mountain. The gorgeous coral reef was itself nothing more than a parasitic ornamentation. If you were to drive your car off the edge of this small island you would not stop falling for seven miles, straight down an underwater cliff to the deepest sea bottom in the world, more than six times as far as you would fall if you tripped over the side of the Grand Canyon at its steepest place.

★　　★　　★

Returning from Guam in the fall of 1974 for my final year of law school, I decided that with an engineering degree I had not wanted and a law degree I did not intend to use, maybe I should write a novel. The thought had been creeping up on me for a year, after a close friend died in a freak accident, falling nine stories from the balcony of an apartment building. Leo Kennedy had joked that I was the literary descendant of Ernest

Hemingway, a fellow boxer, fisherman, and war veteran who had even been wounded in the same leg, and that I needed to follow Papa's path and thus become a writer. The American political system was paralyzed by the Watergate debates. The wheels were coming off the Vietnam War. The military and our Vietnam veterans were in total disrepute. And while on Guam, immersed in the jungle heat and the familiar smells and sounds of the tropics, my mind had begun thinking intensely of my time in Vietnam. I began compiling a sheaf of notes, and one afternoon while sitting in a class on constitutional law, I began writing my Vietnam novel *Fields of Fire*.

Entering the large classroom that seated more than a hundred law students, I perched myself as always in the back row. The professor began a lecture on the War Powers Act, and without provocation the class erupted with vitriol about the evils of everything associated with the Vietnam War. I had become accustomed to the pervasive antiwar feelings at Georgetown Law, but the intensity of the comments during this hour stunned me. The discussion, meant to focus on the constitutionality of a piece of legislation that applied to a whole range of future military actions, became little more than an animated condemnation of the war and the people who had fought it. Negative views about Vietnam were standard fare, but the flood of derogatory comments about those who had served was something different. The propaganda ministries in Hanoi could not have been more one-sided and unfair.

I had left a Marine Corps in which almost everyone had served in Vietnam and entered a law school where almost no one had even seen the inside of a military base. It was already "intuitively obvious to the casual observer," to quote a favorite law school phrase, that the Baby Boom generation had cracked apart along class lines. But during this hour-long hate-in an unstoppable revulsion crept up my spine. Smart people who did not even know anyone in the military were attacking their own age peers as fascists, rapists, murderers, drug addicts, and moral morons. In their obliviousness they did not seem to realize that they were talking about me and a few others in their presence and, more important, a lot of people we cared about who were now dead or maimed. To argue with them would have been like spitting into the wind. In the row just in front of me, one of the few Vietnam veterans I knew at Georgetown Law raised his hand, asking to speak. Angered by the comments, he looked back at me to see if I was going to say anything. In a private signal I shook my head, warning him off, and he lowered his hand.

They ranted. I watched and listened and learned. These were the things that many of them were saying at the lunch tables and in the hallways when I was not present, now shouted openly in a class where each remark seemed to invite yet another. They had no referent other than college classrooms or antiwar rallies or articles and TV shows featuring others who shared their views. Then another thought crossed my mind. What would this conversation sound like if each of them had spent even a month inside an infantry unit in a place like the An Hoa Basin? Meaning no one any malice and setting aside the politics of the war itself, if they were truly honest, what would they now be saying about the complex environment and the people who had fought this war?

Lacking other options, I opened up my spiral notebook and began to write. Once I started I could not stop. Despite my course load, day after day, week after week, at my study desk or at home, I wrote. And as I wrote they all became Will Goodrich, the Harvard genius (ironically nicknamed The Senator) who had dropped out of college on a dare and enlisted in the Marine Corps, with the vague promise from a recruiter that he could spend two years playing French horn in the Marine Band. Doomed by his intellect to become the naive but earnest moral conscience among a platoon of tough Marines in Vietnam, Will Goodrich would return to Harvard after being badly wounded and would remain the moral conscience among a sea of intellectually gifted but politically agitated and socially insulated elites. And the price that he paid in both places was to be mistrusted and shunned in each.

The novel was bigger than Will Goodrich. As I wrote it, the story became an escalating moral drama with a carefully drawn cast of nearly a dozen Marines, each of whom had a different background and a varying reaction to the brutality of the battlefield, even though in combat itself they were united as a cohesive platoon. In the early months I would work on a scene for hours, thinking that I had just painted a Monet, only to realize upon rereading that I had drawn nothing more than a primitive Stick Man.

I persisted, rereading the great novelists, this time in what I viewed to be a private tutorial from the masters, with an architectural eye rather than for enjoyment. Curious about an analogy that Hemingway had drawn in his memoir *A Moveable Feast* between his writing and the paintings of Cézanne, I began studying the French Impressionists. One afternoon while strolling through the National Gallery of Art I saw a striking, emotive landscape on a far wall. Looking at it, I decided that if Hemingway had painted, this could have been his landscape. In an unexplainable but emotionally logical way the landscape reminded me of the opening paragraphs of Hemingway's novel *A Farewell to Arms*. And walking up to the painting I saw that it was a Cézanne.

I had learned something, through a process that I could not yet put into words. After a few weeks of reading and thinking and revisiting that landscape I could articulate how the physical descriptions of Hemingway's novels and the art of Cézanne worked from a common premise. Hemingway had learned from Cézanne, and I had learned from both. With this realization my fledgling novel became richer in texture and my self-confidence as a writer grew, as did my resolve. I had to finish it. I did not want to see myself thirty years later pulling out a few hundred unpublished pages from a desk drawer and lamenting that if I had only stayed with it, I could have produced a lasting piece of art. In my final year of law school I decided against interviewing for legal work or taking the Bar (although I would take the District of Columbia Bar exam two

years later). I stretched my schedule in order to extend my GI Bill coverage into the fall, postponing my graduation from law school to October.

The writing went on long past October and into the next year. In the
end I wrote the novel seven times, cover to cover.

During the summer of 1975, not long after the fall of Saigon, I threw
my camping gear into my car and slowly made my way south toward
Florida along old U.S. Highway 17. Cooking C rations and sleeping on
the ground, I drove reflectively past the swamps and tobacco fields, stopping now and then in little, forgotten towns in eastern Virginia, North
and South Carolina, and Georgia. Finally I entered Florida. My parents
were living in a termite-bitten old grove house in Lakeland that my father
had decided to renovate. The house had been condemned by the county.
On a whim my father had saved it from destruction, buying it for a pittance. He had done magical things with the old home, redesigning it from
floorboards to eaves and lining the walls of the extended kitchen area with
unfinished panels of cypress. The raw, rustic wood was beautiful in its
natural state. It also filled the home with a serene and comforting aroma.

He and my mother had moved to Lakeland from their original retirement place in Cocoa Beach, at first renting a nearby house while he
did the initial demolition and construction on the grove home, soon
moving into the home itself. Nearly two dozen citrus trees covered the
expansive yard. My father liked to say that he moved from Cocoa Beach
to Lakeland because he loved the oranges but that after a year of picking
up spoiled fruit that fell from the trees he left because he was sick of the
oranges.

In the side yard my mother had put in an expansive garden, rich with
tomatoes, cantaloupes, peppers, and squash. With my dad's military
service now behind him, my mother had begun missing her childhood
haunts in Arkansas. My parents were making ever more frequent trips
back to the little town of Searcy and to her home village of Kensett. During one visit my mother had nostalgically bought more than a dozen

strawberry plants at a nursery in nearby Judsonia, transplanting them into her garden in Lakeland. And so there was now a quiet karma in my mother's garden, the closing of a circle, turned into a minor triumph. When she was hardly more than a child she had chopped cotton in the sweltering summer heat, ricked firewood taken from absentee farms in the middle of the night, and picked a lot of strawberries in Judsonia, which then claimed the title of the Strawberry Capital of America. Strawberry plants that once had grown in Arkansas now flourished in her Florida yard, their roots thriving in the rich dark soil that for decades had nurtured orange groves. As she picked a few strawberries in the early-morning quiet my mother could be reminded of the journey that had taken her to a place where she now could toss a few into a bowl purely for her own pleasure, to be mixed in with other fruit and cream for a leisurely breakfast.

Arkansas had been a harsh taskmaster to my mother's family all those years ago, but there were also strong memories that had defined her and still called out to her. Perhaps she simply had begun to yearn for the steam-baked, melodic rhythms that had spawned her. Perhaps, now that my father's military career was over and her children were grown, she was looking for a permanent emotional and ancestral anchor even if it meant embracing at the same time all of the still visible and heartrending reminders of the very struggles she had overcome.

There was something else, less visible but just as telling. The head-spinning transitions of geography, family, and profession had dominated not only my parents' waking hours but also those of all four of their children. Since the age of eighteen my mother had carried not only her own load but also the spiritual well-being of our entire family. As patient and even-tempered as a benevolent priest, there was no burden that my mother could not lift from the shoulders of others, including every one of her children. And there was no personal issue, however jaw-dropping or revealing, that she would not willingly listen to and discuss in order to render careful, balanced advice. In this role my mother was strong and never judgmental, her reassuring tones a magnet for anyone who had a problem or who wished merely to vent his anger and frustration. But over time her very strength seemed to wear her down. The phone lines to the Webb house in Florida were rarely quiet. Every one of us went to her, piling our disappointments, fears, and aspirations onto her. At the same time, few of us asked if she had her own lamentations or tried to sense her own frustrations. Like Billie, the strong, uncomplaining oarsman of the lifeboat in Stephen Crane's famed short story "The Open Boat," as the years went by, my mother rowed everyone else to shore, at the price of her exhaustion.

Once he rebuilt the grove house in Lakeland my father would make good money by immediately selling it. My parents would then move back to Cocoa Beach, only a block up the street from where they had lived before, this time renting a gorgeous but dilapidated waterfront house as my father designed and built yet another home that bordered a canal just down the street. These moves comprised something of a Webb family record, as my parents managed to relocate five times in the space of four years, with three of those five homes on the same relatively short block in Cocoa Beach.

It took a few more years but finally my mother drew the line. My dad could have the Florida sun. He could have the nice house and the boat on the canal, and the mullet jumping and the manatee slowly swimming by. One morning she announced that she was going back to Arkansas, and that if my dad wanted to come, that was fine. And she did. And he did come with her, understanding that since she had moved more than thirty times for him, he had to make the biggest and in some ways the most painful move of his life for her. There was little in Arkansas that my father enjoyed. He never stopped dreaming of someday moving back to Florida. But my mother was now back home.

None of this had yet happened in the summer of 1975.

To my parents' chagrin I was writing but unemployed. To my father's further consternation I seemed to have abandoned a life's preparation as a leader in order to pursue the pipe dream of being a novelist. Out fishing one morning we had an animated debate. "Who would you rather be?" I finally asked him, "Teddy Roosevelt or Ernest Hemingway?"

"Roosevelt!" he said immediately. "He fought the robber barons. He built the Great White Fleet. He saved the wilderness. What did Hemingway do? He wrote some stories and raised a bunch of cats that didn't have any tails."

Writing novels seemed like a pretty good idea in the days just after the fall of Saigon. The presidency had just gone through its worst crisis in American history. The Vietnam War had ended horribly as the world unsympathetically watched the final convulsions of an incipient democracy on TV while they drank their beers and ate their evening meals. The aftermath of medical challenges and unanticipated career changes had brought constant turbulence to my personal life. And all the while, Jim Chiara and I were still pursuing what we viewed to be some justice in Sam Green's case, now with a petition for clemency.

One night while I was visiting my parents in Lakeland, Jim Chiara contacted me. Sam Green had killed himself.

At a time when bad news had become the norm, Sam Green's suicide took me completely by surprise. Disgusted and disenchanted with the entire direction of the country and of everything that had in the slightest way touched Vietnam, I paced in the darkness of my parents' living room, breaking into a bitter rant. Finally I awakened my four-year-old daughter, Amy, packed my Coleman tent and my camping gear inside my car, and drove off into the darkness. Following flat, misty back roads into the swamplands of Alligator Alley, I did not know where I was going and I did not really care. At dawn I saw a roadside sign and turned into a campground next to a lake. It was raining. I pitched my tent during the heavy storm and camped there for three days, talking to no one except for Amy. In her little-girl way Amy patiently tended to me as I sat in the mud, sulking and thinking and cooking old C rations over a Sterno stove. It rained a lot, but I was oblivious. I knew what it was like to eat C rations in the rain and then to curl up wet but warm inside a poncho liner. I had no radio. Cell phones did not exist. But I did not want to listen to the constant bad news or to talk to anybody, anyway.

I ran out of food. I was not in the mood to fish. Finally I rolled up my wet tent, packed my gear, and tossed it back inside the car along with Amy. There were no answers in a rainy campground at the edge of Lake Griffin. I had learned long ago that when bad things happened, inaction was the worst alternative of all. And I had learned more recently that bitterness brought with it nothing more than self-defeating bile.

Jim Chiara and I had exhausted all direct legal remedies in the Sam Green appeal. But after much correspondence, three years later I was given the rare opportunity to personally argue Green's case before a formal assemblage of the Board for the Correction of Naval Records. The BCNR could not reverse Green's conviction, and since he was dead, clemency was not particularly relevant. But as much as was then possible, we finally cleared Sam Green's name. It gave me no small amount of pleasure to call his mother in Cleveland and to inform her that her son's Dishonorable Discharge from the Marine Corps had been reversed, and that his records now reflected that he had served under honorable conditions.

She sent me a Christmas card that year: "My son Samuel, Jr. is happy in Heaven and grave about this."

★   ★   ★

During October 1975, six months after the fall of Saigon and two months after Sam Green took his life, things started to slowly turn around. Through a random series of events I started working with Ted Purdy, one of the great book editors of his time, who although then retired mentored me through a series of edits on the manuscript. Purdy, a Yale alumnus, held a literary pedigree as a noted editor and reviewer that went back more than fifty years, including having been editor in chief of both Putnam and Coward, McCann publishing houses. He had lived in Paris during much of the 1920s, the famous era just after World War I that had spawned many of the great writers of the so-called Lost Generation, including Ernest Hemingway and F. Scott Fitzgerald. He had edited and published Willard Motley's 1947 book-of-the-year *Knock on Any Door* and then later discovered Leon Uris, editing and publishing that former Marine's landmark World War II novel *Battle Cry*. Purdy's strong belief that *Fields of Fire* was not just a book but a serious work of literature, and that my life's calling was to become a major novelist, sustained me through a period of financial and professional uncertainty.

Post-Vietnam fatigue throughout American society meant it was not an ideal time to be selling a book about combat during a war that had just ended badly and that many people simply wanted to forget. *Fields of Fire* was rejected by a dozen publishers before it was finally published in 1978. For much of the time I was jobless. But Purdy's certainty constantly reassured me. And despite these uncertainties, I had not completely disappeared.

As the national bicentennial approached, in July 1976 the Vietnam Veterans Civic Council, an organization sponsored under the auspices of the Veterans Administration, selected me for a bicentennial award designed to publicly recognize the service of an "outstanding veteran." The Council had solicited recommendations from major employers, government agencies, and universities. To my surprise the Georgetown University Law Center had nominated me for the award, partly because of my Vietnam service, partly due to my book on America's strategy in the Pacific, and partly as a result of my efforts on behalf of Sam Green.

During the award ceremony, in front of an audience of several hundred people, I made an impromptu speech about the travails and challenges of Vietnam veterans. In early August the speech was published as a featured editorial in the *Washington Post* underneath a silhouette of American soldiers on patrol and the title "The Invisible Vietnam

Veteran." A key phrase was the pointed challenge "The very people who once called on us to bleed are now whispering that we should be ashamed of our scars. Well, I'm not ashamed of mine."

Serendipitously (or perhaps not), on the day before the *Washington Post* ran my "Invisible Vietnam Veteran" article I received a phone call from Aunt Carolyn, telling me that Granny had died. No one at the *Washington Post* had informed me that the article was even being considered, much less being published, making it a complete surprise to open up the newspaper the next morning and see the article at the center of the editorial page. It was as if Granny had somehow intervened and in her final hours willed it to happen. If nothing else, the publication of the article on the day after her death imbued me with a special determination never to apologize and never to forget our family's journey.

The presidential campaign of 1976 was kicking into full gear. Based on the *Washington Post* article I was asked to debate a draft evader on a local television show regarding candidate Jimmy Carter's proposal to give blanket amnesty to every person who had avoided the draft during the war. During the debate I pointed out that no president in history had elevated every single draft evader to the level of moral purist without an examination of the reasons for which he had violated federal law. As I left the studio, former congressman Bill Ayres, chairman of Gerald Ford's veterans program, called the TV station and asked me to meet with him. I warned him that I was not a Republican, but I agreed to discuss veterans' issues.

A World War II veteran, during his twenty years in Congress Bill Ayres had been known as something of a rascally hellion, but his passion for helping veterans was genuine and he was politically smart. My views had been clearly stated: We all had made decisions during that agonizing war. Jimmy Carter could not give back the arms or the legs or the lives of those who had obeyed the law and served and paid the price. However well-meaning, Carter was not healing the wounds with his proposal; he was deepening them. Following a long meeting with Ayres I agreed to become the national cochair of Vietnam Veterans for Ford, traveling, debating, and writing as part of the campaign.

Although Ford lost the election, in early 1977 I was offered a position as a full committee counsel on the staff of the House Committee on Veterans Affairs, hired by Congressman John Paul Hammerschmidt, the first Republican to be elected to federal office from Arkansas since just after the Civil War. Not incidentally, during the 1974 post-Watergate election sweeps just after Nixon's resignation, Hammerschmidt had beaten back a challenge from a young Democratic upstart named Bill Clinton. But also not incidentally, my mother was from Arkansas, and the different paths that Clinton and I had taken during the Vietnam War could not have more clearly represented the raw schism within the Baby Boom generation itself.

I had not sought the position, but I quickly grew into it. In rather short order I became chief minority counsel to the committee. A new time and mood was taking hold in the Congress as the country began moving forward from the bitterness of Vietnam and Watergate. On the Veterans Committee, Democratic and Republican Party labels were largely set aside. Our dedicated staffs led the way as we focused on the vitally important issues of veterans' benefits and on the emerging challenges of such issues as Agent Orange, post-traumatic stress, and the future of the VA hospital system.

In the summer of 1977, on the day before I finally took the District of Columbia Bar exam, I received a letter from John Kirk, the editor in chief at Prentice-Hall, indicating a desire to publish *Fields of Fire* as a major novel. Kirk, a Harvard alumnus and a Navy veteran of the Korean War, made the point in his letter that the defining war novels of every generation seemed always to cut against the grain of prevailing orthodoxy. In his view *Fields of Fire*, while apolitical and brutally honest, defended on every page the validity of military service at a time when our veterans were being demeaned and frequently defamed, and could become known as the definitive novel from the Vietnam War. My advance was small, but true to his word, on July 10, 1978, Kirk got *Fields of Fire* on the cover of *Publishers Weekly*, billed as "The Greatest War Novel in a Generation." When the novel was published in September, he sent me on a major coast-to-coast book tour.

Bantam quickly bought the paperback rights for six figures, taking the novel off the auction block with a preemptive bid by one of its top executives, World War II Marine veteran Marc Jaffe, and later promoted it heavily at the insistence of editor in chief Lou Satz, who announced that *Fields of Fire* would become the "Lou Satz book of the year." It became a selection of the Book-of-the-Month and Military Book clubs and was a finalist for that year's Hemingway Award. A bestseller in hardback and paperback, *Fields of Fire* was also the first Vietnam novel to become a bestseller in the United Kingdom. Twenty years later the Military Book Club printed a special edition, calling *Fields of Fire* "a savage, moving story that holds a place among America's military classics." Thanks to the loyalty of Ted Purdy and the support of John Kirk, Marc Jaffe, and Lou Satz, the book found its place and is still selling today.

The novel, combined with my military experience and my professional work on behalf of veterans, gave me a sudden forum in both literary and political circles. I was now doing hundreds of interviews. Having spent the previous two years compiling a database of little-known statistics about every aspect of the Vietnam War, I seized the chance to insert a factually accurate picture of the war and the people who fought it into the American political debate.

And so, as I had waited for a civilian career to find me, two had found me almost at the same time. But these were not compatible careers. In America literary and political careers are in every sense of the word contradictory. Thus began a process, repeated several times over the decades, of trying to decide which professional aspiration to pursue. My answer, as it had been since I left the Marine Corps, was to pursue anything that seemed interesting and to continue to do so again and again until one option overcame the others.

The years passed. A conundrum emerged. I would write for a while and miss the challenges of leadership and the sense of mission that attends public service. Then I would return to government for a while until I missed the freedom and creative energy of writing. I thought that someday one of these callings might clearly prevail over the other, but such a professional deus ex machina has never appeared.

In France literary writers have always been revered, their politics irrelevant to an appreciation of their art. Inside the British system Winston Churchill had been able to pursue both writing and politics, allowing him to earn a comfortable living as a writer, even while maintaining office as a member of Parliament. In the American system these two career paths are fundamentally incompatible. Good literature by definition hates simplicity, reveling in life's ambiguities in order to render the complicated nature of human truth. Politics demands simplicity in order to boil down all of those ambiguities into quick sound bites in order to justify controversial yes or no votes, where an agreement with 50.1 percent of a piece of legislation still brings with it a 100 percent yes vote.

As my professional endeavors moved back and forth between these two different and often antagonistic worlds, they often raised questions and hackles among the luminaries in both. The literary and journalistic world is rightly leery of being manipulated by politicians, making it difficult for someone with a political moniker to be considered a legitimate literary figure. On the political side, when you are running for high office it is not the greatest feeling in the world to wake up in the morning and see a few ribald scenes from one of your novels highlighted on the front page of the *Drudge Report*.

Thankfully America remains a country where persistence in multiple professional endeavors is respected as perhaps the ultimate expression of personal independence. By contrast, many of my Japanese friends become confused and even embarrassed when I try to explain that my eclectic professional journey is not a disgrace. In Japan changing jobs and particularly professions is often a sign of failure, and loss of face.

Yes, I studied engineering, long ago. I became an infantry Marine. I studied law. I was a military planner. I became a novelist. I served as a full committee counsel in the U.S. Congress. I taught poetry and the novel at the Naval Academy. I became a journalist, traveling through much of East Asia, in war-torn Beirut, and later in Afghanistan. I was the first American journalist ever allowed to report from inside the Japanese prison system. I served as assistant secretary of defense and Secretary of the Navy. I worked in Hollywood. I was a fellow at Harvard's Institute of Politics. As a business consultant I took American companies into Vietnam. As an ethnographer I wrote a two-thousand-year cultural history of the Scots-Irish people. And among other endeavors I became a U.S. senator.

Okay, I'm still trying to figure out what civilians do for a living.

Over the years spanning the 1970s to today, this journey has also brought me some of the greatest joys and the most frustrating exasperations of my life. I have raised five children and one stepchild born in four different decades. Baby Boomers have been a transitional generation in sexual roles and marital relations, and I, like many, carry the regrets and scars to prove it. But I also have come away with the ultimate blessing: to love and be loved by a woman whose strength, resilience, and intellect surprise me every day and whose judgment I seek on every matter, large or small.

At the age of seven, as South Vietnam fell to the final invasion from the North, my wife Hong Le escaped from Vietnam, along with her entire extended family, which included seven children. Adrift at sea for several days, they were finally scooped up out of the fishing boat on which she had escaped by the U.S. Navy and brought to a refugee camp on Guam. Eventually transferred to another refugee camp at Fort Chaffee, Arkansas, Hong's family was then sponsored by the St. Pius X Catholic Church parish in Greensboro, North Carolina, where they lived before finally settling in New Orleans.

When they left Vietnam, none of Hong's family could speak a word of English, and throughout her childhood Vietnamese was the only language spoken at home. They were not merely immigrants, although immigrants they surely were, in the best traditions of our country. They were also refugees, torn from a fairly stable environment in the seacoast town of Vung Tau by the sudden end of a war, unable to plan their relocation to another country or to prepare for it, emotionally and financially. Nor were they "takers," to borrow an unfortunate characterization that crept into a recent presidential campaign; energetic and determined, Hong's family quickly became "givers" and proud Americans. Hong's Social Security statements reflect her earnings from the time she was eleven years old, working in a shrimp-processing plant outside New Orleans. A dedicated student, she was among the first few Vietnamese to gain entry into the Benjamin Franklin magnet high school in New Orleans. Studying on scholarships and working as a court interpreter, she eventually graduated from the University of Michigan's prestigious Asia Studies Program as well as Cornell Law School.

No-nonsense tough and demandingly loyal, Hong likes to tease me that she is my granny's soul mate. And she is probably right.

* _Chapter Twelve_ *

AUNT LENA'S TEST

I have traveled all over the world, but the view from the terrace of my writing office in Rosslyn, Virginia, is the most inspiring sight I have ever seen.

Just below me as I stand on the eighth-floor balcony is the famed Marine Corps War Memorial, recapturing the moment in February 1945 when the Marines planted the American flag atop Mount Suribachi during the battle for Iwo Jima. Every Tuesday evening during the summer months, hundreds of onlookers pack the Memorial grounds as the Marine Corps hosts a full dress parade, replete with its precision-marching Silent Drill Platoon, the Marine Band, and its Drum and Bugle Corps. Having proudly served our Corps, as did my brother and my son, I enjoy a special perch on the terrace at Prospect House, a front-row seat, year after year, to watch the timeless continuity of its martial traditions.

Southward to my right is Arlington National Cemetery, America's most sacred burial grounds. Clearly visible on the far side of the

354

Cemetery is the Pentagon, that five-sided Puzzle Palace. Farther in the distance, hugging the Potomac River, are the busy runways of Reagan National Airport. In the other direction, off to the north, between the towering buildings of Rosslyn I can see the Georgetown skyline and the dome of the National Cathedral. Closer to me is the infamous Watergate apartment complex, whose very name reminds us of Richard Nixon's bitter fate, and just across the river is the Kennedy Center. Finally, to the east, on the other side of the stone-walled Roosevelt and Memorial bridges, my gaze can traverse the National Mall, from the Lincoln Memorial near the Potomac River to the Washington Monument a mile or so away, then its end point where it reaches the magnificent dome and outer edifices of the U.S. Capitol itself.

I never grow tired of taking in the beauty and the historic resonance of these national symbols. They speak to the remarkable journey of our country, but they are also personal. I spent five years in the Pentagon, one as a Marine and four as a senior executive during the Reagan administration. Years later, on the morning of the 9/11 attacks, I happened to be visiting "The Building" for a private breakfast with the commandant of the Marine Corps, leaving minutes after learning that the Twin Towers had been attacked and only moments before the Pentagon itself was hit. I walk every weekend through Arlington National Cemetery, past familiar graves and memorials. Many friends and former colleagues are buried in Arlington, as are both my parents.

But it is the Capitol Building that always captures my mood, my attention, and, lately, my most serious thoughts. Inside that building is the Senate floor, a place of awe-inspiring history, a chamber often filled with sound and fury, but also, to be honest, a place where in recent years a whole lot of high-level escape and evasion has been going on. And therein lies the conundrum, the seemingly unsolvable dilemma, the undeniable conflict in emotions for many who have served in the Congress in recent decades. As I contemplate the Capitol Building on the horizon, I feel a sense of gratitude for having had the honor of serving inside it as a U.S. senator. But that sense of pride is mingled with regret that I was unable to do enough, that both political parties have become frozen by money and interest groups into awkward positions and false debates that do not fully reflect the concerns of our citizens. Our political system has become paralyzed. It is no wonder that such a large percentage of the American people have lost their respect for and their trust of our national leadership.

The Capitol also stands as a symbol of my own unplanned journey. As I stare at it from the balcony of my writing office I remember how many thousand times I stood on the northern porch of the Capitol Building, just off the Senate floor, staring westward toward Virginia as I made phone calls or simply took a break during some interminable debate. For just as clearly as I can see the Capitol from my writing office, in those moments I could always see my writing office from the Capitol. When things in the Senate became especially disagreeable or tedious, I would think of the welcome solitude of my writing office and the sense of accomplishment I have always felt in putting words together to tell a story that just might affect as many lives as the mundane legislation that is so often the order of the day in the Congress.

I did not choose either of these professions, but I have been blessed to find success in both. Such has been the irony of my completely unpredicted professional career: that one of these callings never superseded the other, that I loved both but neither to the exclusion of the other, and that while involved in one I always missed the sense of accomplishment and participation that I felt in the other. Leadership has always been my natural calling, while writing has been my refuge, for me the singular place where I can sort out my views and clearly state them.

People in and out of politics often ask why I decided not to run for reelection to the Senate. Commentators speculate that I became frustrated with the tedium, that I hated fund-raising, and that while I enjoyed governance I did not like the ornamentations of politics. Each one of those conclusions holds a particle of truth. But the main reason that I decided not to run again was that by spending another six years or more as a member of that paralyzed body I faced the Hobson's choice of either turning into a perennial scold or surrendering a part of my individuality to the uncontrollable, collective nature of group politics. I was not ready to do either.

Others, particularly those who have made politics their career, take a different, fully understandable approach. While in office every senator enjoys the status of minor royalty. Whether or not any among them will inherit the grand legacy of a Daniel Webster or the longevity of a Robert Byrd, most appreciate that the credibility of American democracy rests upon their shoulders with everything they do. Even as they struggle daily with jammed schedules, fund-raisers, telephone calls begging for campaign donations, tedious committee hearings, endless photo opportunities with visiting delegations visiting from home, and no small share of meaningless "gotcha" votes on the Senate floor, they cannot escape the reality that for the moment they are American democracy's definers. And strange as it may seem during some of the Senate's more pretentious debates, they are also its highest tier of practitioners.

Make no mistake: politicians at this level of governance are a shrewd and largely intelligent bunch. The seemingly mindless pirouettes you see on the news shows from a senator with, say, an Ivy League degree or a Fulbright Scholarship are hardly the result of mental incapacity or outright personal corruption. Rather they emanate from that most basic human instinct, the desire to survive and to remain in power, boiled down to the cost-benefit analysis of what must be given up in order to remain viable in a transactional world such as politics, where there is often a price to be paid. And you will always hear the same heartfelt justification, even in the private whispers of a personal conversation:

I need to survive in order to continue to do good things. No matter how much I hate this particular vote, I would hate even more to vote with the other side. Besides, I can always undo it down the road with another vote that will cancel this one out. And unless it violates my conscience (which I would never do, you know that), sometimes taking a position that I couldn't really otherwise swallow is necessary in order to stay in office. How can I do any good if I don't get reelected?

Let's be honest. This is not just in politics. Almost everything in life requires some kind of trade-off. We all negotiate on issues large and small, even if it involves the simple matter of whether you or your spouse is going to pick up your kid from soccer practice. On the other hand, political issues are indisputably in a category all their own. A political leader's foremost role is stewardship of the public good. Any decision made while in public office might affect not only one's personal future but, more important, the long-term health of the country itself.

I came to the Senate with no illusions. During my campaign for office and at every possible opportunity after I was elected, I sought to highlight our country's dangerous descent into a society where the elites at the very top have increasingly moved away from everyone else, until America threatens to become a modern-day version of a banana republic. I arrived with a full appreciation of our political process, gained over many years from a wide variety of professional perspectives. I have taken risks, sometimes making money and sometimes losing it, and between the two, to state the obvious, it feels a lot better to be making money. I did not come to the Senate to soak the rich or to punish the powerful. I want everybody to have the chance to become one or the other or maybe both. There is nothing wrong with being rich. Almost every American dreams of it, and it is a healthy dream for our country, as long as the riches and the influence are fairly earned.

But in recent years, preceding and following my time in the Senate, I have worried about the atrophy of another part of what it means to be an American: that we have thrived on a guarantee of fairness as well as opportunity, that our leaders have a moral duty to protect the weak and the vulnerable and also the dream-seekers, and that we must never allow the very rich to become our masters. America was founded on a rebellion against royalty in whatever form it might reveal itself and on a guarantee that mere wealth should never be allowed to dictate the political direction of the country. Nothing would doom the American Dream more quickly than the establishment of a permanent, removed aristocracy, and quite frankly we are on the brink of allowing exactly that to happen. The never-ending debate of how a society must balance an individual's personal freedom with his larger obligation to community and country has marked every civilization for thousands of years. But our unusual political system holds as its premise the belief that there should be no special access to the corridors of power other than through the force of argument and the rewards of individual talent.

Putting boundaries on the misuse of influence by our most fortunate citizens without unfairly penalizing success is not a contradiction in terms. People from all over the world have always clamored to come to America so that they might be allowed to succeed. But the operative word is *fair*. Americans by and large do not envy wealth, nor do they cringe before power. But they have the right to expect our government leaders to ensure that we live inside a system that guarantees true fairness.

Recent years have called that guarantee into question. When I graduated from the Naval Academy in 1968 the average corporate executive made twenty times the salary of his workers. Today that multiple is around four hundred. The reasons are complicated, but it is an axiom in Washington that when money talks, politicians too often balk. Political campaigns need to be funded. The wealthy and the inordinately successful have their own ways of defining the reasons they have achieved the American Dream. For many, it is easy and often convenient to forget the political and economic structure that enabled their success and thus the obligations that every successful American incurs to the greater good as a result. This is not a war that pits our rich against our poor. The silent losers, for more than four decades, have been those workers and small business owners in the middle, who have been paying an inordinate share of the tax bills to keep our system on track.

It is not political bomb-throwing to point out the truth that those who wish to preserve this uncomfortable tilting of the table against our working people have the most money to spend on a wide variety of political fronts, while others who wish for more fundamental fairness lack the financial resources to back up their concerns, causing them to lose their influence in the corridors of power. Having spent most of my professional life as a sole proprietor, I know the frustrations of this reality.

For our own societal health, we need to find a better way.

This reality has shaped my political career and will continue to inform it. The vast unearned disparities between those at the very top and even our middle class were the principal focus of my rebuttal to President George W. Bush's State of the Union address in 2007, outweighing even our foreign policy blunders in the Middle East. The stagnation of communities and of true opportunity at the very bottom of our social scale was one of the strongest motivations behind my years-long attempts to reform our criminal justice system. The continuing policies that blatantly protect the advantages of our corporate and financial elites impelled my attempt to impose a windfall-profits tax on those who benefited from the government's bailout of the financial sector following the economic crash of 2008 and 2009. Tellingly, it was no accident that senior leadership of both the Democratic and Republican parties deliberately prevented even a vote on this legislation because an open vote would have required our politicians to take a stand and either confront our financial elites or admit that they live and work under their thumbs. The clear unfairness of a system that taxes capital gains at a rate far less than ordinary income led me to oppose any increase in taxes on earned income but to favor taxing capital gains at the same rate that those who actually work for their income are required to pay. Bemoaned and criticized by today's minions on Wall Street and the Chamber of Commerce, this is hardly a revolutionary concept. President Ronald Reagan favored its implementation in 1986.

I held these beliefs before deciding to run for the Senate, and I hold them still. Despite the deliberate distractions on social issues that take up so much of every media day, an elected official's positions on these issues provide a litmus test on how seriously committed he or she is to bringing true fairness to our society.

Over the years as I watched so many of our political leaders talk and dance around the issue of fairness, I developed what I came to call the Great-Aunt Lena Test.

Lena, one of twelve children, was my granny's youngest sister. Although spending part of her early adulthood in Memphis, she lived most of her life in the tiny hamlet of Kensett, Arkansas, where my mother herself was born. I made Lena a promise many years ago, and I have always done my best to keep it.

Aunt Lena never had any children of her own. As the years progressed, I became her favored nephew. In August 1976 I drove down to Arkansas, carrying the burden and the honor of delivering the eulogy at Granny's funeral. On the evening I arrived in Kensett I paid my respects to Lena, who was now herself widowed and alone. I could sense a strange unease in her as we sat, silently watching each other across the expanse of her sparsely furnished living room. It was so quiet that I could hear the bug zapper in her side yard, popping and snapping like a distant firefight as it fried whole flocks of Arkansas mosquitoes rising up in the damp evening air from the nearby ponds and swamps. Inside Lena's living room the loudest noise was the creaking of her rocking chair as she pushed the bare hardwood floor with her toes. I had known her my whole life, but sitting across from her at that moment I had somehow become a different, quizzical creature to her.

She rocked back and forth, measuring me with her bright, intelligent eyes. Finally a small, knowing smirk crossed her face. "So you've been to law school," she said, greatly unimpressed. "Did they teach you how to *lie* yet?"

Seven months later I returned to Kensett to visit with her again. I was now working for Congressman John Paul Hammerschmidt. Having made a speech for him in Hot Springs the night before, I left my motel at five-thirty in the morning and drove nearly two hours so that I might take Aunt Lena to breakfast. These were the days before cell phones, so I had called her from a pay phone in nearby Searcy, announcing that I had arrived to buy her some biscuits and gravy at the locally famous Harding's Restaurant.

Unimpressed, she had rebuked me. "I already ate," she said grudgingly, it now being all of seven o'clock in the morning.

This, I will admit, confused me, coming from the woman who had showered me with more than a few family treasures over the years. "Well, how about if I just come by to say hello?"

"If you want to."

Twenty minutes later I turned onto the small street that bordered her house. Aunt Lena didn't even let me inside. She stormed out of the front door as soon as the car pulled into her narrow gravel driveway, leaving me no doubt that she had been watching from her window and waiting for me to arrive. She was a fiery ball of indignation, five feet high and plump, wearing light-blue slippers and a white cotton house robe. She had curled her grey hair tight against her scalp with rollers and bobby pins, probably last night before she went to bed. And for some reason that I could not figure out, she was carrying a broom handle.

Now eighty years old, Aunt Lena carefully made her way down from the porch one step at a time. Her eyes never left me. She was carrying the broom handle like a scepter or maybe a spear. There was a little cinder-block-walled goldfish pond in her front yard just off the porch. It was late March, but overnight a thin layer of ice had covered the pond. She stopped at the edge of the pond as I walked toward her, still watching me as if I were an invader. Then she suddenly turned away from me and jammed the broom handle into the middle of the pond.

I was fine with that. At least she had finally stopped staring at me. "Froze last night," she said when I reached her, as if we had just left each other in her front yard the day before. She gazed intently into the water, ignoring me, moving the broom handle around the pond with both hands as if it were a large spoon.

"What are you doing?" I asked, for it did seem peculiar.

"You can't let the ice kill off them goldfish."

"No, you can't," I admitted. "I see the point of that."

If she had been a weaker-willed woman Aunt Lena would have allowed herself to shiver and complain, standing there in her thin robe and sockless slippers. As it was, she was in total self-control. A sudden hard stare froze me as if I had been caught in the flash of an old-time camera. "How is *Washington*?" she said, as if it were an accusation.

I shrugged helplessly, giving up. "Okay. What did I do wrong, Aunt Lena?"

She was ready for that. In fact I had just walked into a long-considered ambush. "How can you do this?" she asked querulously. "Getting involved in politics up there in the Congress with that bunch? And then working for a *Republican*?"

She waved the broom handle into the air. "Only one of them is any good. Every time I see that man Jimmy Carter on TV I see the blood of Jesus Christ, dripping off the cross onto his back. Did you ever notice? Jimmy Carter, Jesus Christ, both with the same initials?"

I didn't want to keep her going, but I was tempted to point out that Johnny Cash had the same initials too. And he was from Arkansas. "Aunt Lena," I began, but she cut me off.

"You'll forget us anyway," she said. This was her real point. "They all do. Wear a pretty tie, get a big head, get a nice salary, make all those promises, and then lie through your teeth so you can stay up there."

"I already live up there, Aunt Lena."

"You always were a back-talker," she said. "Don't be disrespectful. The point is, none of them career politicians up there in Washington really remember us, James Henry Webb Junior. They don't care. What are we to them, except trash? We don't swing any state when they vote for president. We don't have the money to scare them or to make them respect us. The people who pretend they know the history, they are somehow afraid to utter the truth. And here's the truth: if you're poor and white you're out of sight. That's what bothers me. What are you going to do to set them straight? Or are you too worried about having a job?"

To put it mildly, her angry, helpless words perplexed me. Deep inside me I knew she was motivated not by hatred or resentment but by a confused sense of justice. And there was more. Inside the intensity of Aunt Lena's gaze I saw my granny, now dead less than a year, reflected in the ageless mirror of my young memories, standing before me with the same near-violet eyes and the same buttermilk skin before the wrinkles had begun to set in, back when I was a child, while she brushed the cowlicks from my hair and sent me off to school. *Someday you're going to be famous, Jimmy Webb, and they're going to make a movie about your life. Now, you behave, you hear me? I don't want to see anything bad in that movie.*

"Aunt Lena, it's just a job I got. I'm not a congressman."

She tilted her soft face away from me, a silent rebuke. The cold had seeped inside her robe. She stifled a shiver, adamant that she would not show me any form of weakness. Finally she pointed toward the fields that stretched forever from the other side of the cemetery that began just across the road that bordered her yard. The morning fog clung to the weeds and the cow pies and the high grass of the pastures. A thin herd of cattle nosed their way right up to the barbed-wire fence that marked the far boundary of the Kensett Cemetery. If it had not been for the fence the cattle would have been filling their cuds from the grass that grew atop my own grandparents' graves. They grazed contentedly in the dew-filled morning meadow, just as they had done in the years of my childhood and even before that, in the time that my mother and Lena and Granny had strolled among the trees and the thick grass and the anthills, wondering what was on the other side of the far fields and if there really was a place called California.

But to Aunt Lena out here in her little house in Kensett, time truly stood still. This day itself could have been a hundred years ago. That was her power. It had been her fate. And in some ways it would always be my burden.

"I remember when your mama and her sister Eunice came back to the house on a hot afternoon not long after her daddy, your grandpa, died of sorrow and a stroke on the same day that your mama's older brother had died of a raging fever a few years before. Eunice said she felt sick and queasy. She was only eight. She and your mama had drank out of a water barrel in the yard behind somebody's house just down the street there. Eunice crumpled up that night and later she died of typhoid fever. Did you hear of anybody lately who died in America of typhoid fever, Jimmy? And your mama always blamed herself for having lived when Eunice died, I don't know why. So your grandpa died and the boy died and Eunice died, and when she was just a baby her older sister had already died of a fever in the middle of the night, some sickness that nobody could identify with the name of a disease. All we knew was that your granny woke us up in the middle of the night and told us we needed to kiss her little baby good-bye. I still remember that. Just kiss the baby good-bye was all that your granny said. So we all lined up to kiss her. That baby's forehead was hot as a frying pan when I put my lips to it. And the next day we were still waiting for the doctor who never came."

Aunt Lena nodded toward the cemetery. "She's buried right over yonder, you know that, just next to your granny and your granddaddy, and the boy and Eunice." She gave me a look. "And soon I will be too."

"I have visited those graves," I said.

"And you'll visit mine too, I guess. Although I doubt you'll come here very often, from the evidence I see." Lena shrugged. "The difference between you and me is that every morning when I wake up I can look right there—right there, and I can see them. And I think about them."

"I think about them every day, Aunt Lena."

"A little bit." She did not budge an inch. "But not in the same way. You never could, because if you did you would not stop talking about it, even up there in Washington, just like I can never stop talking about it down here, even if I'm talking to myself, in my own mind. It's different if you only think about it when you can't always see it. Your mama got out, and she met your daddy, and then along the way came you. And who would ever have thought it that my sister Georgia would have a grandson who could be born out of all of this confusion and then go to law school and work in the *United States Congress?*"

She was looking toward the cemetery as she talked. "Jimmy Webb, I don't know how to say this. I'm so proud of you, but you also make me feel disappointed."

"I will do my best, Aunt Lena," I said. "I do mean that."

"Maybe," she said. "I think you just might sell out. That's a pretty big circus up there. If you do, you will have to face yourself on Judgment Day, but I am not going to let you off the hook that easy. Do those people that you work with and those others who give everybody the money even care a little bit about what we went through? Would caring about it get an airplane built? Would it make them a profit on their prescription drug legislation? Would it get their kids into a special college? Would it get them a government contract to go blow things up in some foreign country? Does anybody up there even know that when we settled out here there was not even a road or a school or a hospital, and that it only got worse over time? That when me and your granny and even your mama was growing up we went barefoot, picking wild poke salat in the spring so we would have some greens to eat, and brushing our teeth with twigs? Do they know that we could not even tell when the so-called Great Depression hit because people back here were already so far down, there was nothing left to take from us, black and white alike? Did they ever hear the word *pellagra?* How about *typhoid fever* and *cholera?*

"No, they don't know any of that," she said, looking at me with a mix of regret and disgust. "The memory of it is all gone now, just like a dream dies at the opening of day. And who should be reminding them? You, Jimmy Webb! Your granny, my big sister, is calling out from her grave. What are you going to give her?"

She had knocked me speechless, as if somebody had hit me in the back of the head with a baseball bat that I never saw coming. "Aunt Lena, there is not a day that goes by when I don't remember my granny. I'm not God. I'm just one little peckerwood who lucked out and got a job up there in the Congress."

"And how many people from our family ever did that? I'm watching you. And when you make me proud you can come back inside my house."

She walked away, not even looking back. I grew a little sad as I climbed back inside the rental car and backed out of her gravel driveway. Still ignoring me, she labored up the porch steps and opened the door to her well-kept little house. She had won and she knew it. She had retained her fierce and unvanquished pride. Her house, small and simple as it was, was now off-limits to me, no matter what my title. I was banned from her premises, as unwelcome as a hill of fire ants. And just to make the point she slammed the door behind her, disappearing inside.

It occurred to me, driving back toward the airport at Memphis, that all I really needed to do in order to regain her respect was to make her proud and to make her understand that no matter the seductions of that place called Washington, I would never change who I was or what I believed.

We later did make up. A few months after my visit, Aunt Lena sent me a little pewter elephant with its trunk high in the air and a circle on its back where you could store your matchsticks, which she told me she had found at a flea market. She passed away at the age of ninety-one, but it was before I ran for office in Virginia as a Democrat, and by that time half of Arkansas had already become Republican. More important, Aunt Lena's admonition stuck with me from the moment she turned away and carried her broom handle back inside her house, leaving me shivering and alone as I stood next to the goldfish pond in her front yard. Stupid me. I had been so full of my upward success that I had forgotten to reassure her about what I was going to do with it.

You'll forget us anyway. Lie through your teeth so you can stay up there.

And so from time to time, when debating the merits of one policy or another, I have given myself the Great Aunt Lena Test: *What do you think, Mister Webb? Would Aunt Lena let you in her house today?* And that became the same unspoken question that I daily put before my colleagues as I watched and listened to so many debates during times of stress and turmoil.

In our country's mansions there are many rooms. But when you speak, when you listen, when you rant in favor or in opposition to one bill or another, when you vote on this policy or that, and especially when you are asking for political contributions to assist you in your journey, here is the easily answered test:

Whose house is it that you're trying to get inside?

Acknowledgments

I would like to express my appreciation for the professionals at Simon & Schuster for all of the work that has gone into the preparation and publication of this memoir. Not unlike a ship at sea, there are many unseen brains and hands at work when a book needs to be edited, artistically designed, publicized, marketed, and sold. I am deeply grateful to Jonathan Karp for his perceptive insights and encouragement and also for the times he personally made himself available as the book progressed. And it has been an enormous pleasure to have worked with Alice Mayhew, whose skills as a talented, no-nonsense editor were proved again and again. Alice, you are the best. You would have been a great drill sergeant.

Thanks also to Alice's key assistant Jonathan Cox and to Simon Green, my agent and my friend, for helping to shepherd the book along.

A special thanks to my friend and classmate Captain Gordon Peterson, USN (Ret'd), for his help in rounding up statistics used in the chapters about the Naval Academy. Gordon gave our country thirty years of service as a helicopter pilot and public affairs specialist, then served another six years as my key legislative assistant on the Senate Armed Services Committee. There is no better "details" person in the business.

And again, I would like to recognize the enormous personal and professional load carried by my wife Hong Le during the difficult and emotionally draining months that it took to write this book. Hong Le understands America with an incisiveness that often comes from the fresh eyes of a refugee, having unexpectedly lost a homeland and looking at a new country from the outside, trying to figure out its mechanics as she is moving in. It was she who believed so strongly that I should write my book *Born Fighting*. And it has been she who has been the greatest supporter of the decision to write this memoir.

Index

About the Author

James Webb, former senator from Virginia, has been a combat Marine, a committee counsel in the Congress, an assistant secretary of defense and Secretary of the Navy, an Emmy Award–winning journalist, a filmmaker, and the author of ten books. Mr. Webb has six children and lives in Northern Virginia with his wife Hong Le, who was born in Vietnam and is a graduate of Cornell Law School.